Capturing Campaign Dynamics

Capturing Campaign Dynamics, 2000 and 2004

The National Annenberg Election Survey

DANIEL ROMER, KATE KENSKI,
KENNETH WINNEG,
CHRISTOPHER ADASIEWICZ, AND
KATHLEEN HALL JAMIESON

PENN

University of Pennsylvania Press

Philadelphia

Copyright © 2006 University of Pennsylvania Press
All rights reserved
Printed in the United States of America on acid-free paper

10 9 8 7 6 5 4 3 2 1

Published by
University of Pennsylvania Press
Philadelphia, Pennsylvania 19104-4112

Library of Congress Cataloging-in-Publication Data

Capturing campaign dynamics, 2000 and 2004 : the national Annenberg election survey /
edited by Daniel Romer . . . [et al.].
   p. cm.
  ISBN-13: 978-0-8122-1944-9 (pbk : alk. paper)
  ISBN-10: 0-8122-1944-9 (pbk : alk. paper)
  Includes bibliographical references and index.
   1. United States. Congress—Elections, 2004. 2. United States. Congress—Elections,
2000. 3. Elections—United States. 4. Voting—United States. 5. United States—
Politics and government—1993–2001. 6. United States—Politics and government—
2001. I. Romer, Daniel, 1946–
JK1968 2004.C37 2006
324.973'0929—dc22   2006045672

Contents

Preface

The National Annenberg Election Survey (NAES) of the 2000 presidential election was a landmark in the history of American political opinion polling. Never before had so intense a study been conducted of the public's day-to-day reactions to the political events of a U.S. presidential election and its extended contestation in the courts. The rolling cross-sectional (RCS) design of the survey allows one to study campaign dynamics in a way that has seldom been possible in U.S. elections. Richard Johnston and his colleagues perfected this design in their studies of Canadian national elections, and he collaborated with Kathleen Hall Jamieson in designing the 2000 NAES. The 2004 survey followed the same strategy, and we provide the data from both studies in *Capturing Campaign Dynamics*.

The book's predecessor explored ways to summarize and analyze the data from this massive survey. Here we provide most of the same material with significant additions. First, we provide more background regarding exploratory and descriptive statistics that can be used in initial analyses of the survey (Chapter 5). We hope this chapter serves as a bridge to the more complex material on multivariate methods in later chapters. Chapter 10 provides additional examples of ways to analyze trends in voter knowledge during the 2004 campaign. This chapter is intended to highlight some of the innovative analyses one can undertake to understand campaign dynamics even in small segments of the population.

Much of the book is based on a course taught by Dan Romer and Kate Kenski on the analysis of the RCS design at the Annenberg Summer Institute on Methods and Statistics at the University of Pennsylvania. The course was designed as a practical guide to analyzing the survey rather than a rigorous examination of the statistical underpinnings of data analysis. The presentation assumes that the reader is familiar with basic statistical concepts such as significance testing, but we review some of this material in Chapter 5. In addition, important concepts are reviewed when necessary, and an appendix of technical terms is provided as a reference for readers. Because chapters were written by different members of the study team, including graduate students from the Annenberg

School for Communication, we credit them for the chapters to which they contributed. A brief overview of the plan of the book will help readers find the material that is most useful to them.

In Chaper 1, Kathleen Hall Jamieson and Kate Kenski discuss the motivating premise of the NAES, that a more complete record of the public's reaction to U.S. presidential elections will help answer important questions about the influence of campaign events on the electorate. Despite the skepticism often expressed about the importance of election campaigns, Jamieson and Kenski provide compelling evidence for the usefulness (and limits) of the NAES in understanding events over the course of a presidential campaign. They also provide some intriguing examples of similarities and differences in media use and political discussion across the last two presidential campaigns.

In Chapter 2, Kenneth Winneg, Kate Kenski, and Christopher Adasiewicz provide an overview of the surveys for both 2000 and 2004. Not only do they describe the main RCS datafile, but they also review the many smaller panel and cross-sectional studies that were conducted during each election. In addition, they describe other files that provide helpful methodological information for the use of the dataset, such as demographic weights and response rates for the survey. They also discuss practical considerations surrounding the use of these measures.

In Chapter 3, Kate Kenski reviews important concepts in survey and research design and shows how they apply to the design of different survey methodologies for the study of elections. In particular, the strengths and weaknesses of the RCS design are discussed in relation to other survey methods, such as simple cross-sectional and panel studies.

In Chapter 4, Kenski discusses the underlying strategy of the RCS design and the specific sampling and interviewing protocols that ensure comparable samples and questioning on each day of the survey. These procedures enable researchers to study change attributable to events during the election campaign rather than to changing features of the survey methodology.

In Chapter 5, Natalie Jomini Stroud and Daniel Romer review univariate and exploratory data analytic strategies that may be useful to readers before progressing to more complex analyses. In addition, several fundamental techniques such as crosstabulation and correlation are discussed with specific examples that apply these methods to the NAES.

In Chapter 6, Kenski reviews the importance of graphical analysis of survey data. In particular, graphic displays permit the researcher to identify trends in the data and potential violations of assumptions that might be made in subsequent data analysis. She also discusses some strategies for smoothing data to identify trends over time.

In Chapter 7, Romer reviews the use of linear and logistic regression for the analysis of cross-sectional data. He reviews the assumptions one makes in using these analyses to identify causal relations in survey data. He also discusses strategies for studying aggregate changes that unfold over time and the effects of voter experiences that might moderate these effects.

Chapter 8 by Kenski and Romer reviews strategies for the analysis of panel data. The NAES contains several panels that were designed to permit the study of important election events such as presidential debates. Strategies to permit stronger causal inferences from this design are discussed using examples from the NAES.

Chapter 9 by Romer provides an overview of the use of time series analysis for the NAES. This analysis uses data aggregated at the daily level to study effects of events during the election campaign or relations between variables measured on a daily basis. Many of the analytic techniques are borrowed from the literature on economic forecasting and may be more novel for readers than the approaches discussed in earlier chapters.

Chapter 10 by Dannagal Goldthwaite Young, Russell Tisinger, Kenski, and Romer examines the use of the NAES to study trends in segments of the population that might be too small to analyze in most cross-sectional surveys even with large samples. The authors provide examples of trend analyses in knowledge acquisition in late and early primary states as well as in late night comedy show audiences (e.g., *The Daily Show*) during the 2004 election year.

As noted earlier, a brief appendix of technical terms is provided so that readers can easily find definitions of concepts. The appendix is organized by chapter and by topic to help readers see the connections between concepts.

The codebook for the datasets found on the CD-ROM was written by Christopher Adasiewicz, who also helped coordinate the implementation of the survey.

NAES data are provided in the format used by the Statistical Package for the Social Sciences (SPSS), and most of the analyses we present use this program. However, we do not discuss specific details for using SPSS or other statistical programs for data analysis. Readers who are unfamiliar with SPSS or other statistical packages should consult the manuals of those programs for information about the procedures needed to run them.

We do not recommend the use of any particular statistical package for analysis of the NAES. For the analysis covered in Chapter 9, readers will want to use packages that have specific procedures for time series analysis. SPSS can accommodate all the analyses if the package includes the Trends module. Other packages that can also be used for time series data include the Statistical Analysis System (SAS), STATA, Eviews, and Matlab.

Give and Take with Our Readers

Another new feature to the NAES will be the opportunity for readers to post questions and comments online regarding the survey and this book. We invite readers to send us questions or comments about analyses they have conducted, problems they have encountered, or interesting findings they want to share with others. We will post these comments and our responses in a timely fashion. This mechanism will be available at www.annenbergpublicpolicycenter.org/naes/index.htm. We look forward to hearing from you.

Chapter 1
Why the National Annenberg
Election Survey?

KATHLEEN HALL JAMIESON AND KATE KENSKI

Do Campaigns Matter?

The presupposition of the National Annenberg Election Survey (NAES) is that understanding campaign dynamics is important because campaigns do matter. Campaigns matter because they elect and because they forecast the positions the president will champion and the leadership capacities he or she will display in office. Much of the survey research on elections has asked: What determines individual voting decisions, and what determines who is elected? While important, these questions ignore the fact that campaigns are designed to elect someone who will lead. Survey questions about the character and competence of a candidate are not simply a vehicle for assessing comparative strategic advantages in gaining votes, but also a means of ascertaining what the public expects of the person who is elected. Nor is an understanding of issue positions of value merely in surmising why one candidate gained more votes, either popular or electoral, than the other. Conducting elections that forecast governance should be a goal of a democracy. Understanding what the public has and has not learned increases understanding of the expectations the citizenry brings to a presidency and at the same time invites us to identify ways to increase learning in campaigns.

What voters know about the candidates and their positions matters because the relationship among campaigning, voting, and governance makes it possible for the citizenry to hold those it elects accountable. By devoting considerable space to questions about what the public learned about candidates and their stands on issues, NAES presupposes that accurate learning about both candidate similarities and differences is as important a goal for elections as actually deciding who wins or loses. The presence of an extensive battery of issue questions makes it possible to ask: Where did the campaigns confuse and where did they clarify the candidates' stands, and what did voters believe that the campaign of the winner had forecast for governance?

Of course, outcome matters as well. Scholars have long debated whether campaigns really make a difference to the outcome of elections. The first few decades of political research tended to find that there were two types of voters: those who decided before the campaigns began and those who decided at the last minute. Most fell into the former category, leaving researchers with the conclusion that few were truly affected by campaigns. "Despite the many differences among countries and from election to election," wrote communication scholar Elihu Katz, "typically about 80 per cent, or more, of the voters have made up their minds about their vote before the campaign begins, that is at least several months prior to the election" (1971, 306).

Many models from political science suggest that one need not use information collected during a campaign to forecast the winner (for an overview of these models see Holbrook 1996). Using economic indicators and presidential approval ratings prior to general election campaigns, the winners of several presidential elections have been predicted accurately. The 2000 presidential election is one of those elections in which the models failed. By most accounts, Al Gore should have won decisively.[1] *Washington Post* political correspondent David Broder (2001) observes that

a number of these political scientists have developed the notion that all that posturing and planning by candidates and managers, all the debate preparation, all the frantic flying from media market to media market and all the money spent from Labor Day to Election Day basically are wasted motions. Presidential elections, they maintain, are determined by fundamental factors, such as the performance of the economy earlier in the election year or the approval rating of the incumbent president or the degree of competition within the incumbent party's primaries.

Because all these are measurable before Labor Day, they say, they can predict with confidence the outcome of the vote. It turns out they can't. These scholars' models missed Gore's minuscule 50.2 percent margin in the two-party popular vote by a statistical mile. (B7)

Some scholars argue that campaigns have an effect on voter choice by directing public opinion toward an equilibrium of candidate support that is determined prior to the campaign. "Campaigns do matter; they play a very important role in shaping public opinion during an election year and they contribute to the ultimate outcome," notes political scientist Thomas Holbrook. "But at the same time it is important to recognize that the political and economic context of the election can place parameters on the potential effect of the campaign" (1996, 158).

With the increased means of targeting voters and the weakened state of political party identification over the past few decades, researchers have found that greater numbers of the voters are making decisions during campaigns. In their investigation of when citizens decide, Steven Chaffee and Rajiv Nath Rimal (1996) found that "The determining factors are likely to arise from specific circumstances, such as the number of candidates, availability of key information, and campaign tactics" (277). The variables that affect time of voting decision vary from one election to another. A similar conclusion was reached by J. David Gopoian and Sissie Hadjiharalambous (1994), who found that across five presidential elections, "these data convincingly demonstrate that the events associated with particular campaigns are the major determinants of the composition of the late deciding electorate of a specific election" (71). Because there is always the possibility that a campaign will affect vote choice, the prospect of studying campaigns should not be dismissed before the campaigns have begun.

Samuel Popkin (1991) maintains that campaigns matter because they provide information about political candidates to voters. He states: "There is no denying that misperception is always present in campaigns. But it is also clear that campaign communications do affect choices, and that they generally make voters more, not less, accurate in their perceptions of candidates and issues" (40).

Many variables can be used as a test of whether or not campaigns matter. Do campaigns enhance citizens' interest in government and public affairs? Do Americans learn about candidate issue positions during political campaigns? Do campaigns affect vote choice? Regardless of the criteria used to determine whether or not campaigns matters, if one does not have data collected daily, some of these effects may be missed.

Locating Decisive Moments

Historians of presidential campaigns have long speculated about the importance of certain moments that may have turned the outcome in one direction rather than another. Unspoken in their analysis is the assumption that the outcome of presidential campaigns is not a foregone conclusion, that some moments are consequential where others are not, and that determining which moments mattered is important in making sense of whom and how we elect and what it all means for those who govern and are governed.

Locked away in private archives are surveys conducted daily for presidential candidates, but the kinds of daily tracking available from public polls offer answers to very few questions. For example, unanswered questions concerning the 1960 presidential campaign abound. Did Eisenhower's noncommittal response to a press conference question about

Nixon's influence damage Nixon's chances? Did Kennedy's interven-tion to release Martin Luther King, Jr., from jail swing substantial votes his way? These are the sorts of information one might hope to glean from a well-done daily survey of the national public.

More questions follow from these. Did the Democratic ad excerpting Eisenhower's press conference create an impact separable from that of the press conference statement itself? Was any effect on black voters cre-ated by the news play of the action to free King or by the campaign com-munication that followed, or was any impact created from a synergy of news and ads? Larger social issues were at play in 1960 as well. How wide-spread was public awareness of, interest in, and responsiveness to Nixon's Quaker heritage and Kennedy's Catholic one? Did public accep-tance of a Catholic or a Quaker president increase as the campaign pro-gressed? Did any change in acceptance of a non-Protestant president extend beyond Catholics and Quakers?

Depending on their point of view, different scholars have featured the importance of different events in Kennedy's election. Unsurprisingly, the communication scholars who produced research for Sidney Kraus's *The Great Debates* (1962) saw the first debate as potentially decisive. By contrast, scholars focused on Kennedy's civil rights legacy emphasized the importance of the King endorsement (Wofford 1980).

Had a survey been in the field daily in the general election of 1960, could it have sorted any of this out? First some history. Asked in a nation-ally televised press conference if he could give us an example of a major idea of Richard Nixon's that he had adopted, incumbent president Dwight D. Eisenhower responded, "If you give me a week I might think of one. I don't remember." That moment was replayed in ads by Ken-nedy against Nixon in the 1960 campaign (Jamieson 1996). Did that magnified moment move votes, and if so, were the numbers sufficient to give Kennedy the presidency?

Other factors favoring a Kennedy victory may also have been at work. That the black vote would go to Kennedy in 1960 was not a foregone conclusion. The Eisenhower administration had, after all, approved the first major civil rights act since reconstruction and had backed desegre-gation efforts with federal troops. At the same time, blacks, who are over-whelmingly Baptist, identified with a religious group fearful of the prospect of electing a Catholic president.

Had Kennedy carried the percent of the black vote garnered by Ste-venson in 1956, he would have lost the election. In Illinois, for example, which Kennedy carried by 9,000 votes, over a quarter of a million blacks voted for the Massachusetts senator.

Many historians believe that a shift toward Kennedy was precipitated by his call to Coretta King and his brother's call to a local judge—actions that, taken together, were credited by many in the civil rights movement with securing Martin Luther King's release from jail, where he was being held on charges stemming from a civil rights protest. What role if any did news coverage play? After all, once outside prison King stated, "I am deeply indebted to Senator Kennedy, who served as a great force in making my release possible. For him to be that courageous shows that he is really acting upon principle and not expediency." Did it matter that King's father told his congregation and with it the press, "I had expected to vote against Senator Kennedy because of his religion. . . . It took courage to call my daughter-in-law at a time like this. He has the moral courage to stand up for what he knows is right. I've got all my votes and I've got a suitcase and I'm going to take them up there and dump them in his lap." Did it matter that two million pamphlets containing endorsements from King were distributed outside black churches? What of the possible impact of ads carried on black radio? In one, civil rights leader Dr. Ralph Abernathy said that it was time "for all of us to take off our Nixon buttons because Kennedy did something great and wonderful when he personally called Mrs. Coretta King and helped free Dr. Martin Luther King Jr . . . .Mr. Nixon could have helped but he refused to even comment on the case. Since Kennedy showed his great concern to humanity when he acted first without counting the cost, he has my whole hearted support. This is the kind of man we need at this hour" (Jamieson 1996).

The religious dynamic in 1960 has also produced reams of speculation. In the two Eisenhower elections of the 1950s, the Catholic vote split 50–50 between the parties (Campbell, Converse, Miller, and Stokes 1966). One open question in 1960 was, Would Kennedy draw higher than expected numbers of votes from Catholics and drive Protestants even more into the embrace of the Republican party? Ultimately Catholics voted 80–20 for Kennedy in 1960. "Calculating the normal vote to be expected of Catholics," Angus Campbell and his colleagues concluded that "one would expect at least a 63 per cent Democratic margin among Catholics. The difference between 63 per cent and the 80 per cent which Kennedy achieved can provisionally be taken as an estimate of the increment in Democratic votes among Catholics above that which the normal Protestant Democratic presidential candidate could have expected" (87–88).

Working from a model inhospitable to communication effects and relying on data incapable of capturing them, Campbell and his colleagues could not address such questions as: Did Kennedy succeed in reframing questions of religion into ones of tolerance? Did messages from conservative Protestant ministers, arguing that a vote for Kennedy was a vote for the Pope, energize Catholic voters? What, if any, was the effect on Catholics and Protestants of Kennedy's speech to Baptist ministers at the Greater Houston Ministerial Association? To what extent was the impact of that event magnified by the repeated airing of it in predominantly Catholic areas that had defected to the Republicans in 1956? Higher than expected Catholic turnout in those regions may have been produced by simple religious identification. Alternatively, the Kennedy message may have capitalized on religious identification in ways that produced increased turnout and a vote shift to the Democrat.

Would a survey such as NAES, a survey designed to capture campaign dynamics, have helped address the questions raised by the 1960 campaign? The answers indicate the potential and limitations of the NAES. The NAES uses a daily rolling cross-sectional (RCS) design to track changes in public opinion. The details of the design will be discussed in subsequent chapters. If consumption of news were tracked, exposure to the Eisenhower press conference assessed, and the media placement of the Democratic ad replaying the Eisenhower press conference logged, a daily sample of 300 voters might have been sufficient to sort out the effects of the press conference and the ad. Tracking changes in public acceptance of a Catholic or a Quaker as a prospective president would also have posed no problem. Similarly, the impact of the King endorsement on the population of white voters could have been assessed.

However, confirming the effect of King's endorsement on the black vote would have been impossible. Not only was this a relatively small population, but since potential black voters were widely disenfranchised in the South, the number able to vote was disproportionately low. Answering the question, "Did the King endorsement give Kennedy Illinois?" poses the same problem we faced in Florida in the 2000 election. The size of the sample we drew in 2000 from any one state at any one point in time was simply too small to permit generalization to the state as a whole. And the number of African American voters drawn from within that sample created the equivalent of anecdotal evidence.

Even if well done and improved every four years, NAES will leave unanswered a large number of tantalizing questions. However, three characteristics of contemporary politics make it possible to use NAES to help sort out the impact of some forms of communication such as ads, news, and debates. First, ad effects can be teased out because in most recent presidential general elections about half of the country received no paid presidential advertising. Second, debate effects can be isolated because a large part of the potential audience does not watch most of any debate. Third, the influence of news can be assessed because there are large differences in the amount of news watched and read by different parts of the public. If those effects change over time, daily tracking may capture the movement. So, for example, by comparing those who reported watching the first general election debate of 2000 to those who consumed news but not the debate, we can answer the question: Did the debate affect perceptions of Gore, or was the change in those perceptions reported in the national surveys only evident in nonviewers? Did the effect of debate viewing decay over time? By examining Gore's standing day to day in the time period leading up to the first debate, we also can answer the question: Was his standing dropping in response to news coverage that preceded the debate, or did the decline begin with his first head-to-head confrontation with George W. Bush? Because presidential debates are so tightly clustered, so that there are only a few days between one debate and another, it is, of course, difficult to isolate the effect of a single debate. This problem compounds the difficulty of asking, What effect did President George W. Bush's petulant performance in the first debate of 2004 have on perceptions of him or his ability to lead?

Do Communication Dynamics Exist, and, If So, Can the Rolling Cross-Sectional Design Find Them?

By giving us the tools to assess campaign dynamics, the design of the NAES allows us to study ways in which changes in exposure affect the other factors at play in a an election. Scholars have argued that many individuals do not pay much attention to politics between elections. As Election Day draws near, people begin paying more attention to politics. How much do people in the United States watch and read campaign news during presidential elections? Does exposure vary over time, or is it constant? Is it the same for different types of media? From December 1999 to January 2001 and from October 2003 to November 2004, the periods covered by the NAES rolling cross-sections, exposure to news varied across time and by medium. NAES respondents were asked how many days in the past week they had watched network and cable news.[2] They were also asked whether they had looked at information on the Internet about the presidential campaign.[3] Figures 1.1 and 1.2 show the responses to these television news and Internet exposure questions across the general election at the daily level. Seven-day centered moving averages are used to smooth the data and reveal the campaign dynamics.[4] Interestingly, many people watched more television news about presidential politics after Election Day 2000, when the election was still undecided, than immediately before.[5] In both graphs, Internet exposure to information about the presidential campaign increased as Election Day approached.

What about other types of exposure to information? How did talking about politics vary across the elections? Since online exposure to political information increased during the campaign, it would not be surpris-

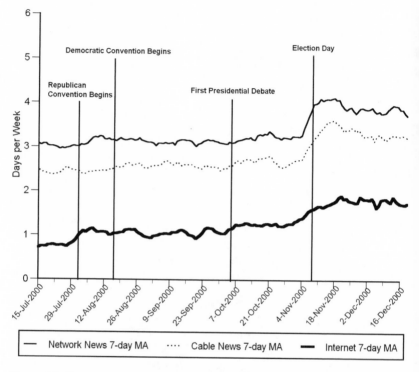

Figure 1.1. Exposure to network news, cable news, and presidential candidate information on the Internet from July 15 to December 19, 2000 (MA, moving average).

ing if political conversation also increased as Election Day approached. Figures 1.3 and 1.4 make further use of the data by looking at political discussion across the general elections. Respondents were asked how many days in the past week they had discussed politics with their family or friends.[6] They were also asked whether they had discussed politics with people at work or on the Internet.[7] As Election Day approached in both elections, talking about politics with various types of discussion partners increased. In 2000, after Election Day failed to produce a decisive presidential winner, talking about politics increased greatly. These examples demonstrate that media exposure and talking about politics were not stable variables across the presidential campaigns. The RCS design has made it possible to capture the dynamic nature of these phenomena.

While communication dynamics exist, so too do unanticipated moments that elicit communication. An RCS design makes it possible to

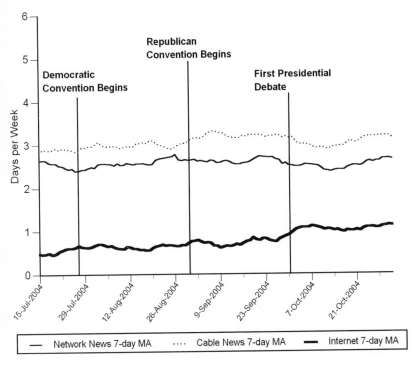

Figure 1.2. Exposure to network news, cable news, and presidential candidate information on the Internet from July 15 to November 1, 2004 (MA, moving average).

capture these moments. Who would have foreseen that the fate of a Cuban child, a decision about releasing oil from the petroleum reserve, or a conviction for driving under the influence of alcohol would play roles in the 2000 election? Who would have foreseen the emergence of the so-called Swift Boat Veterans for Truth or Michael Moore's *Fahrenheit 9/11* in 2004, or anticipated the Abu Ghraib prison scandal, the Chechen attack in the school in Beslan, or the last minute appearance of a tape by Osama bin Laden? Making sense of such occurrences requires a survey that is in the field daily. If perceptions of the state of the economy are assumed to play an important role in the process by which voters make decisions, then having the ongoing capacity to capture shifts in public perception is important as well.

Nearly fifty years ago Carl Hovland observed that cross-sectional surveys were unlikely to find short-term persuasion and opinion change (Hovland 1959). They are also unable to tie the impact of specific events to shifts in attitude. For example, writing about the 1988 campaign,

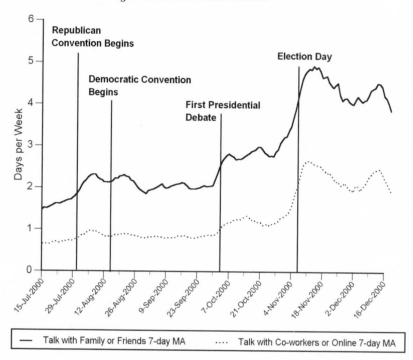

Figure 1.3. Talking about politics with family or friends and with coworkers or online from July 15 to December 19, 2000 (MA, moving average).

Abramson, Aldrich, and Rohde argued that "the vice-presidential candidates had an effect on the candidates, and vice versa" (1991, 530). They draw their evidence from the fact that between September and November that year George H. W. Bush dropped four points in favorability among Gallup respondents, Michael Dukakis and Dan Quayle dropped six, but Lloyd Bentsen jumped by five. What their data can't tell is what role, if any, the debates played in producing those changes.

Even when the method involved located communication effects, scholars who weren't looking for them missed them. Becker, McCombs, and McLeod (1975) showed that the pioneering Columbia researchers Lazarsfeld, Berelson, and Gaudet (1944) and Berelson, Lazarsfeld, and McPhee (1954) overlooked the fact that, among voters who were exposed to media messages in opposition to their predispositions, substantial persuasion occurred. In addition, the early studies showed an agenda-setting effect, although the scholars conducting the studies didn't interpret it as such. In fact, media exposure increased.

If communication in campaigns mattered, most cross-sectional

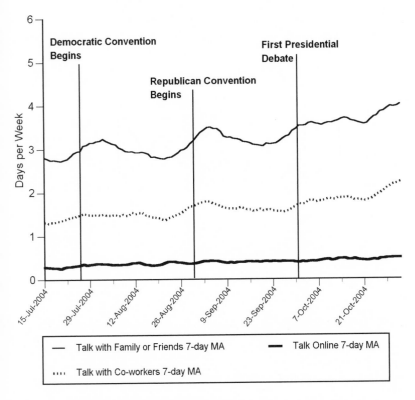

Figure 1.4. Talking about politics with family or friends, with coworkers, or online from July 15 to November 1, 2004 (MA, moving average).

designs were ill equipped to capture or explain that fact. In 1984 the National Election Studies (NES) planning committee responded to these concerns with a weekly RCS design.[8] Decades after the first election studies, those who looked for communication effects through the lens provided by an RCS design found them. In their path-breaking studies of Canadian elections, Richard Johnston, André Blais, Henry E. Brady, and Jean Crête (1992) confirmed that the RCS could detect debate effects. Drawing on the lessons he and his colleagues learned in their Canadian work, Richard Johnston wrote the protocols for the NAES and supervised their implementation in 2000.

Begun in November 1999 and carried through inauguration day 2001, the first National Annenberg Election Survey was an attempt to transcend the limitations of cross-sectional surveys with a daily assessment of the knowledge, dispositions, beliefs and behavior of the U.S. electorate. The NAES was implemented again for the 2004 presidential campaign, with interviews beginning in October 2003 and ending in mid-November 2004. The survey was designed to ascertain how elections work and to permit scholars to draw inferences about the ways in which they forecast governance. In 2004, NAES data were released regularly to the press and public on the Annenberg Public Policy Center (APPC) website, a process directed by former *New York Times* reporter Adam Clymer. These press releases, as well as the NAES 2000 and 2004 data and documentation, are on the disk accompanying this book. In the following chapters, Daniel Romer, Kate Kenski, Kenneth Winneg, Christopher Adasiewicz, Dannagal Goldthwaite Young, Russell Tisinger, and Natalie Jomini Stroud explain the design and uses of the NAES.

Notes

1. The March 2001 volume of *PS: Political Science & Politics* 34 (1) contains articles that discuss how political science models faired in predicting the 2000 election.
2. Network news: for 2000, see variable cE01, for 2004, see variable cEA01. Cable news: for 2000, see variable cE02, for 2004, see variable cEA03.
3. The wording of the Internet questions changed from 2000 to 2004. In 2000, respondents were asked: "How many days in the past week did you see information about the campaign for president online?" (cE21). After the election, they were asked: "How many days in the past week did you see information about presidential politics online?" (cE22). In 2004, they were asked: "How many days in the past week did you access information about the campaign for president online?" (cEA22). Individuals who answered that they did not have Internet access in response to a previous question were coded as 0, meaning that they had not seen or did not access information about the campaign for president or presidential politics online. In 2000, the Internet access question was cE20, and in 2004, it was cEA21.
4. The process of smoothing data will be discussed in Chapter 6.
5. In 2000, the RCS was extended past Election Day because the outcome of the election was not resolved until mid-December.
6. For 2000, see variable cK05. For 2004, see variable cKB01.
7. In 2000, a single question about discussing politics with co-workers or online was asked (cK09). In 2004, we assessed political talk with co-workers (cKB03) separately from political talk online (cKB05). If respondents did not have Internet access (cEA22), they were coded as talking politics online 0 days per week.
8. The 1984 American National Election Study was conducted by the Center for Political Studies of the Institute for Social Research, under the general direction of Warren E. Miller. Santa Traugott was the director of studies. Board members during the planning phase of the 1984 NES included Ray Wolfinger (chair), Richard A. Brody, Heinz Eulau, Morris P. Fiorina, Stanley Kelley, Jr., Donald R. Kinder, David R. Mayhew, Warren E. Miller (ex officio), David O. Sears, and Merrill Shanks. The 1984 NES planning committee included several NES board members (Kinder, chair, Brody, Kelley, Miller, ex officio, Sears, and

Wolfinger) and three other scholars, Stanley Feldman, Ethel Klein, and Steven
J. Rosenstone.

References

Abramson, Paul R., John H. Aldrich, and David,W. Rohde. 1991. *Change and Continuity in the 1988 Elections*. Washington, D.C.: Congressional Quarterly.
Becker, Lee B., Maxwell A. McCombs, and Jack M. McLeod. 1975. The Development of Political Cognitions. In Steven H. Chaffee, ed., *Political Communication*. London: Sage.
Berelson, Bernard R., Paul F. Lazarsfeld, and William N. McPhee. 1954. *Voting: A Study of Opinion Formation in a Presidential Campaign*. Chicago: University of Chicago Press.
Broder, David S. 2001. Why Election Predictors Bombed. *Washington Post*, April 8, B7.
Campbell, Angus, Philip E. Converse, Warren E. Miller, and Donald E. Stokes. 1966. *Elections and the Political Order*. New York: John Wiley.
Chaffee, Steven H. and Rajiv Nath Rimal. 1996. Time of Vote Decision and Openness to Persuasion. In Diana C. Mutz, Paul M. Sniderman, and Richard A. Brody, eds., *Political Persuasion and Attitude Change*. Ann Arbor: University of Michigan Press. 267–91.
Gopoian, J. David and Sissie Hadjiharalambous. 1994. Late-Deciding Voters in Presidential Elections. *Political Behavior* 16 (1): 55–78.
Holbrook, Thomas M. 1996. *Do Campaigns Matter?* Thousand Oaks, Calif.: Sage.
Hovland, Carl. 1959. Reconciling Conflicting Results Derived from Experimental and Survey Studies of Attitude Change. *American Psychologist* 14: 8–17.
Jamieson, Kathleen H. 1996. *Packaging the Presidency*. New York: Oxford University Press.
Johnston, Richard, André Blais, Henry E. Brady, and Jean Crête. 1992. *Letting the People Decide: Dynamics of a Canadian Election*. Stanford, Calif.: Stanford University Press.
Katz, Elihu. 1971. Platforms and Windows: Broadcasting's Role in Election Campaigns. *Journalism Quarterly* 48: 304–14.
Kraus, Sidney. 1962. *The Great Debates*. Bloomington: Indiana University Press.
Lazarsfeld, Paul F., Bernard Berelson, and Hazel Gaudet. 1944. *The People's choice*. New York: Columbia University Press.
Miller, Warren E. and the National Election Studies. 1999. NATIONAL ELECTION STUDIES, 1984 Continuous Monitoring Project [dataset]. Ann Arbor: University of Michigan, Center for Political Studies [producer and distributor].
Popkin, Samuel L. 1991. *The Reasoning Voter: Communication and Persuasion in Presidential Campaigns*. Chicago: University of Chicago Press.
Wofford, Harris. 1980. *Of Kennedys and Kings*. New York: Farrar, Straus and Giroux.

Chapter 2
NAES Datasets, Survey Procedures, and Content

Kenneth Winneg, Kate Kenski, and Christopher Adasiewicz

The 2000 and 2004 National Annenberg Election Surveys are the largest academic public opinion studies of the American electorate ever conducted within a campaign cycle. Adults in the United States were interviewed by telephone about their beliefs, attitudes, intentions, and behavior relevant to the 2000 and 2004 presidential campaigns. Interviews were conducted with 79,458 respondents in 2000 and with 86,276 respondents in 2004. Because some respondents were interviewed more than once for the panel studies, in total, 100,626 interviews were conducted in 2000 and 98,711 in 2004. The surveys were commissioned by the Annenberg Public Policy Center (APPC) of the University of Pennsylvania under the direction of Kathleen Hall Jamieson. In this chapter, we provide an overview of the RCS, panel, and supplemental surveys and introduce readers to the content of the 2000 and 2004 NAES.

Datasets Overview

From a research design perspective, the most innovative feature of the NAES is the national rolling cross-section (RCS) study, which ran nearly continuously from mid-December 1999 to mid-January 2001 (NAES00) and from early October 2003 to mid-November 2004 (NAES04). In 2000, 58,373 respondents were interviewed in the national RCS as shown in Table 2.1. In the 2004 national RCS, 81,422 respondents were interviewed. Additional pre-primary RCS studies were conducted in Iowa, New Hampshire, and the Super Tuesday and Second Tuesday states in 2000, and traditional cross-sections were conducted in South Carolina and Michigan before the 2000 primaries. A RCS study was also conducted in New Hampshire in 2004.

The 2000 and 2004 NAES also contained panel surveys around key

TABLE 2.1. OVERVIEW OF THE NAES STUDIES

Study (RCS = rolling cross-section CS = cross-section)	2000		2004	
	Interviewing dates (dates 2000 unless noted)	Sample size	Interviewing dates (dates 2004 unless noted)	Sample size
National RCS	Dec. 14, 1999–Jan. 19, 2001	58,373	Oct. 7, 2003–Nov. 16, 2004	81,422
Preprimary state oversamples				
Iowa RCS	Dec. 14, 1999–Jan. 23, 2000	3,173	–	–
New Hampshire RCS	Dec. 14, 1999–Jan. 31, 2000	3,814	Jan. 8–Feb. 3	3,454
Super Tuesday States RCS	Jan. 4–March 6	6,627	–	–
Second Tuesday States RCS	Feb. 28–March 13	1,591	–	–
South Carolina CS	Feb. 1–18	1,171	–	–
Michigan CS	Feb. 15–21	388	–	–
Panels—before and after primary elections, conventions, debates, and the general election	*See Table 2.2*	21,168	*See Table 2.2*	11,977
Supplemental studies				
November 1999 National RCS	Nov. 8–Dec. 13, 1999	2,486	–	–
New Hampshire Post-Primary RCS	Feb. 2–22	1,835	–	–
Active Military Household CS	–	–	Sept. 22–Oct. 5	656
Pre-Inauguration CS	–	–	Jan. 11–16, 2005	1,202
Total interviews		100,626		98,711
Total respondents		79,458		86,276

See the 2000 and 2004 codebooks for detailed information on each study.

campaign events, as shown in Table 2.2. Some respondents were reinterviewed to form pre-post panels around the Democratic and Republican conventions, the general election debates in the fall, and the general elections. In addition, the 2000 NAES included five pre-post primary panels.

The 2004 NAES included two stand-alone surveys related to the 2004 presidential campaign. These surveys included a survey of active military personnel and their family members and a pre-inaugural cross-section survey completed in January 2005. In 2000, add-on studies included a November 1999 cross-section and a New Hampshire post-primary cross-section.

The NAES CD-ROM includes the national RCS studies from both 2000 and 2004, the panel studies from 2000 and 2004, all the supplemental primary studies from 2000, the supplemental New Hampshire primary study from 2004, and the stand-alone studies from 2004. In addition, the CD-ROM contains all the NAES survey results press releases from the 2004 campaign along with the sample weights applied to the data discussed in those releases. The CD-ROM also contains codebooks for 2000 and 2004 that provide detailed information about each NAES dataset. The codebooks contain catalogs of every variable in the datasets and the questionnaires that were used to interview respondents. Table 2.3 summarizes the average daily interviewing for the continuous national RCS in 2000 and 2004.

Sampling and Interviewing Protocols

Phone work for the 2004 NAES studies was conducted by Schulman, Ronca, & Bucuvalas, Inc., (SRBI) from their facilities in New York, Fort Myers, Florida, and West Long Branch, New Jersey. Phone work for the NAES 2000 studies, with the exception of the South Carolina and Michigan studies, was also conducted by SRBI; the 2000 South Carolina and Michigan studies were conducted by Princeton Data Source of Fredericksburg, Virginia. In both 2000 and 2004, phone work was supervised by APPC. In 2000, APPC worked in conjunction with Princeton Survey Research Associates of Washington, D.C.

CROSS-SECTION STUDIES

We sampled respondents for cross-section studies through a random-digit dialing process. First, we generated a list of random 10-digit numbers, and interviewers dialed these numbers to determine which were working household phones. Second, at each household, interviewers randomly chose a respondent from among the household's adult resi-

Table 2.2. Panel Studies

Study	2000			2004		
	Interviewing dates (dates 2000 unless noted)			Interviewing dates (dates 2004 unless noted)		
	Pre-event initial interview	Post-event reinterview	Sample size	Pre-event initial interview	Post-event Reinterview	Sample size
Pre-post primary election						
Iowa	Dec. 14, 1999–Jan. 23, 2000	Jan. 26–Feb. 17	1,596	—	—	—
New Hampshire	Dec. 14, 1999–Jan. 31, 2000	Feb. 2–27	1,900	—	—	—
Super Tuesday states	Jan. 4–March 6	March 10–April 6	3,853	—	—	—
South Carolina	Feb. 1–18	Feb. 23–March 8	503	—	—	—
Michigan	Feb. 15–21	Feb. 24–March 8	145	—	—	—
Pre-post conventions						
Republican	July 21–30	Aug. 4–13	1,197	Aug. 20–29	Sept. 3–13	1,049
Democratic	Aug. 4–13	Aug. 18–27	1,230	July 16–25	July 30–Aug. 8	1,016
Pre-post debates	Sept. 21–Oct. 2	Oct. 4–10	1,514	—	—	—
	Oct. 4–10	Oct. 12–16	670	—	—	—
	July 21–30, Aug. 4–13, Oct. 12–16	Oct. 18–31	2,052	Sept. 20–29	Oct. 14–24	1,248
Pre-post general election	Jan. 3–Nov. 6	Nov. 11–Dec. 7	6,508	July 15–Nov. 1	Nov. 4–Dec. 28	8,664

See the 2000 and 2004 codebooks for detailed information on each study.

TABLE 2.3. NATIONAL RCS DAILY INTERVIEWING

| | 2000 | | | 2004 | |
| | Interviews completed | | | Interviews completed | |
Month	Total	Daily average	Month	Total	Daily average
			Oct. 7–31, 2003	1,536	61
			November	4,682	161
Dec. 14–30*, 1999	882	59	December	5,541	198
January 2000	2,311	80	January 2004	5,032	168
February	2,779	96	February	5,665	195
March	3,262	105	March	4,245	137
April	1,810	60	April	3,613	125
May	1,507	49	May	8,313	268
June	1,422	47	June	4,236	141
July	7,131	246	July	7,306	244
August	9,571	309	August	8,969	289
September	9,218	307	September	9,007	300
October	9,617	310	October	11,200	361
November	4,841	173	Nov. 1, 3–16	2,077	138
December	2,993	107			
Jan. 2–19, 2001	1,029	57			
Total	58,373			81,422	

*Daily averages are based on the total number of interviewing days in the month, which excluded major holidays and the day of the general election. See the 2000 and 2004 codebooks for more information.

dents. (Additional steps were involved in sampling respondents for the Active Military Household Cross-Section in 2004; see below.) This process is the generally accepted method for sampling respondents for public surveys by telephone, because it covers every household in the country with a phone, and avoids the incompleteness and inaccuracy of most published telephone directories.

The list of random 10-digit numbers was provided by Survey Sampling, Inc., of Westport, Connecticut. The first eight digits of each number—representing area code, exchange, and bank—were generated proportional to telephone company estimates of the number of working household phones in each combination of area code, exchange, and bank. The last two digits of each number were generated entirely at random. Known cell phone numbers were deleted prior to dialing, as required by federal regulations.

Upon dialing a number, interviewers attempted to determine if it was a household. Numbers that were not in service or were business or government phones were set aside. When interviewers reached a household, they asked to speak with an adult age 18 or older, and then asked this person to give the number of adult residents in the household so that one could be chosen at random to be the survey respondent. If there was only one adult in the household, he or she was chosen as the survey respondent. If there were two adults, one was randomly selected by age; the interviewer asked to speak with either the younger or older adult. If there were three adults, the interviewer asked to speak with the youngest, middle, or oldest adult. If there were four or more adults, one was randomly selected for the survey by birthday; the interviewer asked to speak with either the adult who most recently celebrated a birthday or the one who would have a birthday next.

We were aggressive in repeatedly dialing numbers to attempt to determine which were working household phones, and choose respondents and complete interviews. After numbers were dialed for the first time, they were scheduled to be redialed as needed, up to a total of 18 dials over 14 days. In many cases, dialing a number resulted in no answer, a busy signal, or the call being forwarded to an answering machine, and in these cases, the number was typically scheduled to be called again, no later than the next day. In other cases, the person who answered the phone requested a specific date and time for the interviewer to call back. If the person who answered the phone refused to participate, the number was scheduled to be called back, typically a few days later, by an interviewer specially trained in eliciting participation (refusal conversion). In addition, if a respondent started and then broke off an interview, he or she was called back in an attempt to restart and finish the interview. After a second refusal or break-off, a number was not dialed again.

ROLLING CROSS-SECTION DIALING PROTOCOL

For rolling cross-section studies, we followed a strict protocol for when to add new randomly generated phone numbers to the sample of numbers that interviewers were dialing, when to make initial and repeat dials to each number, and when to retire numbers and stop dialing them. New numbers were added to the sample daily, at a fixed ratio to the number of completed interviews that were desired—1:6 in 2000 and 1:9 in 2004. The day that a number was added, up to two dials were made. Over the subsequent three days (days 2–4), up to two dials were made each day. Over the next 10 days (days 5–14), up to one dial was made each day. After 18 dials over 14 days, the number was retired, and no more dials were made, even if the number was known to be a working household phone, and additional dials could have potentially yielded a completed interview. This strict protocol helped to stabilize fluctuation in the composition of the sample of respondents interviewed on any single day. (For a detailed discussion of the rolling cross-section dialing protocol and methodology overall, see Chapter 4.)

2004 MILITARY SURVEY

The 2004 Active Military Household Cross-Section consists of interviews with 656 members of households where at least one household member was currently serving in the U.S. military at the time of the survey. Of these 656 respondents, 372 were themselves actively serving in the military, while 284 were residents of households where someone else was actively serving.

We identified respondents for the military survey through the national RCS. Between February 13 and September 29, we asked national RCS respondents if they or any member of their household currently served in the military. Out of 48,626 respondents interviewed for the national RCS during this period, 1,396 (2.9%) were found to be living in active military households. All these households were redialed for the military survey. Upon recontacting an active military household, we first attempted to speak with an active military member. If this was not possible because he or she was away for the duration of the survey, we attempted to speak with another member of the household, trying first to re-interview the person who participated in the initial national RCS interviewing (assuming that this person was not the active military member who was away). The 2004 codebook on the CD-ROM describes the military survey sampling procedure in detail.

PANEL STUDIES

We sampled respondents for panel studies by selecting respondents who had been interviewed for a cross-section study prior to a campaign event and attempting to re-interview them after the event. The 2000 and 2004 codebooks on the CD-ROM describe which cross-section respondents were selected for re-interviewing for each panel. For example, we sampled respondents for the pre-post panel around the Republican convention by attempting to re-interview every respondent who had been interviewed for the national RCS during the 10 days before the start of the convention.

Typically, panel re-interviews needed to be completed on a rapid turnaround, for example, within 10 days after a campaign event. In these cases, interviewers began dialing all the phone numbers at once, and kept redialing them as necessary until the end of the re-interview period. Refusal and break-off conversions were attempted as with cross-section studies (see above). When the re-interview period was longer, the maximum number of dialings was capped at 18 dials over 14 days.

RESPONSE RATES

The question of a survey's response rate is of significant concern to any researcher employing survey data, particularly data gathered via telephone. A response rate is a measure of the percentage of telephone numbers released into the field that resulted in a completed interview. While low response rates are of concern to researchers, a low response rate does not necessarily indicate a biased sample (Groves and Couper 1998).

While in-person surveys typically obtain higher response rates than telephone surveys, carrying out a survey the size and scope of the NAES using in-person interviews would be prohibitively expensive and time-consuming. Response rates for the 2000 and 2004 NAES were comparable to those obtained by most contemporary telephone surveys in both the cooperation rate, which is the percentage of households that agreed to participate in the survey once they had been successfully reached by an interviewer, and the overall response rate, which accounts for both refusals and potential participants whom interviewers were unable to contact despite repeated attempts.

For the 2000 national Rolling Cross-Section, the cooperation rate was 53 percent, and the overall response rate was 25–31 percent. For the 2004 national RCS, the cooperation rate was 54 percent, and the overall response rate was 22–25 percent. In both years, overall the response rate is given as a range to account for the different formulas that can be used to calculate the total number of households eligible for a survey. The slight decrease in overall response rate between 2000 and 2004 reflects a secular trend. It is becoming more difficult to contact Americans for telephone surveys because of their increasing resistance to taking calls from callers with whom they are unfamiliar, and because of increasing use of technology to block such calls. More information about response rate, including calculations for panels and other NAES studies, is available on the CD-ROM.

SAMPLE WEIGHTING

Despite the best efforts, the composition of telephone surveys does not always reflect the composition of the actual population that they are designed to represent as accurately as researchers would like. Although telephone numbers used in the NAES were randomly sampled to maximize the representativeness of the survey to adults in the nation overall, not everyone who was sampled agreed to participate in the survey as demonstrated by the response rates. Survey nonresponse can be problematic because it has the potential to bias population estimates (Lohr 1999). For example, in the 2000 NAES, 55.3 percent of respondents in the national RCS were female, while U.S. Census Bureau estimates maintain that in 2000, 51.7 percent of adults in the U.S. population were female. In other words, it appears that women were more likely to take part in interviews than were men. This can be problematic when looking at variables on which males and females differ, such as party identification. Females tend to identify with the Democratic Party more than do men. If a survey over-represents women, the results from the survey may contain a Democratic bias, unless the survey estimates are adjusted through weights. Furthermore, while most people in the United States live in households with telephones, an estimated 5.9 percent of households did not have telephones in November 2000 (Federal Communications Commission 2004). Consequently, these individuals did not make it into the sample frame of the NAES. Because discrepancies can occur between the kinds of people who participate in a survey and the composition of the population to which one wants to generalize, survey researchers often apply weights to their datasets to compensate for the discrepancies before conducting descriptive analyses. If one is conducting multivariate analyses and demographic controls are used, weights may not be needed.

Sample weights readjust the roles that cases play in the analyses. If a sample contains more women than are actually present in a population, weights can be created so that the female cases are downweighted and the male cases given more weight. When conducting analyses, one should create weights that are tailored to the dataset one is analyzing. Over the 2004 campaign season, the APPC put forth 83 press releases containing NAES analyses on the presidential campaign. For each segment of the NAES data used, unique sets of weights were created. The press releases are included on the CD-ROM. The weights used for each of these press releases are also included, so that students can practice replicating the analyses, and researchers can use the weights for their own projects. The weights take into account household size, number of telephone lines into the residence, geographic region, sex, race, age, and education. To use the weights, one must match the weights to the appropriate NAES files using the KEY variable, which is a case identifier. It is important to remember that the weights were created for particular segments (date specific) of data. It would not be appropriate, for example, to use the weights created for the entire dataset overall if one plans to analyze the data from January only.

Consensus in the public opinion community has not been reached on how weights should be constructed. For example, some people weight their data by party identification, while others strongly oppose such an approach. Therefore, researchers should give considerable thought before weighting their data. For researchers who plan to weight their data by demographic variables, the U.S. Census Bureau website (www-.census.gov) provides data on the U.S. population, and these are summarized in Table 2.4. Their projections can be used to create weights tailored to the segments of data that are of interest to the researcher.

Missing Data

In the data collection process, respondents occasionally do not answer questions posed to them, producing missing information in the datasets. While efforts are made to minimize the presence of missing data, respondents may be inclined to say that they "don't know" how to respond to a given survey question. Sometimes, respondents simply refuse to give a response to a particular question. In general, the NAES survey documentation denotes "don't know" responses as 998 and refused responses as 999 as the variable values.

Before analyzing data, researchers must make some choices regarding how missing responses will be handled. In some cases, researchers are able to take care of missing data through recoding. Often, researchers employ conventional methods, such as listwise or pairwise deletion. Other missing data approaches include creating dummy variables for the missing data and incorporating those dummies in models, using maximum likelihood estimation, or employing multiple imputation techniques. The type of missing data method selected depends on the assumptions that one makes about the data that are missing (see Allison 2002 for a description of the various types of methods used to handle missing data). When the missing data on a variable are unrelated to the other variables in the dataset, the missing responses are said to be *missing completely at random* (MCAR). If the missing data are MCAR, the remaining subset of the data can be treated as a simple random sample of the original dataset. While having missing data is never ideal, when the missing data are MCAR, the potential problems that may ensue have to do with the decreased sample size and thus power, but researchers do not have to worry that their estimates will be biased. But if the missing data are systemically associated with other variables in the dataset, the missing information could bias the estimates. The missing data approach should therefore be chosen with care.

Researchers analyzing the NAES data should note that not all questions on the survey were asked of all respondents. In some cases, questions were only asked of respondents who gave certain responses to prior

TABLE 2.4. NATIONAL WEIGHTING TARGETS, PERCENTAGE OF TOTAL POPULATION

2000

Sex and age	Male	Female
18–24	6.3	6.4
25–34	9.3	9.7
35–44	11.1	11.3
45–54	8.6	9.2
55–64	5.6	6.1
65+	7.0	9.5

Sex and education	Male	Female
Less than high school	8.0	8.4
High school graduate	16.8	19.9
Some college	10.9	12.4
College graduate	12.1	11.5

Age and education	18–34	35–54	55+
Less than high school	4.8	4.4	7.3
High school graduate	10.7	15.1	10.9
Some college	9.5	9.1	4.8
College graduate	6.7	11.7	5.3

Race	Total
White	84.5
Black	11.2
Other	4.3

Ethnicity	Total
Non-Hispanic	90.3
Hispanic	9.7

Region	Total
Northeast	19.6
Midwest	23.8
South	35.3
West	21.3

2004

Sex and age	Male	Female
18–24	6.3	6.3
25–34	9.0	9.1
35–44	10.2	10.6
45–54	9.2	9.8
55–64	6.3	6.8
65+	6.9	9.4

Sex and education	Male	Female
Less than high school	7.8	7.8
High school graduate	16.6	19.1
Some college	10.8	12.5
College graduate	12.7	12.6

Age and education	18–34	35–54	55+
Less than high school	4.9	4.3	6.4
High school graduate	10.1	14.4	11.3
Some college	9.1	9.0	5.2
College graduate	6.7	12.2	6.4

Race and ethnicity	Total
Non-Hispanic white	71.9
Non-Hispanic black	10.7
Hispanic	11.8
Other non-Hispanic	5.5

Region	Total
Northeast	19.4
Midwest	23.1
South	35.8
West	21.6

Source: Bureau of the Census

questions in the survey. For example, in 2004, only respondents who did not consider themselves Democrats or Republicans were asked: "Do you think of yourself as closer to the Republican or Democratic Party?" Other questions were asked only to a random selection of respondents. For example, when it came to assessing candidate traits such as how well "cares about people like me" or "strong leader" applied to George W. Bush or John Kerry in 2004, only a random two-thirds of respondents were asked these questions. The random question splits were necessary to ensure that several types of questions could be asked. Therefore, before performing analyses, researchers must take the sample splits into consideration because the sample splits will affect the sample size and thus power of the analyses performed.

The CD-ROM

The CD-ROM contains the complete files from both the 2000 and 2004 NAES. The data files are in both SPSS format and tab-delimited format, which users can import into other statistical packages. The codebook files contain catalogs of every variable in the datasets and the questionnaires. Table 2.5 lists the contents and names of each data file on the CD-ROM.

The codebook files on the CD-ROM can be read with a PDF reader such as Adobe Acrobat. Both the 2000 and 2004 Codebooks present the detailed information for every question asked in all the NAES surveys, organized by subject area. Supplemental codebook sections contain the various versions of the questionnaire in the form they were asked by the interviewers. This will allow researchers to see the order in which questions are asked.

The codebooks will allow the researchers to view the full text of the questions, response categories, the timing of questions, and form splits where they occurred. They contain a number of tables that summarize major groups of questions to help researchers easily find the items in which they are interested. The CD-ROM also contains a search engine, called NAES Search that gives the researcher the opportunity to search for items in the codebook using a simple keyword search.

Furthermore, the CD-ROM contains the press releases that came from NAES during the 2004 campaign year. Finally, as a way for researchers to examine the data associated with the release, the CD-ROM also contains the sample weights used in each release.

The Questionnaire

This section provides an overview of the content of the national cross-section and panel surveys. A brief description of the stand-alone surveys

TABLE 2.5. CD-ROM FILES

NAES 2004
  Cross-Section Studies
    National Rolling Cross-Section
      CdBkNRCS.pdf (codebook)
      DataNRCS.sav (SPSS data)
      DataNRCS.txt (ASCII data)
    New Hampshire Rolling Cross-Section
      CdBkNHRC.pdf
      DataNHRC.sav
      DataNHRC.txt
    Military Cross-Section
      CdBkMili.pdf
      DataMili.sav
      DataMili.txt
    Inauguration Cross-Section
      CdBkInau.pdf
      DataInau.sav
      Datanau.txt
  Panel Studies
    Democratic Convention Panel
      CdBkDCon.pdf
      DataDCon.sav
      DataDCon.txt
    Republican Convention Panel
      CdBkRCon.pdf
      DataRCon.sav
      DataRCon.txt
    Debates Panel
      CdBkDeb.pdf
      DataDeb.sav
      DataDeb.txt
    General Election Panel
      CdBkElec.pdf
      DataElec.sav
      DataElec.txt

---

will follow. The 2000 and 2004 codebooks on the CD-ROM provide detailed information on every question asked.

NATIONAL ROLLING CROSS-SECTION SURVEY

The national RCS is a dynamic survey designed to serve two important, yet sometimes conflicting, functions. First, it was structured to maximize the number of questions asked consistently throughout the field period in order to perform and maintain its time series function. Second, it was purposely kept flexible enough to react to and measure the day-to-day

TABLE 2.5 (CONTINUED)

		Contents	File Name
NAES 2000			
Cross-section studies		Interviewing December 14, 1999–April 3, 2000	CS000403.zip
	National Rolling Cross-Section	April 4–July 17	CS000717.zip
		July 18–September 4	CS000904.zip
		September 5–October 2	CS001002.zip
		October 3–November 6	CS001106.zip
		November 8–January 19, 2001	CS010119.zip
		Iowa pre-presidential primary election cross-section	IACS.zip
		New Hampshire pre-primary	NHCS.zip
		Super Tuesday states	SUPERCS.zip
		Second Tuesday states	SECCS.zip
		South Carolina pre-Republican presidential primary	SCCS.zip
		Michigan pre-Republican presidential primary	MICS.zip
Panel studies		Iowa pre-post presidential primary election panel	IAPNL.zip
		New Hampshire pre-post primary	NHPNL.zip
		Super Tuesday states	SUPERPNL.zip
		South Carolina pre-post Republican primary	SCPNL.zip
		Michigan pre-post Republican primary	MIPNL.zip
		Pre-post Republican convention	GOPPNL.zip
		Pre-post Democratic convention	DEMPNL.zip
		Pre-post October 3 Bush-Gore Debate	DEB03OCT.zip
		Pre-post October 11 debate	DEB11OCT.zip
		Pre-post October 17 debate	DEB17OCT.zip
		Pre-post general election	ELECPNL.zip
		New Hampshire post-primary cross-section	NHPOSTCS.zip

changes in the campaign and capture noncampaign news issues that, nevertheless, could have some impact on the campaign. To that end, we created a survey document that met both these needs by containing a core set of questions that remained on the survey throughout the field period and a set of questions with a finite life on the survey. However, in some cases, questions came on and off the survey at different times based on the relevance of the question or questions to a specific point in the campaign.

Furthermore, in order to accommodate the very large number of questions that were part of the core and those which were placed on the survey temporarily, we found it necessary to have "split samples" for certain questions. That is, we presented questions either to the entire sample, two-thirds of the sample, half of the sample, one-third of the sample, or one-fourth of the sample. The advantage of creating sample splits in the survey is that it increases the number of questions appearing on the survey. This ensures the widest possible variety of question and affords NAES with maximum flexibility. However, we have been very careful in creating the split questions to allow for reliable sample sizes for all questions. The codebooks on the CD-ROM indicate which questions were subject to split samples, and contain tables summarizing how split samples were applied to different groups of questions at different points in the campaign.

Table 2.6 outlines the categories of variables in the NAES04 dataset.

EVALUATIONS OF CANDIDATES, POLITICAL FIGURES, AND GROUPS

As the presidential campaign progresses it is critical to track evolving opinions of candidates, political figures, and groups that are in some way part of the campaign. These evaluations are an underlying component of NAES. The NAES included items evaluating the presidential candidates and other political figures on a number of dimensions. These included feeling thermometer ratings, ratings of candidates on a series of trait attributes, perceptions of candidates' ideologies, and specific to George W. Bush in 2004, an evaluation of his job performance as president.

Feeling Thermometer. To gauge a general impression of respondents' feelings about the candidates, respondents were asked to rate the candidates on so-called "feeling thermometers." In 2000, candidates were rated on a zero to 100 point scale. The 2004 survey, however, included a feeling thermometer using a zero to ten scale. After conducting careful analyses of 2000 NAES data, we determined that collapsing the scale to a zero to ten scale would make little difference in overall evaluation, yet would be easier to implement via the telephone than a zero to 100 point scale.

If a respondent was completely unaware of the political figure or group, then the interviewer coded the response as a 101 in 2000 and as an 11 in 2004. If a respondent had heard of the political figure or group but indicated they did not know enough to evaluate, then the interviewer coded the response as a 102 in 2000 and as a 12 in 2004. These responses were used to create an awareness variable that measures how well a candidate was known. If respondents were deemed unaware of the candidate, then they were not asked to rate the candidate on the trait

TABLE 2.6. VARIABLE CATEGORIES

- **General opinions of candidates, political figures, and groups**
  - Favorability and approval
  - Character traits and ideology
  - Emotional reaction to candidates
- **Policy issues—opinions and knowledge** *(see Table 2.7)*
- **Candidates' biographies—opinions and knowledge** *(e.g., Kerry's Vietnam record)*
- **Media—exposure and opinions**
  - TV news
  - Newspapers
  - Talk radio
  - Late-night comedy
  - Online political information
  - Opinions of media overall
- **Political discourse—exposure and opinions**
  - Debates—primary and general election
  - Conventions
  - Ads
  - Contact with campaigns *(e.g., phone calls or direct mail)*
  - Other political discourse *(e.g., major speeches, candidate appearances on TV interview shows)*
  - Opinions of political discourse overall
- **Political participation—attitudes and behaviors**
  - Interest in politics and the campaign
  - Discussion of politics
  - Involvement in campaigning *(e.g., attended rally, donated money)*

- **Orientation to politics**
  - Ideology
  - Confidence in institutions
  - Political efficacy and cynicism
  - General political knowledge
- **Candidates' chances and endorsements—opinions and knowledge**
- **Voting behavior and attitudes**
  - Voter registration
  - Presidential primary—intended and actual vote
  - General election—intended and actual vote
  - Voting in past elections
  - General voting attitudes and influences
  - Opinions of female candidates
  - Opinions of proposed voting reforms
- **Opinions of election outcome** *(extensive questioning in 2000)*
  - Legitimacy and significance of election
  - Vote count accuracy
  - Disputed 2000 vote
  - Transition from Clinton to Bush *(2000 only)*
- **Congressional election—opinions of candidates and voting**
- **Demographics**
  - Sex, age, education, and income
  - Employment
  - Ethnicity, citizenship, and residency
  - Religion
  - Military service *(extensive questioning in 2004)*
  - Gun ownership
  - Household composition and location

This table is a summary—see the 2000 and 2004 codebooks for detailed information. The 2004 codebook contains a chart listing comparable variables between 2000 and 2004.

and candidate ideology evaluation variables. As candidates dropped out of the race, they were dropped from the feeling thermometer, the trait, and candidate ideology variables list.

In 2004, we also asked respondents separately to rate the job that Bush was doing as president, and to rate Bush as a person.

Trait Evaluation. The 2004 NAES expanded the list of trait descriptions considerably from 2000.[1] The traits are attributes used to describe the candidate in some way. For example, a trait could be a positive trait, such as "optimistic," or a negative trait, such as "reckless." During the primaries, NAES sought to maximize the sample size for each candidate while staying within the thirty-minute time constraint of the survey. In 2004, we did this by devising a method by which two of the six top Democratic presidential candidates[2] were randomly selected for each survey to be evaluated on the traits. However, all respondents evaluated George W. Bush on the traits since he was the only Republican in the race. The six Democrats evaluated were John Kerry, John Edwards, Howard Dean, Wesley Clark, Joe Lieberman, and Richard Gephardt. When John Kerry's final opponent, John Edwards, dropped out on March 3, all respondents were asked to evaluate only Kerry and Bush from that point on. Over the course of the 2004 campaign, up to twenty-five traits were part of the battery. These included, "cares about people like me," "inspiring," "strong leader," "trustworthy," "shares my values," "knowledgeable," "steady," "says one thing, does another," "optimistic," and "effective."

Candidate Ideology. Respondents also assessed where they believed the candidates fell on the ideological spectrum. The scale ranged from very conservative to very liberal. During the 2000 primaries respondents rated the ideology of the Republican candidates, Bush, John McCain, and Steve Forbes, and the Democratic candidates, Al Gore and Bill Bradley. Respondents rated Bush and Gore during the general election period. In 2004, respondents evaluated all six of the top Democrats on ideology during the primaries until each dropped out. As of March 3, respondents evaluated only Kerry and Bush. As of April 21, independent candidate Ralph Nader was added to the list of candidates evaluated on ideology (until September 12).

POLICY ISSUES AND THE STATE OF THE NATION: MEASURING KNOWLEDGE AND OPINION

An important part of capturing campaign dynamics includes tracking changes in the direction people see the country heading, what people

TABLE 2.7. POLICY SUBJECTS

- **Economic issues**
  - Taxes
  - Budget and deficit
  - Labor
  - Trade
- **Health and human issues**
  - Health care and insurance, including Medicare
  - Social Security
  - Education
  - Poverty
- **Foreign affairs**
  - Military defense
  - Iraq *(2004 only)*
  - Terrorism and homeland security *(2004 only)*
  - Immigration

- **Social issues**
  - Abortion
  - Stem cell research *(2004 only)*
  - Gay rights *(extensive questioning in 2004)*
  - Other civil rights issues *(2000 only)*
  - Gun control and crime
- **Energy and environment**
- **Legal and ethical issues**
  - Lawsuits and regulation
  - Money in politics *(2000 only)*
- **Supreme Court** *(2004 only)*

This table is a summary—see the 2000 and 2004 codebooks for detailed information. The 2004 codebook contains a chart listing comparable variables between 2000 and 2004.

feel are the most important problems facing the nation, and how people perceive the state of the economy. Additionally, it is important to understand where people stand on the issues that the candidates were discussing or potentially going to discuss during the campaign and to determine how close their positions were to those held by the candidates. In this section, the NAES includes a general question on the direction of the country (NAES04 only) and the country's most important problem. This section also includes respondent issue positions serving several purposes. First, their positions were recorded so researchers could analyze how these positions compared with those of the candidates they supported. These questions used wording comparable to the questions we asked regarding perceptions of candidate stances. Second, the NAES tracked the salience of issues over time. The survey's flexibility allowed us to add or drop questions as issues cropped up during the campaign. Third, in 2004, NAES researchers reported the results of issues stances from time to time in press releases throughout the campaign. The key questions measuring respondent issue stance appeared in the form of either a two-point favor/oppose scale or a five-point favor/oppose scale. In the last two months of the NAES04 survey, all two-point favor/oppose questions were changed to five-point scales. Table 2.7 summarizes the issues addressed by the 2000 and 2004 NAES. In 2000, issues included the economy, taxes, Social Security, education, health insurance, abortion, crime, campaign finance, and gay rights. In 2004, questions in this section covered such issues as a constitutional amendment banning gay marriage, taxes, abortion, prescription drug coverage, health care, gun control, defense, terrorism, education, Social Security privatization, Iraq, homeland security, the Patriot Act, and stem cell research.

Aside from understanding what Americans knew about the issues discussed in the campaign and what their stances were, it is essential to understand what they knew about where the candidates stood on the issues and furthermore, their perceptions of how candidates and political parties performed on issues. Knowledge and perceptions of the candidates combined with demographic and behavioral variables will allow researchers to study the ways by which citizens learn about candidates over the course of the campaign.

In 2004, NAES devoted a battery of questions to tracking and measuring George W. Bush's performance ratings in a variety of areas. Because his first term was strongly defined by terrorism, security, and the war in Iraq, much of the evaluation concentrated on these areas. Items also tracked Bush's performance on handling the nation's economy and the impact of his policies on the economy. Other items tracked respondent perceptions of how the rest of the world viewed the United States as a result of Bush's presidency.

This section also examined where the respondents believed the candidates stood on the issues discussed during the campaign. In addition, during both the primaries and the general election, NAES contained a battery measuring knowledge of candidates' past issue positions. Respondents were asked which candidates held a particular stance and which candidate matched a given biographical description.

In sum, this portion of the survey contained the following types of questions:

- Perception of the direction of the country and the most important problems facing the country
- Perceptions of the nation's economy, assessments of respondent's own economic situation, and outlook for respondent's own and the country's economic future.
- Respondent's own positions on policy issues
- Knowledge of the candidates' policy positions
- Perceptions of the candidates and political parties on issues, including Bush's performance on the economy, Iraq, terrorism, and other issues

MEDIA USE

Underlying much of what the 2004 NAES is trying to accomplish is the ability to analyze media effects over the course of a campaign. The 2000 NAES was among the first to move away from the prior, mostly unsuccessful methods of using post-election cross-sectional surveys to uncover media effects. The NAES is designed to allow the researchers to watch the campaign evolve so that media effects become more apparent. The NAES04 media battery is similar to the 2000 NAES media questions, but the designers have expanded it to include questions on viewing or listening to Spanish language media, Black Entertainment Television, NPR, and *The Daily Show with Jon Stewart.*

The NAES04 continued to employ self-reported media exposure and attention measures of usage of various news media. The NAES asked how many days in the week prior to being interviewed respondents used the following news sources: national broadcast television news, cable news, local television news, newspapers, talk radio, and the Internet. Those who read the newspaper or listened to talk radio were asked which newspaper they read most often or which radio host or program they listened to most often. In addition, respondents were asked how much attention they paid to stories about the presidential campaign in each of these media.

In other sections of the survey, there were questions about media coverage of the candidates. Further, in NAES04 there were specific viewing measures on Michael Moore's movie *Fahrenheit 9/11* and the environmental movie *The Day After Tomorrow.*

POLITICAL DISCOURSE

In the NAES00, there were a number of items gauging respondent exposure to and impressions of the discourse of the candidates and the campaigns. Items focused on the level of attention candidates and campaigns devoted to promoting plans and criticizing opponents, negativity in the campaign relative to previous campaigns, and which candidate, Bush or Gore, was conducting a more negative campaign. Respondents also assigned grades to the candidates and the news media on how they were behaving and covering (in the case of the journalists) the campaigns. Additionally, the 2000 survey contained an item asking respondents to indicate whether they felt they learned enough to cast a vote. In 2004, because of utility (based on earlier analysis) and space limitations, this section was tightened to measure those items deemed most essential to evaluating campaign discourse. The NAES04 included the items on the level of attention candidates and campaigns devoted to promoting plans and criticizing opponents, and whether respondents learned enough in order to make an informed vote choice.

This section also included tracking of awareness and impact of specific media events involving Bush, including an appearance on the program *Meet the Press* in February and his State of the Union speech in January.

ADVERTISEMENTS

In the NAES00, respondents were asked during the general election if they had seen ads for either Bush or Gore. If so, they were asked which candidate had been discussed more in the ads, and whether they could recall whether the ads were saying positive or negative things about the candidates. During the primaries, respondents were asked about specific content in ads that were being discussed in the news or had heavy buys.

In the NAES04, the predominant focus of questions related to advertising was on advertising early in the general election campaign primarily aimed at what the campaigns, journalists, pundits, and scholars called "battleground states." Researchers have been interested in the impact of advertising on voter knowledge and whether voters would be more or less likely to believe deceptive or untrue claims made by the campaigns or others advertising on their behalf. In 2004, much of the money spent on advertising was in the battleground states. At the time, the NAES04 included questions on advertising, there were considered to be 18 battleground states.[3] Using the data from the questions, researchers can assess the level of believability of the claims made in the advertisements among those living in battleground states, where there was wide advertising exposure, and among those not living in the battleground states, where there was limited (national cable and carryover to bordering non-battleground states) to no exposure. The questions measured exposure, learning, and believability of claims. These questions were on the survey for a limited time—between three and six weeks.

Further, two advertising related questions were on the NAES04 for a ten-day period in January 2004. One was an exposure question and the other recorded what voters did upon seeing an advertisement appear on their televisions—watch, turn the channel, fast forward using a digital video recording system, or turn away.

John Kerry's Viet Nam war record was questioned in a series of ads sponsored by the Swift Boat Veterans for Truth (SBVT). The NAES04 included questions about exposure to these ads and the believability of the charges made specifically in them and about Kerry's Viet Nam record in general as part of the section on Candidate Issue Stances and Biographies.

CAMPAIGN EVENTS: DEBATES AND CONVENTIONS

Analysis of the 2000 NAES panel data shows that debates did make a difference. In Chapter 8, Kenski and Romer show that debate viewing affected how much people talked about politics with their friends and family and how they perceived candidates' debate performance. In the 2004 general election campaign, there were three presidential debates and one vice-presidential debate occurring roughly over a two-week period. Because of the attention the news media give to the debates in the days leading up to and following these events, it is an important communication task to measure whether there were any debate effects impacting the direction of the campaign. Following each debate, including the vice-president candidates' debate, the NAES04 asked whether respondents had watched the debate, on which network or cable station they watched, which candidate did best, and did the candidates meet, exceed, or fall short of expectations. Among those who said they did not see the debate, the NAES04 asked whether they had heard or read about the debate and which candidate they thought did best based on what they heard or read.

Items about the Democratic and Republican conventions measured viewing of several speeches made at each convention. In addition, the NAES04 looked at whether respondents watched the conventions on national news programs, local news programs, or political talk shows. This information will help researchers understand where respondents were getting most of their coverage.

Also in 2004, after both conventions ended, an item was placed on the survey for a short period asking which convention was more accurate in portraying the other party. This item will give researchers a means to analyze perceptions each party convention creates for the other party. Panels were also conducted around the party conventions and Election Day. The CD-ROM contains complete details on these panel studies.

CAMPAIGN CONTACT

In the early primary and caucus states, like New Hampshire and Iowa, candidates and campaigns devote considerable amounts of their time and resources in the months leading up to those contests. Similar to the NAES00, the NAES04 was interested in trying to determine the importance of campaign contact in voters' opinions and choices. In New Hampshire, the only state where the NAES04 conducted a primary state oversample, the survey included a question about specific in-person contact with any of the candidates. In all states holding a Democratic primary or caucus before March 10, the NAES04 included questions about other types of campaign contact: general campaign event attendance, phone call from a campaign, direct mail, or e-mail. We focused not solely on communication from specific campaigns, but from interest groups as well.

POLITICAL DISCUSSION

The NAES includes a battery of items by which researchers can assess the degree of political engagement in the social environments in which respondents are situated. These questions measure political discussion with family and friends and with those who are not considered so intimate (coworkers and those online). In 2000, coworkers and those online were not considered separately in the questionnaire. This presents problems when trying to draw distinctions between the two groups. To remedy this, and to recognize the growth of online communities and general Internet access, the NAES04 asked separate questions gauging respondents' level of discussions with coworkers and those online.

In addition to measuring the frequency of political discussion, the NAES04 included questions measuring the general political nature of those discussions: National, state, or local politics. These questions appeared until mid-March 2004.

ORIENTATION TO GOVERNMENT

To help understand the political orientation of the respondents, the NAES asked their party identification and political ideology. The party identification questions included a measure of party strength; ideology was asked using a 5-point spectrum from very liberal to very conservative.

Orientation to government includes trust in government, cynicism, and political efficacy. Questions measured respondents' level of trust in the federal government, generally, and specifically in the branches of the federal government, and in state and local governments. Cynicism items included whether presidents and other political candidates, in general, keep their promises, and specifically in 2004, whether President Bush had kept the promises he made as a candidate. Another cynicism item asked whether presidents make decisions in the nation's best interests. Questions on efficacy included items measuring whether or not "people like me" have a say in what government does and whether or not politics is too complicated to understand. Respondents were also asked whether or not "we all" have a duty to be politically informed, and the importance, efficacy, and satisfaction of voting. In addition, the NAES04 contained a section measuring general political knowledge using questions from the Delli Carpini/Keeter knowledge battery (Delli Carpini and Keeter 1996). These were used as benchmarks against which campaign knowledge could be measured.

ASSESSMENT OF CANDIDATE CHANCES

Perceptions of which candidate is ahead can influence media coverage and voter attitudes, previous research in electoral campaigns has shown. In both the 2000 and 2004 NAES, the dynamic of the process by which candidates were deemed to be ahead, behind, or faltering was captured by two sets of questions. In 2004 an additional question set was added. The first set of questions, implemented during the primary season, asked respondents to rate on a 0 to 100 scale the chances of each candidate for gaining his party's nomination. This question was followed by a question asking the respondent to rate the chances that the candidate would defeat George W. Bush. In the period leading to and including the New Hampshire primary (October 7, 2003 through January 27, 2004), respondents were asked to rate their likelihood of voting for an unnamed Democrat versus George W. Bush. This method was used because most candidates were still relatively unknown to the voting public. After the New Hampshire primary on January 27, the question was changed to match potential Democratic candidates against Bush in a general election trial heat. Two candidates were randomly assigned to this series so that respondents were asked about two potential matchups. Only John Kerry, John Edwards, Howard Dean, and Wesley Clark were included in this group of Democrats. The others either had dropped out already or had poll numbers in the single digits. During the 2004 primaries, a third question asked if the media had determined a front-runner among the Democratic candidates.

VOTING BEHAVIOR

The practice of absentee and early balloting has increased significantly in the United States over the last thirty years. Absentee voting generally refers to the process of casting a ballot at a location other than a voting station on Election Day (Kenski Forthcoming-a). As each state has its own election procedures, absentee voting policies vary from state to state. Early voting generally refers to any procedure by which a voter may cast a ballot before the standard time of poll opening on Election Day (Kenski Forthcoming-b). While the term "early voting" is often used broadly to mean voting before Election Day, it is also used more specifically to refer to voting before Election Day at an election office or designated polling site. In some states, the designated polling sites have been placed in locations of convenience, such as supermarkets or shopping centers. NAES data collected during the two weeks following the election show that one in five general election voters in 2004 reported that they cast their ballots before Election Day—substantially more than in 2000 when approximately 14 percent of voters reported that they cast their ballots early.[4]

Because of the increasing prevalence of absentee and early voting, during the weeks before Election Day when absentee or early voting were options, respondents were asked whether or not they had already cast their ballots for the upcoming primary or general election at the time of the survey interview. The NAES questionnaire did not assume that voters wait until Election Day to cast their ballots. Consequently, when assessing vote preference using the NAES, researchers must recognize that the "vote intention" variable is not the only variable that should be taken into consideration. For students of election campaigns, state adoption of no-fault absentee and early voting practices is consequential because allowing citizens to vote before Election Day changes campaign dynamics. The dynamics of early balloting are explored further in Chapter 6.

In addition to voting behavior related to the current presidential election, NAES asked respondents about voting behavior in the most recent past presidential election (1996 for NAES00 and 2000 for NAES04). Further, NAES04 asked about voting behavior in the 2002 Congressional elections. These measures of past voting behavior will help researchers construct a more complete picture of the electorate.

HOUSE AND SENATE

In 2004, NAES focused primarily on the dynamics of the presidential election campaign and placed much less emphasis than NAES00[5] on the U.S. House and Senate contests. The coverage areas for the presidential contests were so great that there was little space for anything but the most basic House and Senate questions. The NAES04 included questions asking respondents to name their senator and rate their senator on the feeling thermometer scale, if that lawmaker was standing for reelection.

AFTER THE ELECTION

2000 was a unique year in the history of U.S. presidential elections. The election ended in uncertainty and ultimately reached the Supreme

Court before Al Gore conceded. The NAES00 continued throughout the entire postelection period of uncertainty, focusing many of its survey questions on the disputed outcome in Florida. In 2004, the outcome was clear by the day after Election Day. Bush's victory in Ohio gave him enough electoral votes for reelection. The NAES04 remained in the field for 14 days following the November 2 election, mostly to complete the sampling through the proper RCS methodology. The survey instrument generally remained the same during this time, except that the verb tenses in several questions were changed to reflect postelection wording, and questions were added to measure whether respondents felt Bush would do a better job than Kerry handling a variety of policy issue areas now that he had been reelected. In addition, the NAES04 included questions asking about actual vote, when the respondents made up their minds, if they believed their votes were counted fairly, and to rate the honesty of each campaign.

DEMOGRAPHICS

The demographic questions in the 2004 NAES are similar to the demographic questions asked in 2000 with some exceptions. In 2004, the questions on race and ethnicity were changed slightly. Questions about current and past military service were added to reflect the Iraq war and its impact on the campaign and to aid in the development of a separate military survey that the NAES conducted in September 2004. The NAES also grew in the number of questions relating to United States citizenship, adding questions on whether respondents were born in the U.S. and if not, how long they have been living in the country. The NAES added questions about firearm ownership, membership in the NRA, as well as a question about whether the respondent has a friend, colleague or family member who is gay or lesbian (to help in the analysis of civil union and marriage constitutional amendment questions). These questions appeared in the survey along with standard questions on gender, age, education, income, employment, marital status, and the presence of children in the household. Similar to most surveys, the demographic questions were asked at the end of the interview since these questions are typically more intrusive, thus minimizing the impact of a termination of the interview.

The Stand-Alone Studies

The 2000 and 2004 NAES include a number of stand-alone surveys related to the issues raised in the presidential campaign. These include state-specific election cross-section surveys, a survey of active military personnel and family members, and a survey conducted in the week leading up to the presidential inauguration in January 2005. These surveys are described below, briefly, because they contain some unique content features.

STATE-SPECIFIC PRE-PRESIDENTIAL PRIMARY ELECTION CROSS-SECTION STUDIES

During the presidential primary campaigns in 2000 and 2004, the national cross-section was supplemented by state-specific cross-section surveys conducted among residents of key primary states. Interviewing was conducted in the weeks before the states' presidential primary elections. In 2000, theses surveys were conducted in Iowa, Michigan, New Hampshire, South Carolina, the Super Tuesday states, and the Second Tuesday states. In 2000, the races were more competitive and involved primaries of both the Democratic and Republican parties. However, in 2004, the NAES included state supplemental interviews in New Hampshire only. Iowa was not included because caucus procedures differed greatly from the NAES telephone methodology, which is more comparable to a primary or general election. Super Tuesday states were not supplemented because after New Hampshire in 2004 because it became clear that John Kerry was the front-runner and heading for the nomination. The questions exclusive to New Hampshire in 2004 dealt with candidate endorsements, vote in the 2000 New Hampshire primary, and environmental issues specific to New Hampshire.

MILITARY PERSONNEL AND FAMILY SURVEY

From late September through early October 2004, NAES surveyed 656 adults who either had served on active duty between February and October or who were family members of those who served but were unavailable to be interviewed. Their responses can be compared to the responses of 2,436 adults polled nationally from September 27 through October 3. The sample for this separate stand-alone survey was culled from the national rolling cross-section study during the February through September sampling period. The military survey was a combination of many of the questions from the national cross-section and questions specific to the military experience, including the situation in Iraq. The survey did not ask the voting preference of the respondents. The military-specific questions included those that asked about the adequacy of the training and equipping of regular and National Guard/Reserve forces sent to Iraq and Afghanistan, the burden placed on National Guard and Reserve members and their families, reinstituting the draft, accountability in the Abu Ghraib prison abuse scandal, the impact of the media showing images of flag-draped coffins returning to Dover Air Force Base on respect for the troops, veteran health care issues, gays and lesbians in the military, gender issues, satisfaction with military life, and reasons for joining the military. Responses to some of the military questions can be compared to the national cross-section because the NAES04 included a limited number of the military questions on the national cross-section at the same time it was fielding the military survey.

PRE-INAUGURAL SURVEY

The final survey of the 2004 campaign conducted by NAES was the pre-inaugural survey conducted in January 2005 in the days leading to Bush's second inauguration.

This survey serves a final check on citizens' attitudes toward the president, what he has said he would accomplish, and the electoral process, in general. It is a shortened version of the national cross-section, containing many of the questions on policy issues, especially Iraq, evaluation of the president, voting behavior, media use, and political discussion.

Final Remarks

It must be noted that this chapter's description of the variable categories contained in all the NAES surveys are but brief snapshots. To see the full breadth of the 2000 and 2004 National Annenberg Election Surveys, researchers should use the codebook and search engine found on the CD-ROM.

Notes

1. Traits used in NAES00 included "honest," "inspiring," "cares about people like me," "knowledgeable," "provides strong leadership," and "hypocritical."

2. The Democratic candidates included in the trait evaluation were chosen because they had the highest voter preference poll numbers. As the candidates dropped out, the list was reduced accordingly.

3. Arizona, Arkansas, Delaware, Florida, Iowa, Maine, Michigan, Minnesota, Missouri, Nevada, New Hampshire, New Mexico, Ohio, Oregon, Pennsylvania, Washington, West Virginia, and Wisconsin.

4. These estimates were based on weighted data. The findings were based on interviews with 1,334 voting citizens conducted between November 3 and November 16, 2004. The comparable fourteen-day period in 2000 was November 8 through November 21, when 1,649 voting citizens were interviewed. For 2004, the margin of sampling error was plus or minus three percentage points, and for 2000 it was plus or minus two percentage points.

5. NAES00 included items that classified the congressional district and the type of race in that district. NAES00 also asked respondents to name in open ended fashion their representatives and senators as well as their senators' challengers if the senator was standing for reelection. NAES00 asked favorability using the "feeling thermometer" questions and vote intention if interviewed before the election, and actual vote if interviewed afterward.

References

Allison, Paul D. 2002. *Missing Data.* Thousand Oaks, Calif.: Sage.
Delli Carpini, Michael X., and Scott Keeter. 1996. *What Americans Know About Politics and Why It Matters.* New Haven, Conn.: Yale University Press.
Federal Communications Commission. 2004. *Trends in Telephone Service.* Retrieved May 10, 2005 from http://www.fcc.gov/Bureaus/Common_Carrier/Reports/FCC-State_Link/IAD/trend504.pdf.
Groves, Robert M. and Mick P. Couper. 1998. *Nonresponse in Household Interview Surveys.* New York: John Wiley.
Kenski, Kate. Forthcoming-a. "Absentee Voting." In Larry J. Sabato and Howard R. Ernst, eds, *Encyclopedia of American Parties and Elections.* New York: Facts on File.
Kenski, Kate. Forthcoming-b. "Early Voting." In Larry J. Sabato and Howard R. Ernst, eds., *Encyclopedia of American Parties and Elections.* New York: Facts on File.
Lohr, Sharon L. 1999. *Sampling: Design and Analysis.* New York: Duxbury Press.

Chapter 3
Research Designs Concepts for Understanding the Rolling Cross-Section Approach

KATE KENSKI

In this chapter and the next, we will introduce the reader to the rolling cross-sectional (RCS) design and illustrate the types of research that can be conducted with the 2000 National Annenberg Election Survey (NAES). These chapters assume reader familiarity with basic research methods and statistics.[1] However, we review several concepts that are important for analyzing the NAES. We then synthesize the RCS approach and compare it to two other observational research designs commonly used in the study of political campaigns: the repeated cross-sectional design and the panel design.

Basic Concepts in Research Design

Before we discuss the tradeoffs of different research designs, a review of some basic but important concepts is in order. These concepts are important for evaluating which type of design should be used in one's research. Our research should begin, of course, with a question or set of research questions that we want to answer. Sometimes research questions are *descriptive*. Their purpose is to describe the characteristics of a population. How prevalent is A in the population? How many adults in the United States listen to political talk radio? Other research questions are *associative* and deal with the relationships of variables. Is A associated with B? Are respondents' levels of education associated with their exposure to political information on the Internet? Many research questions deal with the *causal relationship* between variables. That is, does A affect or produce changes in B? Does newspaper reading increase respondents' levels of political knowledge about the presidential candidates?

We refer to the concepts of interest as *variables*. A *variable* is an entity that takes on two or more values. These values can be quantitative or qualitative. A *constant*, on the other hand, is an entity that has only one value. It does not vary. When conducting research, we often want to know how concepts relate to one other. Constants are not helpful in trying to figure out how concepts relate to each other. For example, we might have a research question about the relationship between gender and political participation. If we conduct a study in which we survey only women, we cannot answer questions about the relationship between gender and participation because gender in the study is a constant. In order to look at the relationship between gender and participation, we need to interview men as well so that we can compare men's responses to those made by women.

Researchers often identify variables in their studies as either *independent* or *dependent*. An independent variable refers to one that is thought to be the cause or predictor of another. A dependent variable refers to a variable that is the result or outcome. For example, we may ask: Does watching late night comedy increase one's cynicism about the political process? Here, watching late night comedy is hypothesized to produce an effect, increased cynicism. Late night comedy is the independent variable, and cynicism is the dependent variable.

In the social sciences, causal inferences (Does A cause B?) are usually made in probabilistic rather than deterministic terms. We do not restrict our interest only to those matters where A always causes B. We are interested in whether A tends to cause B or is likely to cause B. Unlike descriptive or associative inferences, the case for causality is often difficult to make. Researchers frequently look to John Stuart Mill's criteria for making causal inferences. "Mill held that causal inference depends on three factors: first, the cause has to precede the effect in time; second, the cause and effect have to be related; and third, other explanations of the cause-effect relationship have to be eliminated" (Cook and Campbell 1979, 18).

The first criterion in assessing causality is time. Does A precede B? Temporal sequencing of variables is not always readily apparent and is more evident in some cases than in others. For example, in answering the question, "Are women less knowledgeable about politics than men?" we can be certain that gender precedes political knowledge. It is unlikely that one's level of political knowledge will produce an effect on one's gender. In other situations, the temporal sequencing of variables is difficult to determine. Does political knowledge affect political participation? Or, does political participation affect political knowledge?

The second criterion is association. Is A associated with B? If two variables are not related to one another, then one cannot produce an effect on the other. The level of association between variables can be determined by analyzing how the variables covary. Variables are said to *covary* when the variation in one is related to the variation in the other. Results from cross-tabulations or correlations between two variables let us know how strongly if at all two variables are associated.

The third criterion, ruling out alternative explanations, is the most difficult to achieve. The list of alternative explanations can be endless. But some alternatives are more plausible than others, and it is to these that researchers devote most of their attention. Suppose that we hypothesize that A causes B, and we have met the criteria of temporal sequencing and association. A comes before B in time, and A and B are highly associated. Could there be another explanation, other than A causing B? One might be that a third variable, C, causes both A and B. Suppose C occurs before both A and B. Because C is causing both A and B, it makes it look as if A and B are related. In this situation, C is producing a spurious relationship between A and B. Ruling out alternative explanations involves eliminating potential *confounding variables*. Confounding variables are those that may obscure the relationship between the variables of interest in a given study.

While researchers studying a topic probably have a good sense of many of the potential confounding variables, it is possible that some variables have not been considered. There is rarely a final word in research. Since our knowledge of the world is constantly evolving, the cautious researcher will recognize that there are limitations to every study. It is unlikely that a scholar has thought of everything. No research strategy is perfect. But careful design can increase the likelihood that research will improve our understanding of the world.

Intervening variables help explain the mechanics of the causal relationship between two variables. The independent variable causes variation in the intervening variable, which in turn produces variation in the dependent one. For example, we might want to explore the relationship between respondents' sex and levels of political participation. Because political participation can be defined in different ways, we specify a particular type of participation that we are interested in, such as giving money to the campaigns of candidates. What is the relationship between gender (cW01) and donating money to candidates (cK22)? Does being female influence whether one gives money to political candidates? In the 2000 NAES data collected between October 6 and November 6 ($N = 4,390$), there is an association between gender and giving money to a presidential candidate. More men than women contributed money to presidential candidates (8.1% of men compared to 5.5% of women). This difference was statistically significant (chi-square = 11.537, df = 1, $p = .001$).

Is there something innate about women that makes them less likely to give to political campaigns? Or, are there other variables that might help us explicate the relationship? We know that men and women differ in their socioeconomic status. Men tend to make more money than women on average—a finding confirmed in the NAES. We might hypothesize that men give more money to political candidates because they have more disposable income than women. We can check this contention by looking at the correlation between gender and donating money while controlling for household income (cW28). If the relationship between gender and participation is no longer significant, then evidence suggests that being male affects giving money to presidential candidates because of income differentials between men and women. Results from the NAES support this claim. When controlling for income, the correlation between gender and giving money is not significant.

Making Valid Inferences

In order to gather data about the variables in which we are interested, we develop instruments to measure those variables. These measures are not the true concepts themselves but reflections of the concepts. *Operationalization* is the process by which we define the variable through our selection of an instrument. Spector (1981) warns: "Choice of instruments is as important as any step in an investigation, but too often little attention is given to instrumentation" (20). When analyzing secondary data, the choice is often not up to us. But we can still scrutinize whether the measures in a survey meet our research needs.

We create survey questions to capture the concepts as completely as possible. Often scholarly debates occur over whether or not the measures captured the concepts better than other measures that could have been used. If measures are to be useful, they must be reliable. The *reliability* of a measure is its ability to be replicated. If our survey instruments are inconsistent in the responses that they elicit, then they are of little use. A measure that gives us different results time after time is one that is not reliable and thus does not get at the essence of the concepts that we want to capture. Also, a measure that is not reliable is not going to be valid.

Validity is the ability to measure the essence of the concepts that we want to capture. A valid measure is one that does a good job of getting at the true meaning of our variable. It measures what we want to measure. The truth, of course, is always elusive to some extent. And while we are never sure that we have captured it in its entirety, we try to make sure that we are as close as possible. Cook and Campbell (1979) use the terms "*validity* and *invalidity* to refer to the best available approximation to the truth or falsity of propositions, including propositions about cause" (37).

The *content validity* of measures is crucial. Content validity is sometimes called face validity. On their face, do the measures used in the study seem to measure the concepts in which we are interested? Wording questions properly enhances the validity of one's study.[2]

Problems can occur when questions are not worded consistently across respondents. If interviewers, for example, stray from the survey scripts and change the wording of the questions when they are interviewing different people, then reliability of the responses can be undercut. Problems can also occur when the wording of questions is vague. When the meaning of words is ambiguous, respondents can interpret the meaning of the question in multiple ways. Ambiguous wording in a question challenges the validity of the question because the respondents may have a different idea in mind from the one that researcher wanted to test. For example, for a brief period, the 2000 NAES included a question that was supposed to capture whether people felt it was their civic duty to vote. Respondents were asked: "When you vote do you usually get a feeling of satisfaction from it, or do you only do it because it's your duty?" (cR50). What is the content validity problem with this question? It is unclear whether people make a clear distinction between duty and satisfaction. Must these options be mutually exclusive? Because those who vote because they feel it is their duty might in turn feel satisfied from performing that duty, arguments could be made that the validity of this item is questionable.

Technical jargon should be avoided in the question wording, especially when conducting research on a large or diverse population. Question wording should be simple so that it can be understood by a wide variety of potential survey participants from different educational and cultural backgrounds. Researchers should pay attention to how questions are framed. The wording should be as unbiased as possible, meaning that it does not lead the respondent toward a particular answer.

Even the ordering of questions should be considered before a survey is put into the field. The ordering of questions should be randomized so that it does not affect the outcome of the responses. When possible, consideration should be given to the ordering of responses within questions as well. For example, if one candidate's name always comes before another's, does the ordering benefit or penalize any of the candidates? The NAES randomized the order of several questions to avoid problems that a fixed order might produce.

Sometimes there are socially desirable answers to particular questions. Efforts should be made to minimize social desirability bias. For example, people know that voting is a socially desirable activity. Thus, when asked whether they have voted, many respondents say they have when in fact they may not have. To minimize the social desirability bias about voting, the NAES voting question let respondents know that many people do not get a chance to vote. NAES 2000 respondents were asked: "In talking with people about politics and elections, we often find that they do not get a chance to vote. Did you happen to vote in the November election?" (cR34). Even with the preface that many people do not get a chance to vote, respondents are still likely to say that they have voted when they have not. Although the Federal Election Commission reports that 51.3 percent of the voting age population in the United States voted in the 2000 general election, 75.3 percent of NAES respondents interviewed between November 8 and November 22 said that they had voted in the general election ($N = 2,293$).

Much survey research involves the use of interviewers. Interviewers should be trained before conducting interviews to ensure that they do not influence the responses that the survey participants give. "When interviewers are used, it is important to avoid having them influence the answers respondent[s] give, and at the same time to maximize the accuracy with which questions are answered" (Fowler 1993, 6).

There is often a gap between a measure and the true meaning of a concept that the measure is attempting to represent. In short, there is often some error in our measurements. Sometimes the error is random, meaning that it does not occur in a systematic way. When *random error* occurs, any single response is as likely to be higher than the truth as to be lower. For example, the NAES asked respondents how many days in the past week they watched late night comedy shows, such as David Letterman or Jay Leno (cE10). Looking at the 2000 national cross-sectional data from October 3 to November 6 ($N = 10,808$), respondents watched late night comedy an average of 0.65 days per week (SD = 1.45).[3] Many (76.8%) reported that they had not watched late-night comedy in the past week. If the errors in the survey participants' responses were random, the respondents would be as likely to overreport as to underreport how much they actually watched late night comedy shows. Random errors are a concern because they can affect the precision of our estimates. *Bias* is another type of error, but one that is much harder to deal with. When something is biased, it systematically throws off our estimates. When this occurs, it is difficult to adjust because we are never sure about the exact magnitude of the bias.

When conducting research that involves causal inferences, researchers should be concerned with different types of validity. Cook and Campbell (1979) identify four types: construct, external, statistical conclusion, and internal. These types of validity influence our confidence in making causal inferences. Some of the specific threats to validity that will be mentioned fall into more than one of these four categories. These categories are used to give readers a general overview of potential threats to the validity of their studies.

External validity is the ability to generalize a study to the population that it was intended to reflect. When conducting surveys, we frequently use randomization so that we can generalize our findings. Population parameters are the characteristics of the population that we want to study. We often want to ask questions about populations that are large. Most of the time, it is simply not possible to interview everyone in the population as is done when a *census* is taken. Therefore, we sample members of the population that we wish to study.

A *sample* is a subset of a population. There are different ways to sample members from a population. Some sample methods are better than others when trying to generalize from a sample to a population. The NAES samples are *random samples* of adults in the United States, meaning that the samples are random subsets of the population of adults in the United States. According to Fowler (1993),

The key to good sampling is finding a way to give all (or nearly all) population members the same (or a known) chance of being sampled, and to use probability methods for choosing the sample. Early surveys and polls often relied on samples of convenience or on sampling from lists that excluded significant portions of the population. These did not provide reliable, credible figures. (4)

In any research design, there are always limitations or threats to making valid inferences. The generalizability of a study depends in part on the *sample frame*. The sample frame is the list of members from a population who have a chance of being selected into the sample. The NAES was conducted using random digit dialing (RDD). Households were randomly selected. Procedures were established for randomly selecting adults from the households for interviews. The sample frame consisted of individuals who were living in households that had telephones. Individuals without telephones were not interviewed. "Nationally, this is about 5% of the households; in some areas, particularly central cities or rural areas, the rate of omission may be greater than that" (Fowler 1993, 24). This puts a constraint on the population to which we can generalize.

Selecting a sampling procedure that gives each person in the population a known chance of being interviewed is important for obtaining a representative sample of the population. Once a sample frame has been selected, an equally important issue is nonresponse. Having a good sampling strategy does not by itself justify claiming that the sample is representative of the population to which we want to generalize. Generalizations from our data can be sabotaged by *nonresponse bias*. Nonresponse bias occurs when individuals who have been selected for interviews do not answer the survey and differ from those individuals who do answer it. Researchers typically report response rates or cooperation rates with their studies. Response rates usually refer to the number of people interviewed divided by the number of people sampled. Cooperation rates refer to the proportion of people who were interviewed from people who were contacted. There are different formulas for response and cooperation rates that take into account partial and completed interviews.[4] High response and cooperation rates are desirable. If the response rate of a study is high, it is often assumed that nonresponse bias is less likely to be a problem. This assumption, however, can be faulty. Some incentives that increase response rates also increase bias (see Merkle, Edelman, Dykeman, and Brogan 1998, cited in Blumenthal 2005).

Researchers sometimes try to compensate for these limitations by weighting the data. "Whenever an identifiable group is selected at a different rate from others, weights are needed so that oversampled people are not overrepresented in the sample statistics" (Fowler 1993, 25). If a study underrepresents a segment of the population, weights can be constructed to give cases from the underrepresented segment more weight. While weights may be important when conducting descriptive analyses of populations, there is disagreement over whether these weights are necessary when trying to assess the relationship between variables. There is also debate over how such weights should be constructed. Should weights be based solely on demographic characteristics? Should they be based on how many telephone lines, including cell phones, a respondent has in his or her household? After all, a respondent who lives in a household with multiple telephone lines has a greater chance of being selected into the survey. Should researchers interested in vote choice weight the data by party identification? Some researchers claim that party identification is a stable characteristic, while others argue that party identification is an attitudinal concept that has the potential to fluctuate over the course of a campaign. The issue of weighting is an important one and should be considered by the researcher before she conducts data analysis. The examples used in this book, however, are created from unweighted data so that the reader can replicate them with little difficulty.

Statistical conclusion validity deals with the ability of the study to make conclusions about the covariation of the variables. Were there enough cases in the study to detect an effect that one hypothesized? This is the issue of statistical power. Zaller (2002) argues that power analyses are missing from many published works. He states: "To judge from most published work, whatever survey they are analyzing is plenty big enough to answer the question they are asking. If they get a null result, the normal assumption is that the hypothesis under investigation is weak or wrong" (298). The size of a sample affects the precision of the estimates that can be drawn from it. As sample size increases, the sampling error around estimates decreases. Detecting large effects is easier than detecting small ones. If the effect that one wishes to detect is likely to be small, then one may have to increase the sample size of the study. If there is a lot of variation in the population characteristics that one wishes to detect, then bigger samples will be needed.

The validity of our assertion that one variable causes another depends on whether or not these variables covary. Assuming that one has enough power to detect the effects, is there evidence to suggest that the variation in one variable is related to the variation in another? Cook and Campbell (1979) note:

In many studies, a decision about covariation is made by comparing the degree of covariation and random error observed in the sample data to an a priori specified risk of being wrong in concluding that there is covariation. This risk is specified as a probability level (usually 5%), and we speak of setting α at .05. (40)

The statistical conclusion validity is further enhanced when the magnitude of the variation is large.

Construct validity deals with issues of confounding. Are we appropriately describing or naming the cause of a presumed effect? Some of the issues around question wordings discussed earlier could be considered construct validity problems. The Hawthorne effect is an example of a construct validity problem. This effect occurs when people in a study change their attitudes or behavior because they feel important or special for taking part in the study. "[T]he mere knowledge that one is in a study may affect behavior even if observations are not being made" (Spector 1981, 27). In short, it is not the event or treatment that has brought about the change but some other process instead. Researchers may not be aware of the intervening process that is producing the effect.

Internal validity is the truthfulness of a claim that one variable causes another. Assuming that we have determined that two variables are associated, is there enough evidence in our data to suggest that A produces an effect on B? Harkening back to Mill's criteria for supporting causal inferences, have we ruled out possible alternative explanations? There are many ways that the internal validity of our causal assertions can be threatened. We will discuss just a few of them here.[5]

One threat to internal validity is history. History refers to events that take place during our study that happen at the same time as our purported causes. In searching for campaign effects, researchers often want to see if campaign events produce change in voters' opinions about the candidates. Assuming that effects are found, history hinders our ability to attribute the changes to the campaign events if other events take place during the same time period. Because the opinion changes may have been caused by other events, it is difficult to make solid claims that the campaign events produced the difference in opinions.

In the course of a study, researchers sometimes change the wording of questions. When the wording of questions changes during a study and a change in respondent answers is observed, it is difficult to know whether the change occurred because of some event or because the wording of the questions shifted. This threat to internal validity is also a threat to the construct validity of the measures.

Another threat to internal validity is maturation. "This is a threat when an observed effect might be due to the respondent's growing older, wiser, stronger, more experienced, and the like between the pre-test and posttest and when this maturation is not the treatment of research interest" (Cook and Campbell 1979, 52). When the pretest and posttest are conducted over a short period of time, it is unlikely that maturation will pose a great threat to the internal validity of the study.

The internal validity of a study can be hurt by selection bias. Selection bias occurs when the people in groups differ. For example, we might want to test whether watching the presidential debates enhanced people's scores on the political knowledge items about the issue positions of the presidential candidates. We could compare those people who said that they watched the debates to those who did not. However, debate watchers may differ from non-watchers. People who watch debates are likely to be older, more partisan, and more educated than their counter-parts (Kenski and Stroud 2005). This creates a selection bias problem.

A related selection bias in panel studies is differential subject loss. Panel studies often experience some attrition in study participation. Differential subject loss occurs when the people who drop out of the study are different from those who remain. When effects are observed, we do not know if they would have occurred if the people who dropped out of the study had remained in it.

In studies where the same individuals are interviewed over time and are given the same questions, testing effects may occur. Repeated testing allows respondents to become familiar with the questions. This may affect their performance on the items.

A related problem is interaction of testing and treatment. This problem occurs when the event that we supposed would affect members of the population has an effect on study participants because they took the pretest. For example, the NAES includes several knowledge questions about the issue positions of the presidential candidates. Some respondents were interviewed more than once. The initial interview may have made the respondents more sensitive to information about particular issue positions. If we observe that the accuracy of their responses to these questions has improved, we will not know whether the improvement is attributable to some campaign event, to their familiarity with the questionnaire, or to an interaction of having taken the pretest and being influenced by the campaign event because of it. To the extent that this problem hampers the generalizability of the effect, interaction of testing and treatment may be considered an external validity concern. To compensate, the NAES includes the national RCS data, which can be used as a control for the panel data.

To maximize the validity of a study, researchers should take into account the various threats to which particular research designs are more vulnerable. When conducting surveys, Fowler (1993) contends that researchers should pay attention to three things: (1) the sampling strategy, (2) questionnaire writing, and (3) interviewing techniques. In order for research to be successful, careful planning is required at many levels.

Research Designs That Capture Change

Different designs have been employed to explore the issue of whether or not campaigns produce effects. In any type of research, the causal direction of the variables of interest can be subject to debate. Some research designs, however, make stronger cases for the hypothesized relationship of variables than do others.

The notion of capturing campaign effects suggests that the researcher will study some phenomenon at a minimum of two points in time. After all, in order to see change and attribute it to some event, one has to know what the state of something was prior to the event that is thought to have caused the change.

It is not always possible to collect data over time. A *cross-section* refers to data that have been collected at a single point in time. Some research methods can be used to test inferences about causality from cross-sectional data. While the case for the association between two variables can be made from cross-sectional data, inferences about causality are much harder to make since we are often not sure which variable preceded the other. The strength of the causal inferences made from a single cross-section design is much weaker than the strength of inferences made from data that have been collected over two or more time points.

The study of effects can be performed through experimental as well as non-experimental or observational research designs. Experimental research designs are those studies in which the researcher manipulates the stimuli that the study participants receive. This manipulation is called the treatment and is the independent variable of the study. "Experimental research is explanatory in nature: experiments are conducted primarily to test hypotheses, not to describe some large population or to explore previously uncharted social patterns" (Schutt 1996, 220).

Observational studies, in contrast, are those in which the researcher does not manipulate or intrude upon an environment. When one wants to generalize about a large population, nonexperimental approaches are often preferred. Observational studies, however, have their drawbacks. Because data collected in the field in an observational study are not manipulated, inferring causality is challenging. "For the most part, experimental studies are considered to be more powerful than nonexperimental designs in uncovering causal relationships among variables. This is due to the fact that through control and randomization, potential confounding effects can be removed from a study" (Spector 1981, 20). Through the collection of observational data over time, researchers can strengthen their case that one variable has produced an effect on another.

In analyzing observational data, we often try to control for extraneous factors that might hide the relationships of the variables in which we are interested. But as previously discussed, there are many potential threats to the validity of causal inferences. It is difficult, if not impossible, to control for everything. Experiments have the benefit of randomly assigning study participants to treatments. Assuming that the randomization has worked and the groups are comparable in every way other than the treatment given, when effects are found, they can be attributed to the manipulation. In studying campaign effects, however, it may be difficult to create realistic manipulations. While effects may be witnessed in the laboratory, the setting is often unnatural, hindering the researcher's ability to generalize the effects to the larger population.

In studying campaigns, most of the time we are not merely interested in whether it is possible to produce effects. We want to know whether actual events produced effects on potential voters. The rest of the chapter is devoted to comparing the rolling cross-section design to two commonly used longitudinal designs that are used in observational studies: the repeated cross-sectional design and the panel design.

The *repeated cross-sectional design* is one in which the data have been collected at two or more points in time. The collected data are different samples drawn from the same population. The repeated cross-sectional design is "appropriate when the goal is to determine whether a population has changed over time" (Schutt 1996, 133).

In the *panel design*, the same individuals are interviewed at two or more points. This design allows researchers to track changes in individuals over time. In this design, measures on the pretest are compared to the measures on the posttest to see if significant differences appear. When differences are found, it is often assumed that the observed change was produced by the event or treatment that happened between the panels.

The NAES includes several panel datasets. During the primary season in 2000, panel studies were conducted around the Iowa caucuses, the New Hampshire primary, the South Carolina Republican primary, the Michigan primary, and the Super Tuesday primaries. During the general election campaign, panels were placed around important campaign events including the Republican convention, the Democratic convention, and the presidential debates. In 2000, panels were placed around each of the presidential debates. In 2004, a single panel was placed before and after the debates. Panel studies were also conducted around the general election; the same respondents were interviewed before and after the general elections in both 2000 and 2004.

While the panel design has the capacity to capture change at two or more time points, high costs often prohibit tracking the same individuals several times across the course of an election. Not only can this approach be expensive, but repeated interviewing of the same study respondents can produce participation fatigue and attrition. Repeated cross-sections do not cause the same levels of fatigue as do panel designs. In both designs, researchers have to plan when the waves of data collection will take place. They must have a good sense of when potentially consequential campaigns events are likely to happen.

Many election studies have not been designed to capture campaign dynamics. Even when studies manage to conduct interviews at two time points, this collection is not sufficient to capture the ebb and flow of political campaigns. Holbrook (1996) observes:

One of the problems with studying campaign effects at the individual-level is that most public opinion surveys are not designed with this purpose in mind. The main data source used by students of elections, the biennial National Election Study (NES), is primarily designed to study the effect of partisanship, issues, and personalities on voting behavior. The primary drawback to the NES is that it lacks a dynamic component that would allow for a clear analysis of how campaign events produce changes in political attitudes. In addition, the NES includes very few survey items that are specifically intended to capture the effects of political campaigns. (33–34)

While data collected at two time points may be able to demonstrate change in a population or change in individuals, it is difficult to attribute these changes to any single event.

The *rolling cross-section design* (RCS) allows researchers to track dynamics in a population. The RCS "is a design that facilitates detailed exploration of campaign dynamics. Its essence is to take a one-shot cross-section and distribute interviewing in a controlled way over time" (Johnston and Brady 2002, 283). Although rolling cross-section design is referred to as a distinct approach in this chapter, it is actually a special case of the repeated cross-section design. The RCS design involves taking a series of cross-sections over a period of time. Each cross-section is equally spaced across the time period of interest. In the NAES, cross-sections took place each day. What makes the rolling cross-section unique is the sampling protocol used to ensure that each cross-section is truly random. The details of this protocol and why it works will be explained in Chapter 4. Because each cross-section is random, researchers can aggregate the data to create time series.

The RCS approach is relatively new. It was first used in the 1984 American National Election Study (ANES) and again in an ANES 1988 study of the Super Tuesday primaries. This design was adopted for the Canadian Election Study (CES) in 1988. While the 1984 ANES used weekly cross-sections, the 1988 CES was the first to employ a daily cross-section design.[6]

Figures 3.1, 3.2, and 3.3 illustrate the types of dynamics that can be analyzed by tracking public opinion across the course of an election. In 2000, respondents were asked whether the federal government should spend more money on Social Security benefits, the same as now, less, or no money at all (cBC01). Figure 3.1 shows the percentage of respondents surveyed between July 15 and November 6, 2000 who said they thought the government should spend more money on Social Security. Using a 7-day moving average to smooth out some of the sampling variation, this figure shows that beginning the second week of October, support for increasing government spending on Social Security began to decrease somewhat. Nevertheless, a majority of respondents across this time period supported an increase in Social Security spending.

Figure 3.2 tracks the electorate's understanding of the presidential candidates' positions on investing Social Security contributions in the stock market (cBC07, cBC08). Respondents were asked whether the candidates favored allowing workers to invest some of their Social Security contributions in the stock market. Bush favored the position, while Gore opposed it. Figure 3.2 shows that the percentages of adults answering the candidate issue positions on Social Security correctly increased across the course of the general election.

The situation in Iraq played a large role in the 2004 presidential campaign. Over the course of the entire 2004 RCS, respondents were asked:

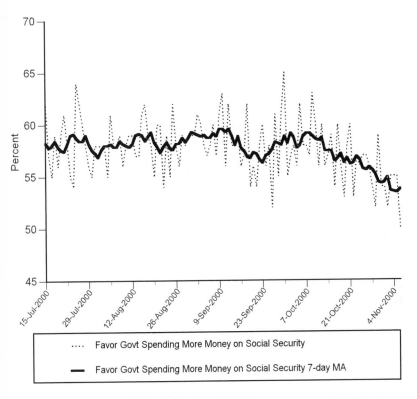

Figure 3.1. Percentage of U.S. adults from July 15 to November 6, 2000 stating that the federal government should spend more money on Social Security benefits (MA, moving average).

"All in all, do you think the situation in Iraq was worth going to war over, or not?" (cCD21). Figure 3.3 illustrates how opinions about Iraq changed between October 21, 2003 and November 1, 2004 among U.S. adults. Feelings toward U.S. involvement in Iraq improved at the end of November 2003 and through the third week of December. Saddam Hussein was captured by U.S. forces on December 13, 2003. But toward the end of December and through the middle of June 2004, the percentage of respondents saying that our involvement in Iraq was worth it declined steadily. A few days before the Democratic national convention, opinions toward Iraq improved. This improvement continued through Election Day.

Tracking the effects of campaigns across time is a function of the study design. Capturing campaign dynamics requires information about a

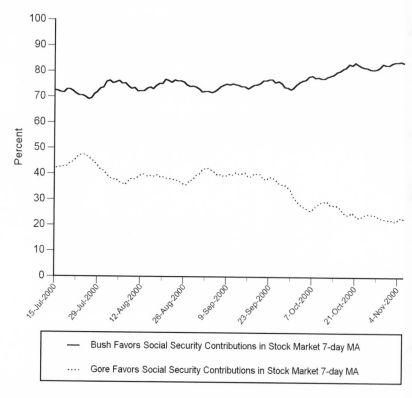

Figure 3.2. Percentage of U.S. adults from July 15 to November 6, 2000 stating that Bush and Gore favor allowing workers to invest Social Security contributions in stock market (MA, moving average).

population across a number of time periods. In the next section, we will compare the RCS design to others commonly used to ascertain campaign effects.

The RCS Approach and the Repeated Cross-Sectional Design

The RCS and repeated cross-sectional designs are similar. Both of these designs allow researchers to generalize about large populations when appropriate sampling strategies have been used. Generalizations made from the RCS approach and repeated cross-sectional designs are restricted to the population level. Some generalizations can also be made about subgroups within the population, assuming that the sample sizes are large enough. Because these designs do not track the same individu-

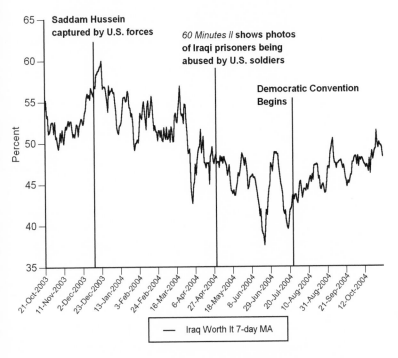

Figure 3.3. Percentage of U.S. adults from October 21, 2003 to November 1, 2004 stating that Iraq was worth it (MA, moving average).

als over time, researchers cannot test hypotheses about individual-level changes.

The RCS approach is essentially a specific type of repeated cross-section design. Repeated cross-sections are used to identify changes in a population between two or more points in time. The repeated cross-sectional design itself does not specify how far apart in time the waves of cross-sections should be conducted. The timing and frequency of the cross-sections are up to the researcher.

In campaign research, repeated cross-sections are usually scheduled before and after an event takes place so that the researcher can argue that the event produced some change in the population under study. Each cross-section is composed of individuals randomly selected from the population. When a *single* cross-sectional study takes place over the course of several days, interviews completed at the beginning of the interviewing process may not be comparable to those completed toward the end of the process. When a single cross-section is being conducted, a list of individuals randomly selected from the population is drawn. The researchers contact individuals on the list throughout the course of the study. Some individuals will respond to the researchers' interview request quickly. Others are harder to reach and will have to be contacted several times before they are interviewed. Because individuals who answer the survey immediately upon being contacted may differ from those who are interviewed only after repeated contact, time within the single cross-section may be related to specific characteristics of the survey respondents.

The rolling cross-sectional design, on the other hand, requires that interviews take place on a set schedule across the time period of interest. The unit of this schedule can vary from study to study. For any particular study, the schedule must remain constant. The NAES was run on a daily release schedule. Rather than working from a single list of randomly selected members of the population, several lists are generated and are released into the field at specified intervals (daily for the NAES) so that the date of the interview is a random event. The smaller the unit of the release schedule, the more sensitive the study is to changes in the environment, assuming that the sample size is large enough. Because of the nature of political campaigns, using the day as the unit of the release schedule makes sense. Many things happen in the news environment daily.

Researchers who rely on repeated cross-section designs may miss important campaign events depending when the cross-sections have been conducted. If a lot of time passes between the repeated cross-sections, it may be difficult to attribute any effects to a specific event.

Because the rolling cross-sectional surveys are in the field for a long and consistent period of time during campaigns and each individual cross-section is random, the data generated from this design can be grouped into larger cross-sections if desired. For those researchers who want to compare the scores of individuals at one period with the scores of other individuals in the population at another period, data from the time points of interest can be grouped and compared. Before conducting analyses on the primary variables of interest, however, the newly constructed cross-sections should be compared to make sure that the demographic variables are comparable.

To demonstrate using the NAES data as repeated cross-sections, the overall evaluations of Al Gore and George Bush were compared before and after the first presidential debate in 2000. For those interested in campaign events, the first presidential debate is a likely focus for a repeated cross-sectional study. The first presidential debate was on October 3. Data collected five days prior to the debate ($N = 1,599$) are compared with data collected 5 days after the debate ($N = 1,511$). To ensure that these cross-sections were comparable on sociodemographic variables, proportions tests and *t*-tests were performed comparing them on gender (cW01), age (cW02), and educational (cW06) composition. No significant differences were found on these variables.

NAES respondents were asked to give overall evaluations of the presidential candidates. These evaluations are sometimes called feeling thermometer ratings. Respondents were asked:

For each of the following people in politics, please tell me if your opinion is favorable or unfavorable using a scale from 0 to 100. Zero means very unfavorable, and 100 means very favorable. Fifty means you do not feel favorable or unfavorable. If you don't know enough about the person to rate him or her, just tell me and we will move to the next one.

Respondents were then asked to evaluate Gore (cA11) and Bush (cA01). Their responses were used to create a new variable based on the difference between these evaluations. This variable is called "Gore minus Bush." When Gore's evaluation is higher than Bush's evaluation, the variable is positive. When Bush is performing better, it is negative. Did the scores on this variable before the debate differ significantly from scores given after the debate? In the five days prior to the debate, the average difference between respondents' Gore and Bush scores was -2.68 ($N = 1,514$). The average "Gore minus Bush" score was -2.20 in the five days after the debate ($N = 1,440$). An independent samples t-test revealed that the difference in the ratings between these two time periods was not statistically significant.

A look at a time series of this variable a few weeks prior to the first presidential debate to a few weeks after the third presidential debate gives a better understanding of the difference between Gore and Bush's evaluations. While the only conclusion that can be reached from the repeated cross-section approach is that there was no difference between them, the RCS approach shows that Gore's evaluations began to fall in mid-September. Around the third week of September, respondents overall gave Bush higher evaluations than Gore. Around the third debate, the difference between Bush and Gore's evaluations grew, with Bush outperforming Gore. After the third debate, Gore's rating began to rise (see Figure 3.4).

The disadvantages of the RCS approach compared to a simpler repeated cross-sectional design are that it requires more planning in the sampling scheme and it costs more than conducting a few cross-sections. The major advantage of the RCS approach compared to a repeated cross-sectional design that only contains a few waves of data is that the RCS approach is more likely to capture changes when they are not necessarily expected.

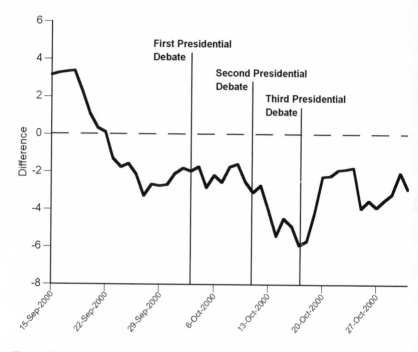

Figure 3.4. Gore minus Bush feeling thermometer evaluations from September 15 to October 31, 2000 (5-day moving average).

The RCS Approach and Panel Designs

The RCS approach and panel designs share the goal of trying to capture changes. The nature of the designs, however, allows different types of generalization to be made. While data collected with the RCS and repeated cross-sectional designs can tell us whether a population has changed over time, data collected with panel designs can tell us whether individuals have done so. There are often times when we would like to argue that group-level data tell us something about individuals' behavior. Making inferences about an individual-level process from group-level data, however, is problematic. Researchers who make inferences about an individual-level process from group data commit what is called an *ecological fallacy*.[7] Panel designs have an advantage over the RCS and repeated cross-sectional designs if the purpose of the research is to monitor changes within individuals. Generalizations should not be made about individual processes when using RCS and repeated cross-sections.

The internal validity threat of history is always a concern to designs that track changes over time. When we observe changes in individuals or in populations, we can never be absolutely certain that a particular event produced the effects. Because the RCS design gives us a wider view of the campaign, we can make stronger claims about when changes occurred. Theoretically, the panel design could also be implemented with the same rigor across the course of the campaign. But in practice, the cost of such an endeavor would be prohibitive. "Keeping track of panel members is expensive, and the likelihood of subject attrition is high. In addition, panel members who are interviewed frequently may tire of the process, which is called 'subject fatigue'" (Schutt 1996, 134).

Because the NAES panels are placed at only two points in time, they can only tell us whether individual changes occurred. They cannot tell us whether the changes were in the process of happening prior to the events around which the panels were placed. "The most obvious shortcoming of this design is that one cannot be certain that some factor or event other than the treatment was responsible for the posttest change" (Spector 1981, 29).

Using the NAES panel data collected around the first presidential debate in 2000, the differences in respondents' evaluations of Gore's honesty can be compared at the individual level. Respondents in this panel were initially interviewed between September 21 and October 2. The postdebate followup interview took place between October 4 and October 10. Looking again at the first presidential debate, the trait ratings of Gore's honesty are analyzed. Respondents were asked to evaluate the presidential candidates on a series of traits through questions, such as "Does the word 'honest' describe Al Gore extremely well, quite well, not too well or not well at all?" (cA13, rA13). Answers were recoded so that "extremely well" and "quite well" responses were grouped together and compared to "not too well" and "not well at all" responses. A proportion comparison test of Gore's honesty ratings revealed that respondents lowered their ratings of Gore from the first panel wave to the second ($N = 1,424$). About 55.6 percent of respondents in the predebate panel said that "honest" described Gore well compared to 51.3 percent in the postdebate panel. This 4.3 percent difference was significant with $p < .01$. If the only data that we collected were panel data, we might have concluded that the first presidential debate had lowered public opinion about Gore's honesty.

How does using the RCS data enhance our understanding of the effects of the first presidential debate? An advantage of the RCS design is that it allows researchers to construct a time series to get a stronger sense of where public opinion was prior to the event. "The advantage of the time series is that one can see the direction in which trends were heading at the time of intervention or treatment. A treatment might inhibit or stop a trend which would not be reflected in a single pretest-posttest comparison" (Spector 1981, 31). Figure 3.5 tracks the percent-

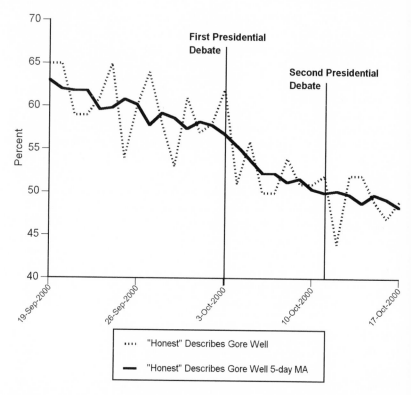

Figure 3.5. Percentage of U.S. adults from September 19 to October 17, 2000 who said "honest" describes Gore very well or extremely well (MA, moving average).

age of respondents who say that "honest" describes Al Gore well. This graph shows that opinions about Gore's honesty were on the decline well before either the first or second presidential debate took place. We cannot conclude that the first presidential debate had no effect on individual-level processes. Because the RCS presents evidence to suggest that the changes in the population were already in motion, however, the claim that the debate caused individuals to lower their opinions about Gore's honesty is weakened.

"Endogenous change is a major problem with before-and-after designs. In panel designs with a single pretest and posttest, any change may be due to testing, maturation, or regression" (Schutt 1996, 245). In an election study in which the panels are conducted over a short period of time, the likelihood of maturation being a threat to internal validity is small.

Testing effects, however, may occur with panel designs. As mentioned earlier, panel designs may sensitize survey participations to the concepts being explored in the survey. Sometimes events may affect survey respondents because the respondents have become sensitized by the pretest questions, creating a testing and treatment interaction. When this problem occurs, the generalizability of our study is stunted. Panel designs do not require having a post-event comparison group that has not received the pretest. Such comparison groups are often a good idea. Because observed changes may be attributed to respondents having been asked questions prior to an event, a comparison group that has not received the pretest and therefore could not have been affected by the pre-event interview is useful. Testing effects from the panels can be explored with the NAES panels by using the national cross-section as a group that did not get the initial set of questions. Before conducting such tests, however, researchers should make sure that the national cross-section respondents are similar on a wide variety of characteristics to those in the panel studies.

Panel attrition is another potential drawback to the panel design. When respondents drop out of a study, the generalizability of the study is diminished if the individuals who drop out are different from those individuals who remain. When we compare the demographics of the first presidential debate panel to that of the national cross-section interviewed at the same time as the debate panel pretest (September 21 to October 2) in 2000, we find that the RCS and panel are statistically equivalent on average household income (cW28) and proportions of females (cW01) and blacks (cW03). Participants in the panel, however, are more likely to report being older (cW02), married (cW08), educated (cW06), and interested in politics (cK01).

When studying the campaign dynamics, one potential shortcoming of the panel approach is that researchers often fail to anticipate important events before they occur. Panels can be placed around known events such as conventions and debates. But if unanticipated events occur, the researcher is out of luck. Some campaign events happened without being forecast.

Conclusion

No research design is flawless. There are always potential threats to the validity of one's research. Each design comes with its own set of constraints. Before selecting a research design, the tradeoffs of the various designs should be considered. Understanding the level of analysis to which one wants to make causal inferences is important. "The units of analysis for a study represent the level of social life on which the research question is focused, such as individuals, groups, towns, or nations. We do not fully understand the variables in a study until we know what units of analysis they refer to" (Schutt 1996, 88). If researchers wish to make inferences about individual-level causal processes, then panel designs should be employed. While the most innovative feature of the NAES is its rolling cross-sectional data, many panels are also contained within the study for those wishing to study individual-level changes.

Capturing campaign dynamics requires a research design that tracks members of the population across the course of the campaign. Presidential candidates create and participate in various campaign events through the campaign season. Campaigns generate advertising and direct mail that target members of the electorate at different times throughout the course of the campaign. News about the candidates is generated every day. While simple repeated cross-sectional designs and the panel designs can capture change, the RCS approach offers researchers data over a longer period of time, giving researchers a wider context in which to understand their results.

Holbrook (1996) notes, "Understanding the effect of any process is difficult if the focus is only on what comes out at the end of the process. Only by expanding the analysis to include studying the dynamics of public opinion during the campaign period can one gain an appreciation for the effect of the campaign" (46). This is precisely the goal of the National Annenberg Election Survey.

Notes

1. Individuals who have not taken an introductory research methods course should consult texts such as Babbie (1995), Cook and Campbell (1979), Schutt (1996), and/or Spector (1981).

2. For more information about the wording of questions, see Sudman and Bradburn (1982).

3. The data used in this example are unweighted. Before making a generalization about the viewing habits of adults in the United States, researchers may want to consider weighting the data.

4. The American Association for Public Opinion Research's *Standard Definitions* should be consulted for more information about response and cooperation rates. This information can be found on the AAPOR website: www.aapor.org

5. Cook and Campbell (1979) provide detailed explanations and examples of different types of threats to the validity.

6. For more information about this important study, see Johnston, Blais, Brady, and Crête (1992).

7. For more information about ecological inferences, see Achen and Shively (1995), King (1997), and Langbein and Lichtman (1978).

References

Achen, Christopher H. and W. Phillips Shively. 1995. *Cross-Level Inference*. Chicago: University of Chicago Press.

American Association for Public Opinion Research. 2000. *Standard Definitions: Final Dispositions of Case Codes and Outcome Rates for Surveys*. Ann Arbor, Mich.: AAPOR.

Babbie, Earl. 1995. *The Practice of Social Research* 7th ed. Belmont, Calif.: Wadsworth.

Cook, Thomas D. and Donald T. Campbell. 1979. *Quasi-Experimentation: Design and Analysis Issues for Field Settings*. Boston: Houghton Mifflin.

Blumenthal, Mark. 2005. Mystery Pollster. May 17.Retrieved November 5, 2005 from http://www.mysterypollster.com/main/2005/week20.

Federal Election Commission. 2002. Voter registration and turnout 2000 [Online]. www.fec.gov (consulted 10/8/02)

Fowler, Floyd J. 1993. *Survey Research Methods*. 2nd ed. Newbury Park, Calif.: Sage.

Holbrook, Thomas M. 1996. *Do Campaigns Matter?*. Thousand Oaks, Calif.: Sage.

Johnston, Richard, André Blais, Henry E. Brady, and Jean Crête. 1992. *Letting the People Decide: Dynamics of a Canadian Election*. Stanford, Calif.: Stanford University Press.

Johnston, Richard and Henry E. Brady. 2002. The Rolling Cross-Section Design. *Electoral Studies* 21: 283–95.

Kenski, Kate, and Natalie Jomini Stroud. 2005. Who Watches Presidential Debates? A Comparative Analysis of Presidential Debate Viewing in 2000 and 2004, *American Behavioral Scientist* 49: 213–28.

King, Gary. 1997. *A Solution to the Ecological Inference Problem: Reconstructing Individual Behavior from Aggregate Data*. Princeton, N.J.: Princeton University Press.

Langbein, Laura Irwin, and Allan J. Lichtman. 1978. *Ecological Inference*. Beverly Hills, Calif.: Sage.

Merkle, Daniel, Murray Edelman, Kathy Dykeman, and Chris Brogan. 1998. An Experimental Study of Ways to Increase Exit Poll Response Rates and Reduce Survey Error. Paper presented at the annual conference of the American Association of Public Opinion Research, St. Louis.

Schutt, Russell K. 1996. *Investigating the Social World: The Process and Practice of Research*. Thousand Oaks, Calif.: Pine Forge Press.

Spector, Paul E. 1981. *Research Designs*. Beverly Hills, Calif.: Sage.

Sudman, Seymour and Norman M. Bradburn. 1982. *Asking Questions: A Practical Guide to Questionnaire Design*. San Francisco: Jossey-Bass.

Zaller, John. 2002. The Statistical Power of Election Studies to Detect Media Exposure Effects in Political Campaigns. *Electoral Studies* 21: 297–329.

Chapter 4

The Rolling Cross-Section Design

KATE KENSKI

This chapter provides details on the rolling cross-sectional design in general and the NAES in particular. Data from the NAES are used to illustrate how we implemented the RCS design. As mentioned in Chapter 3, the rolling cross-section is a series of repeated cross-sections using a sampling plan to ensure that each of the cross-sections is composed of randomly selected members from the population under study. Because the composition of each cross-section is random, researchers can treat the date of interview as a chance event. "Properly done, the date on which a respondent is interviewed is as much a product of random selection as the initial inclusion of that respondent in the sample" (Johnston and Brady 2002, 283). In the case of the NAES, this process allows analysts to aggregate the individual cases to the daily level (or higher aggregates) and look for changes that take place in the electorate over the course of the election season.

Interviews with randomly selected individuals take place throughout the course of a rolling cross-sectional study. The unit of analysis can be either the individual at a single point in time or the population over time. The primary unit of analysis for studying populations over time must be determined before an RCS study begins.

The date of interview is a central concern of the rolling cross-section design. Prior to conducting a RCS study, researchers have to decide what type of schedule they wish to implement. The unit of the schedule can vary from study to study. In one study, researchers may want to track changes that happen on a weekly basis. In another, changes that happen day to day may be the focus. For any particular study, once the unit of the schedule has been chosen, it should remain constant throughout the study.

The NAES rolling cross-sectional design uses *day* as the unit for the schedule. The NAES team chose day because many things happen in the news environment daily. A larger unit, such as week, could have been chosen. In order to capture campaign dynamics and attribute changes in public opinion to particular campaign events, however, day was selected as the unit of the sampling schedule. Generally, a study using a smaller unit for its release schedule will be more sensitive to changes in a dynamic environment than a study that uses larger units. Researchers who prefer to use week as their unit of analysis, moreover, can aggregate data collected on a daily release schedule into weekly sections. If the study has been conducted under a weekly schedule, however, researchers cannot break those data into days and assume that each day of interview is a chance event.

RCS Sample Design

Once a schedule has been chosen, a random sample of members from the population is drawn. Rather than working directly from this initial list of randomly selected members of the population, this list of randomly selected individuals is broken up into several smaller lists called *replicates*. The NAES sample was acquired through random-digit dialing procedures. A list of randomly generated telephone numbers in the United States was made.[1] This list was then broken into several replicates. Just as a telephone number's chance of being selected for the initial list was random, so was the number's chance of being placed into a particular replicate.

A certain number of replicates are released into the field each day, depending on how many interviews researchers want to complete. Schulman, Ronca & Bucuvalas (SRBI), the firm that conducted the RCS fieldwork for the NAES, determined that a 6:1 ratio of sampled telephone numbers to completed interviews was generally needed to produce a target number of interviews in 2000. A 9:1 ratio was needed to produce a target number of interviews in 2004. The number of replicates released each day varied across the NAES study. More replicates were released into the field on days when important events were happening or were likely to occur than on days when little was going on in the campaign environment.

Figure 4.1 shows the number of interviews that were completed each day from December 14, 1999 to January 19, 2001. Averages of between fifty and three hundred interviews were conducted each day for the national RCS study. During the intense periods of the presidential primary campaigns, one hundred national cross-section interviews were completed each day on average. At the end of the primary season around the beginning of April and until the beginning of July, as word of vice-presidential prospects leaked to the press, this average fell to around fifty interviews per day. Because the general election was of great

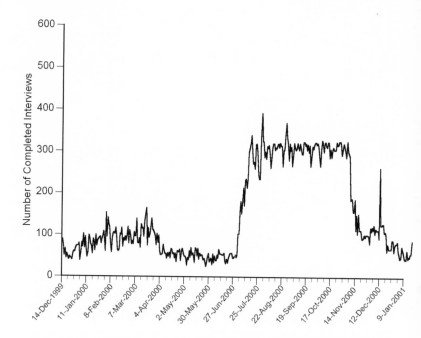

Figure 4.1. Number of interview completions by day in 2000 National RCS.

interest, the NAES allocated more resources to the collection of data around the general election rather than around slower periods, such as the summer when the number of campaign activities were relatively low. In July, the target number of interviews increased, and more replicates were released into the field each day. Around three hundred national cross-section interviews were completed daily from mid-July through the general election. During November and much of December 2000, one hundred national cross-section interviews were completed each day on average. These averages do not include interviews that were done as a part of the panel studies or add-on cross-section studies noted in the NAES codebook.

Similarly, Figure 4.2 shows the number of interviews that were completed each day from October 7, 2003 to November 16, 2004. Again, sample size targets changed from month to month, with larger sample releases occurring around key events. Over sixty individuals were interviewed per day on average during October 2003, while over three hundred sixty individuals were interviewed per day during October 2004.

Comparing Figures 4.1 and 4.2, different patterns emerge. In 2000, the average number of interviews decreased substantially after the pri-

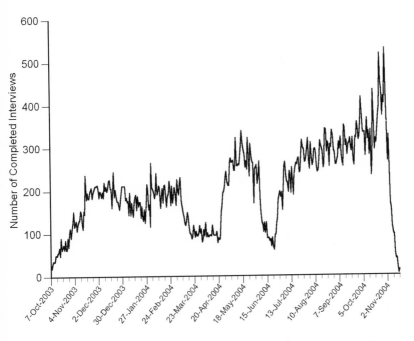

Figure 4.2. Number of interview completions by day in 2004 National RCS.

mary season was effectively over, as it became clear that George W. Bush was going to be selected as the Republican candidate and Al Gore was going to be the Democratic candidate. In the spring of 2004, the number of target interviews never went below a daily average of one hundred interviews, even when it had become clear that John Kerry was the Democratic nominee. We kept the average number of interviews relatively high because campaign and independent expenditure group (527) advertising became heavy in March, suggesting that the general election had already begun (see Winneg, Kenski, and Jamieson 2005). In fact, in 2004, the number of interviews increased from the end of April through the month of May, so that important campaign effects would not be missed.

Selecting a target sample size for each day (or whatever the unit of the release schedule is) depends on three things: (1) the size of the effect that one wants to detect, (2) the project's budget, and (3) the capacity of the call-house(s). Research projects always contain practical as well as theoretical constraints. Implementing a highly sensitive research design can be expensive, especially if the effects that one wants to detect are small. The larger one's sample size, the more precise one's estimates. Each daily cross-section comes with sampling variation. This sampling variation is reduced when the sample size increases.

If one is conducting research on a subset of the population, then the power of that effect on that subpopulation should be determined. If one wants to look at African-Americans, for example, then one should make sure that there are enough cases to find an effect when analyzing the NAES or any dataset. Zaller (2002) observes:

It would also seem that the scholars who consume surveys should make more use of power analysis in their studies, especially in studies which turn up null or trace effects. That is, they should estimate the probability of rejecting the null hypothesis with respect to the particular size of effect they expect, given the model they are using, the characteristics of the variables in it, and the amount of data they have. (323)

Compared to most election studies, the total sample size of the NAES is massive. Nevertheless, to detect small effects for some hypotheses, even the NAES may not be large enough.

Sample Release and Clearance

For RCS designs to work, strict procedures must be worked out so that each telephone number has the same chance of being selected and of producing a completed interview as any other telephone number. Serious effort was made to increase the response rates without compromising the assumption underlying a random sample. For example, people who were initially called on a weekend were not to be pursued more aggressively than people who were initially called on weekdays. The NAES followed a special protocol so that the sample of respondents interviewed on any single day would be as representative of the population as possible. A total of eighteen call attempts were made for every telephone number that was released into the field. The callbacks took place over a period of two weeks. If it was determined that a telephone number was out of service or nonresidential, interviews at that number were not pursued. After a telephone number was released into the field, call attempts were made as follows:

Days 1–4:   2 attempts each day
Days 5–14: 1 attempt each day

There was also a refusal conversion protocol. If a respondent made an initial refusal on days 1–6 from the phone number's release into the field, then the person was called back for potential conversion four days from the initial refusal. If the initial refusal was made on days 7–9, the person was called back on day 10. If the initial refusal took place on days 10–13, the respondent was called back for conversion the next day. And finally, if the initial refusal took place on day 14, then a callback for conversion was made on the same day. If a completed interview did not take place after 14 days of a telephone number having been released into the field, no further contact was initiated.

What is important to note here is that there were strict procedures in place so that no telephone number was treated differently from any of the other numbers selected. Telephone numbers released on Tuesdays were not handled differently from telephone numbers released on Fridays. This protocol ensures that the probability of being interviewed is a random event. By stabilizing the proportion of respondents who completed an interview after having been called only a few times and those who completed an interview after being called numerous times, the representativeness of the daily cross-sections is maximized.

Why is it important that the date of the interview be a random event? If the date of interview is random, then the characteristics of the sample on any given day will not vary systematically. Figure 4.3 shows that if we plot the data across time, there are no systematic patterns of variation in the demographic characteristics, such as gender (cW01) or race (cW03), which should remain stable across the campaign. If we have been consistent in our sampling and interviewing strategy, we would not expect, for example, the number of female or white respondents in the sample to increase or decrease. Because these characteristics do not change in a predictable way, we do not have to worry that they are potential confounding variables to our analyses. When we observe that some variables change in systematic ways across the campaign, we can attribute these patterns to genuine changes in the electorate with greater confidence.

The NAES design allows us to challenge the assumptions of what is and is not stable during the course of the campaign. For example, partisan stability across the campaigns has been questioned. Some polling organizations weight their data by party identification (cV01). If party identification fluctuates across the campaign in a non-random way, however, this strategy may not be wise. Figure 4.4 shows the percentage of the electorate that identified as Independent from mid-July to the end of December 2000. It demonstrates that this percentage is not stable over time. Surveys that are weighted by party identification may be operating under some misconceptions about party identification. Party identification may not be as stable as once thought and could be considered an indicator of the respondents' attitudes toward candidates at a given moment in the campaign. Because we know that the sample characteristics on things that should remain stable, such as gender and race, are in fact stable when we plot them, we are able to make the claim that

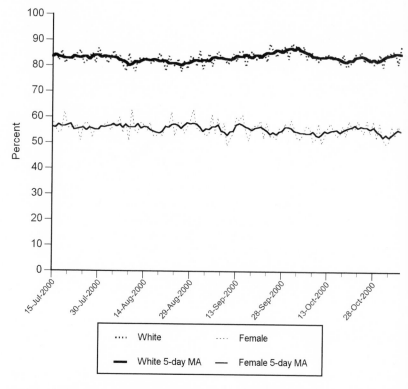

Figure 4.3. Gender and racial composition of national RCS from July 15 to November 6, 2000 (MA, moving average).

party identification changes over the course of the campaign and is not steady.

Call Dispositions

A total of 373,016 telephone numbers were called over the course of the nation cross-section study in 2000. This total includes 12,944 calls made during the initial phase of the study, which began November 8, 1999. Interviews that took place prior to December 14, 1999 were used to test survey questions and work out the kinks in the process of releasing the replicates. It was during this time that the call-house, SRBI, determined how many replicates were needed to complete the target number of interviews for each day. In 2004, a total of 761,089 telephone numbers were called over the course of the national RCS study.

Random-digit dialing, of course, produces many telephone numbers

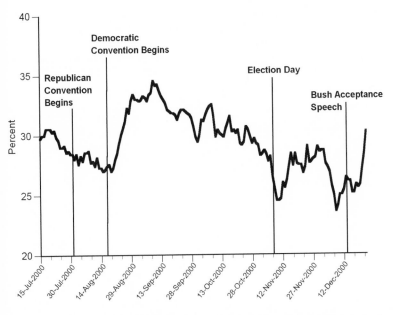

Figure 4.4. Percentage of respondents who identified as Independents during the general election in 2000 (MA, moving average).

that fail to yield completed interviews. When contacting telephone lines randomly generated, final dispositions of the telephone numbers revealed that 34.0 percent of the numbers in 2000 and 50.5 percent in 2004 either were not residential lines or were not in service. Dispositional data are shown in Table 4.1.

There are a number of reasons why individuals must be contacted several times before an interview is completed. In addition to people not being home when called initially, a large percentage of initial call attempts result in the person answering the telephone and telling the survey firm to call back at some other time. Of those telephone interviews that were completed, the average number of calls made to complete the interview was 3.71 (median = 3, SD = 2.99) in 2000 and was 4.07 (median = 3, SD = 3.45) in 2004. Figure 4.5 shows the percentage of the completed interviews that were obtained after a given number of dials in 2000. Most of the interview completions take place in the first few dial attempts. Fewer completions take place the longer a telephone number has been in the field. The farther away in time it is from a number's initial release into the field, the less likely the number will yield a completed interview.

TABLE 4.1. DISPOSITION OF CALLS FOR THE NAES NATIONAL CROSS-SECTIONS

Disposition	2000	2004
Not in service/nonresidential number/ line problems	126,746 (34%)	384,639 (50.5%)
Hang up/call block/dialer hang up		11,171 (1.5%)
No answer/busy	44,357 (11.9%)	52,630 (6.9%)
Answering machine	13,705 (3.7%)	47,993 (6.3%)
Respondent unavailable for all of field /not competent	12,781 (3.4%)	34,992 (4.6%)
Callback	55,278 (14.8%)	76,970 (10.1%)
Refusal	52,184 (14%)	53,861 (7.1%)
Ineligible	5,346 (1.4%)	1,377 (0.2%)
Break-off	1,760 (0.5%)	16,104 (2.1%)
Complete	60,859 (16.3%)	81,422 (10.7%)
Total	373,016	761,089

This pattern is important because respondents who answer the survey in the initial few calls may be different from those who are harder to reach. Because new numbers are released into the field each day, the completed interviews are composed of many people who are reached after a few dials as well as a few people who are reached after many call attempts. When an RCS study begins, the first couple of weeks of interviews will not have this mix of people contacted after a few calls and those contacted after several calls. On the first day of the study, for example, completed interviews will only consist of those individuals who have been called once or twice, based on the NAES protocol. This is why the first few weeks of the NAES data collection should not included when analyzing data across time.

It should be noted that there were thirteen days in the 2000 NAES and eight days in the 2004 NAES when replicates were not released and calls not made because these days fell on national holidays. Telephone calls were not made on

NAES 2000

1999: December 24, December 25, December 31

2000: January 1, January 2, July 3, July 4, November 7, November 23, December 24, December 25, December 31

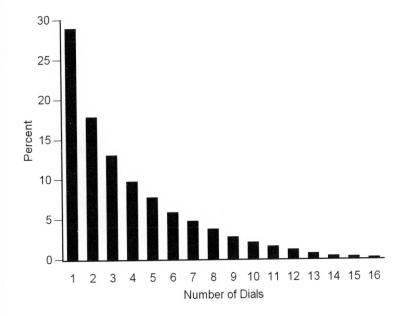

Figure 4.5. Percentage of completed interviews in the national cross-section by number of dials made in 2000.

2001: January 1

NAES 2004
2003: November 27, December 24, December 25, December 31
2004: January 1, April 11, July 4, November 2

Before conducting across-time analyses, researchers should be aware that data are missing on these dates.

Conclusion

The RCS design is a special type of repeated cross-sectional design that uses strict calling protocols. By releasing new lists of people to be interviewed into the field on a regular schedule, this design is able to ensure that each of the cross-sections is composed of randomly selected members from the population under study. If done correctly, the rolling cross-section design should rank at the top of studies that generate the possible random sample for capturing campaign dynamics.

The NAES target sample size varied throughout the study. On those days when large samples were desired, additional replicates were released into the field. Because the general election was of great interest, it was made a priority in resource allocation and sample size in both 2000 and 2004. The larger the sample size, the greater the precision of the estimates generated. When conducting a RCS study, the size of one's sample may be constrained by the research budget. Interviewing large numbers of individuals is expensive. Therefore, researchers with specific hypotheses should perform power analyses to see whether conducting such studies is worth their time, given the resources available.

Note

1. See Chapter 2 or the NAES codebook for more information about the telephone procedures used to construct the NAES sample.

References

Johnston, Richard and Henry E. Brady. 2002. The Rolling Cross-Section Design. *Electoral Studies* 21: 283–95.
Winneg, Kenneth, Kate Kenski, and Kathleen Hall Jamieson. 2005. Detecting the Effects of Deceptive Presidential Advertisements in Spring of 2004. *American Behavioral Scientist* 49: 114–29.
Zaller, John. 2002. The Statistical Power of Election Studies to Detect Media Exposure Effects in Political Campaigns. *Electoral Studies* 21: 297–29.

Chapter 5
Exploratory Analysis

Natalie Jomini Stroud and Daniel Romer

This chapter has two aims. The first is to review exploratory data analysis techniques that can be used to examine the nature of variables. The second aim is to introduce several methods for evaluating relationships between variables. This chapter is meant as a review of basic statistical techniques that should be considered in advance of progressing to the more complex statistical analysis discussed in subsequent chapters. For more information on the concepts from this chapter, the consultation of an introductory statistics text is recommended.

Variable Distributions

When beginning an analysis of data, it is often helpful to look at each variable's *distribution*. As Moore and McCabe (1993) write, "The pattern of a variable is called its distribution. The distribution records the numerical values of the variable and how often each value occurs" (6). Graphical displays, called histograms, provide a visual representation of a variable's distribution. Figure 5.1 shows several histograms of variables that can be found in the NAES data. The histogram in Panel A shows the distribution of the income variable (cWA04). The shape of the distribution is *symmetric* around a single peak near its center. We call such distributions *unimodal* because they have only a single region with the most cases. The *normal* distribution is a prominent example of a unimodal and symmetric distribution.[1] The second panel shows the number of days in the past week that information about the campaign for president was accessed online among Internet users (cEA22). This distribution is highly *skewed* and hence is nonsymmetric. The modal frequency is at the low end of the continuum (most Internet users did not access political information online). Panel C shows the distribution of respondents who watched all, some, or none of the presidential debate on September 30, 2004 between George W. Bush and John Kerry (cFA03). This is a fairly

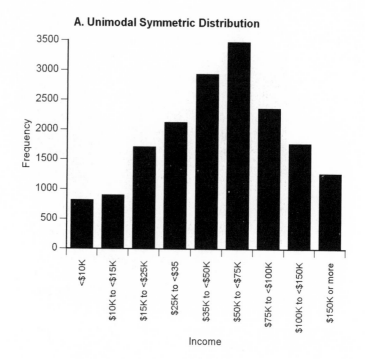

A. Unimodal Symmetric Distribution

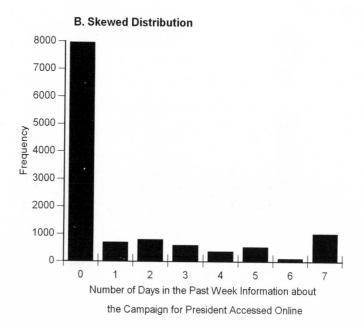

B. Skewed Distribution

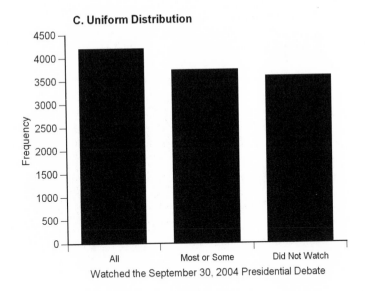

C. Uniform Distribution

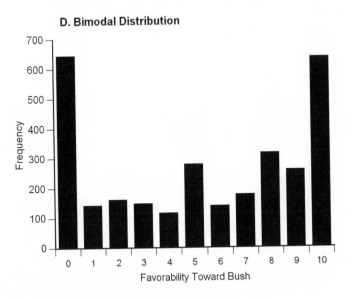

D. Bimodal Distribution

Figure 5.1. Variable distributions.

uniform distribution: approximately the same percentage of respondents answered each of the three categories.[2] It is symmetric but not unimodal. Panel D shows favorability ratings of George W. Bush in the week prior to the election (cAA01). This is an example of a symmetric *bimodal* distribution with two peaks indicating clustering at the extreme values of the continuum. Hence, it would be inappropriate to describe this distribution as having a single modal value. As will be explained in more detail below, knowing the distribution of a variable can help to select appropriate analytic techniques.

Types of Measurement Scales

There are several different types of scales of measurement that one will encounter when conducting analysis using the NAES. The following paragraphs discuss nominal, ordinal, and interval scales of measurement.

Nominal scales (also known as categorical) have no natural ordering. For example, vote intention is often measured on a nominal scale because intentions to vote for one candidate versus intentions to vote for a different candidate are not ordered. We might label the values of a nominal scale as 1 (intends to vote for Kerry) versus 0 (intends to vote for someone else). However, these values are arbitrary and should only be construed as containing nominal information. They simply designate that those people intending to vote for Kerry are equivalent to each other but different from those who intend to vote for someone else. Nominal variables have values that are mutually exclusive and exhaustive (Schutt 1996).

Ordinal scales imply an ordering and hence contain quantitative information; however, the distance between the values is not known. Though not used in the NAES, questions that ask respondents to rank various options produce ordinal variables. For example, one might be asked to rank candidates for president from most to least preferred. The following ranks might be assigned by a respondent to different candidates: 1 (Bush), 2 (Kerry), 3 (Nader). However, the magnitudes of the differences in preference are not specified. One might prefer Bush over the other candidates a great deal or only a small amount. Because of this limitation, it may be misleading to add or subtract ranks (for example to calculate means) since the difference between a rank of 1 and a rank of 2 may not be comparable to the difference between a rank of 2 and a rank of 3.

Interval scales imply an ordering in which the distance between the values is equivalent. Addition and subtraction can be meaningfully applied to interval scales. A classic example of an interval scale is temperature, where, for example, 56°F is ten degrees hotter than 46°F.[3] In the NAES dataset, it is possible to consider the measurement of candidate viability as an interval scale. Respondents were asked to indicate on a scale from 0 to 100 what they thought the chances were that a Democratic candidate would beat out the other candidates to become the Democratic candidate for president (cNA01 through cNA06). One could argue that the difference between scores of 90 and 100 on this scale is the same distance as between 10 and 20.

Although these various scale types seem fixed, there are important exceptions. First, each type is "downwardly compatible." A variable that is measured using one type of scale can be treated as a less restrictive scale in an analysis. Therefore, an interval level scale can be treated as ordinal or nominal when conducting analyses. Further, an ordinal scale can be treated as nominal.

Second, there are instances in which a variable can be redefined to be "upwardly compatible." This can happen when a scale with ordinal properties is used to measure a variable that could be considered an interval scale. In the NAES dataset, education (cWA03) is measured with ordinal characteristics. Respondents are asked to indicate the last grade or class they completed in school. Responses include: grade 8 or lower, some high school with no diploma, high school diploma or equivalent, technical or vocational school after high school, some college with no degree, associate or two-year college degree, four-year college degree, graduate or professional school after college with no degree, and graduate or professional degree. This scale could reasonably be recoded to approximate an interval-level scale by assigning each category a value corresponding to the number of years spent in school. For example, some college may be assigned a value of 14 years of schooling and obtaining a four-year college degree may be assigned to a value of 16 years.

It is important to note that the degree to which these scale types should guide analysis has been debated. Lord (1953) provides a classic example of how a variable can be assigned to different levels. Lord notes that one could consider the numbers on football jerseys as nominal— each designates a player without any order. On the other hand, faced with an accusation that lowerclassmen are receiving lower numbers, one could treat the jersey numbers as interval data and use statistical tests to evaluate the claim. Velleman and Wilkinson (1993) argue that there are other considerations in determining scale type besides a priori assumptions. They note "the scale type of data may be determined in part by the questions we ask of the data or the purposes for which we intend it" (70). Hence, it is perhaps best to consider the objectives of one's analysis before defining the level of one's data.

Most of the variables used in the NAES are measured at a level at least as high as ordinal but not necessarily at the interval level, including the viability example discussed earlier. By this, we mean that they clearly contain ordinal information, but we may not know how well they satisfy the condition of equal intervals between scale values. For example, local television news viewing in the past week (cEA06) is measured on a scale from 0 to 7 days. If the variable were interval, then the difference between watching local television news no days versus one day per week would be the same as the difference between watching local television news six days versus seven days in the prior week. It is possible; however, that the variable is ordinal in that the difference between watching local television news zero days versus one day per week is much larger than the difference between watching local television news six versus seven days per week.

As another example, the NAES asks respondents how much attention they paid to "stories about the campaign for president on national network or cable TV news" (cEA05). The response options to this question include: a great deal of attention, some, not much, or none. Although the categories are ordered, the distance between the categories may not be equivalent. The difference between "a great deal of attention" and "some" could be quite large. It could be the difference between listening attentively whenever a political topic is covered (a great deal) and occasionally glancing at the television screen when politics is on (some). The difference between people saying "not much" compared to "none," however, may be very small. "Not much" could mean remembering President Bush was on the news a few nights ago, but little else, while "none" could mean no recall of seeing President Bush. Alternatively, it is also possible that the attention variable is an interval scale—perhaps the difference between "not much" and "none" is identical to the distance between "some" and "a great deal."

There has been much discussion as to whether ordinal scales can be treated as interval for statistical analysis (see for example Johnson and Creech 1983; Zumbo and Zimmerman 1993). Indeed, in many cases, it is impossible to know for sure whether a variable meets the requirements of an interval scale. Throughout this book, we often treat variables as interval scales. We do so because, oftentimes, deviations from the assumption of equal intervals will not have a large impact on our conclusions. One reason for this is that all variables are measured with a certain amount of random error. As discussed in Chapter 3, these errors reduce precision but do not bias results in a systematic fashion. Deviations from the equal interval assumption of interval measurement can be treated as one such source of error.

To illustrate how deviations from scale assumptions can be treated as error, suppose that you had both an ordinal- and an interval-scale measure of the same variable so that you could compare the two. Figure 5.2 depicts several possible combinations of these measures with the same ordinal scale but different interval scale values. In Panel A, the ordinal scale exactly matches the interval scale. Here, the ordinal and interval scales are equivalent. In Panel B, the distance between values 1 and 2 is larger than the distance between other values. The result is a slight nonlinearity in the relation between scales. However, the basic linear relation is preserved, and analyses using the ordinal scale would likely produce very similar results to the interval scale. In Panel C, there are two distances that are larger than others. As a result, in some cases, the ordinal scores are too low compared to the interval scale (1 and 3) and in others they are too large (2 and 4). Nevertheless, the basic linear relation remains. Finally, in Panel D, we see a more pronounced deviation at one end of the scale: the distance between values 0 and 1 is very large compared to the other distances. In this case, the error is more systematic and might lead to misleading conclusions if analyses were conducted with the ordinal rather than interval scale of measurement.

What is striking about the examples in Figure 5.2 is that despite failures to meet the equal interval assumption in several cases, the ordinal scale still retains the essential *monotonic* relation (steadily increasing or decreasing) with an underlying interval scale. Hence, one will have to decide how much precision is needed to analyze a variable. It may be the case that ordinal data are sufficient to support the analyses one wishes to conduct. One solution to this dilemma is to plot the ordinal variable against another variable that should be linearly related to it. If the relation were observed to be nonlinear, a researcher could collapse ordinal categories that appear to have smaller distances. For example, in Panel C, one could collapse values 0 and 1, 2 and 3, and 4 and 5 in order to have a variable with three values that more closely produces a linear relationship.

Tukey (1977) discusses other procedures for transforming variables to make their relations with related variables more linear. He shows how power, square root, and log transformations can be used to rescale a variable so that it has a straight-line relationship with theoretically related variables. In Chapter 7, we also discuss the use of logistic regression analysis. This analysis can be conducted by transforming the values of a dependent variable into a scale with only two values (high and low). Given the wide range of options for analyzing data, it is clear that no matter what the scale level, one can find an appropriate technique to identify relationships between variables.

A.

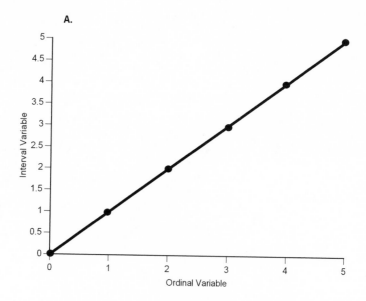

B.

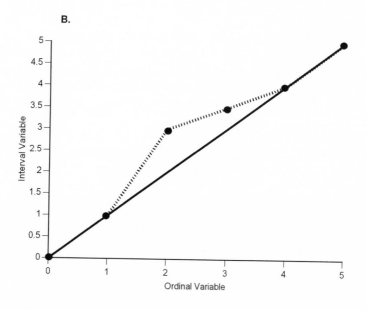

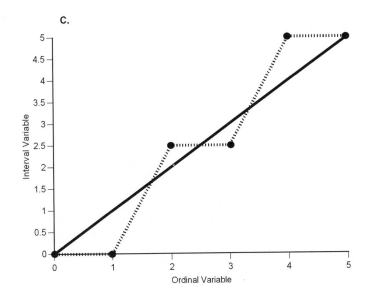

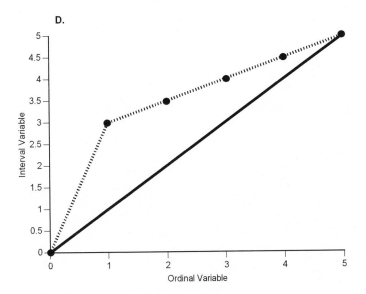

Figure 5.2 Ordinal and interval data graphically displayed. Solid lines indicate perfect match between ordinal and internal scale (first panel). Other panels show various types of discrepancy between the two scale types (versus solid lines).

TABLE 5.1. FREQUENCY DISTRIBUTION OF ATTENTION TO NEWSPAPER ARTICLES ABOUT THE CAMPAIGN FOR PRESIDENT (SEPTEMBER 6–NOVEMBER 1, 2004)

Variable values	Frequency	Percent	Cumulative percent
1 (A great deal of attention)	3,745	25.5	25.5
2 (Some)	6,415	43.8	69.3
3 (Not much)	2,881	19.7	89.0
4 (None)	1,617	11.0	100.0
Total	14,658	100.0	

How to Describe Distributions: Univariate Statistics

It is often useful to convey information about a variable's distribution by calculating descriptive statistics. The computation of *univariate* statistics depends on a variable's scale type and distribution. Univariate statistics can include measures of a variable's central tendency, such as the mean, and measures of the dispersion of the values around the central tendency, such as the standard deviation.

The *mode*, one measure of central tendency, is particularly appropriate for nominal variables. It indicates the category with the largest frequency. For example, in the unweighted distribution of party identification (cMA01) between Labor Day and November 1, 2004 in the NAES04, the modal value is Democrat because the largest percentage of respondents (33.6%) identifies as Democrats, compared to 32.6 percent Republicans, 27.2 percent Independents, and 6.6 percent identifying as something else.[4]

The *median* is a measure of central tendency appropriate for ordinal variables or interval variables with skewed distributions. The median is the value midway between the top and bottom half of the distribution. For any distribution, it is possible to order the values from lowest to highest and to calculate the *cumulative* number of cases as the values increase in size. For example, in Table 5.1 there are 3,745 cases for value 1 and 6,415 cases for value 2. This yields a cumulative frequency of 3,745 + 6,415 = 10,160 for value 2. The median is the value of the variable for the first case that exceeds 50 percent of the cumulative distribution. In small distributions, this is easy to calculate. In large distributions with many cases per value, it is a little more complex.

Table 5.1 shows the distribution for attention to newspaper articles about the campaign for president (cEA13) among those who read the newspaper at least once in the prior week. The median can be found by determining the scale location of the variable at the 50th *percentile*, the location at 50 percent of the cumulative distribution. Looking at the cumulative percentage column in Table 5.1, 50 percent is crossed in the "some" category. However, this category contains about 44 percent of the cases. To identify the median more precisely, we can *interpolate* its value. Technically speaking, each value on a scale represents a range of scores with the value lying in the middle of the range. The value 1, a great deal of attention, lies in the middle of 0.5 to 1.5. The value 2 (some attention) goes from 1.5 to 2.5. Since the beginning of the second value starts with 25.5 percent of the cases, we can locate the 50th percentile by finding the case in the range from 1.5 to 2.5 that adds another 24.5 percent of cases, which in this case is .245 × 14,658 or 3,591 cases. This is typically done by assuming that cases are spread evenly within a scale value. Hence, the 50th percentile occurs when 3,591/6,415 of the cases in the second scale value have occurred, or .56 of the way from the beginning of the scale value's range: 1.5 + .56 = 2.06. The median for this distribution is 2.06, which is a little more than some of the time.

The *mean*, denoted $\bar{x}$, is the average value of the distribution calculated by multiplying each value by its frequency divided by the total number of cases in the distribution. In notation, it is written as

$$\sum x_i \, (f_i \, / \, N),$$

in which the summation operator $\sum$ takes the sum over each of the k values of x ($i = 1$ to k) multiplied by its frequency f_i divided by the total number of cases in the distribution N. The mean is an appropriate measure of central tendency for interval variables. For example, for the survey question asking respondents how many days in the past week they watched a 24-hour cable news channel (cEA03), the mean response between Labor Day and Election Day was 3.13 days. As previously noted, the central tendency for skewed distributions is often better conveyed by the median because the mean can change drastically based on extreme values. For example, consider the highly skewed online political information variable from Figure 5.1. The mean response for this variable between Labor Day and Election Day is 1.33 days. Alternatively, the median of the variable is closer to 0, which more accurately reflects the distribution. When the median is lower or higher than the value of the mean, this is an indication that the variable is skewed. For normal distributions, the mean and the median are identical.

In addition to a measure of central tendency, it is also of interest to understand how dispersed the values of a variable are around the center. The *interquartile range* can be used to assess the dispersion of values around the median. To calculate the interquartile range, first find the median (the first score above the 50th percentile). Then, calculate the 25th and 75th percentiles. For example, if you have a distribution with the values {1, 2, 3, 3, 4, 5, 6, 6, 7, 8, 9}, 5 is the median. The 25th percentile (the median of the distribution to the left of the median) is 3. The 75th percentile (the median of the distribution to the right of the median) is 7. The interquartile range is 7 − 3 = 4.

The *standard deviation* S is a measure of dispersion around the mean. This metric, appropriate for nonskewed interval level variables, can be computed using the following formula:

$$S = \sqrt{[(\sum (x_i - \bar{x})^2)/(N - 1)]}.$$

The square of the standard deviation is known as the *variance*. For the measure of how many days in the past week respondents watched a 24-hour cable news channel, the standard deviation is 2.86. Returning to the question asking respondents how many days in the past week they accessed information about the campaign for president online, the standard deviation for this variable is 2.25 while the interquartile range is 2. As with the measure of central tendency, using the interquartile range may be more appropriate since the variable is heavily skewed.

Bivariate Descriptions of Variables

For any two variables, it is often of interest to evaluate whether or not there is a relationship between them. As one variable increases, does the other decline? Does one group have more favorable attitudes toward a candidate compared to another? For example, one may be interested in whether viewers of FOX, CNN, and MSNBC differed in their vote intentions. Or one may want to compare attitudes toward Democratic presidential nominee John Kerry before and after the Democratic National Convention. This section will review several methods for analyzing relationships between two variables, known as *bivariate relationships*.

The analysis of bivariate relationships is sensitive to each variable's scale level and distribution. Statistics associated with bivariate relationships can help to determine the magnitude of the relationship and whether it is statistically significant. Although there are many possibilities for evaluating bivariate relationships, this section will focus on three: crosstabulation (with associated measures of association), analysis of differences in means, and scatterplots (with associated tests of correlation).

Crosstabulation

Crosstabulation allows one to analyze the relationship between nominal or higher level variables. A crosstabulation is a table with one variable defining the rows and the other the columns. For example, using the

TABLE 5.2. CROSSTABULATION OF MOST WATCHED CABLE NEWS NETWORK AND
TWO-PARTY VOTE INTENTION (SEPTEMBER 6–NOVEMBER 1, 2004).

Vote intention	FOX N (%)	CNN N (%)	MSNBC N (%)	Total N (%)
Bush	3,113 (79.7%)	1,782 (36.4)	546 (40.1)	5,441 (53.5)
Kerry	795 (20.3)	3,117 (63.6)	815 (59.9)	4,727 (46.5)
Total	3,908 (100.0)	4,899 (100.0)	1,361 (100.0)	10,168 (100.0)

Cell entries contain N and percentage of respondents in each column.

NAES, crosstabulations would be appropriate if you were interested in
looking at differences in major party vote intention (cRC14) between
those who watched different cable news stations (cEA04). Each cell contains a frequency count of the number of people defined by the row and
column of the two variables. In Table 5.2, for example, 3,113 respondents who identified FOX as their most watched cable news network
intended to vote for Bush. Crosstabulations also typically include percentages associated with each cell based on either row totals or column
totals. In Table 5.2, 79.7 percent of those who watched FOX most often
intended to vote for Bush.

By comparing the column percentage within a cell to the corresponding percentage in the total column, it is possible to assess the relationships between the variables. For example, 79.7 percent of Bush vote
intenders among FOX viewers is much larger than the 53.5 percent of
Bush intenders in the entire sample. Overall, Table 5.2 shows that those
who identify FOX as their most watched cable news network were more
likely to say that they intended to vote for Bush than those who identified other cable news networks as their most watched stations. Further,
those who identified CNN or MSNBC as their most watched station were
more likely to say that they intended to vote for Kerry. Mere inspection,
however, does not give an indication of *statistical significance*, the degree
to which the data in the table could have arisen by chance. When evaluating the relationship between two nominal variables, one statistic used
for determining whether the relationship is significant is known as the
Pearson chi-square statistic. This statistic is computed using the following
formula:

$$\chi^2 = \Sigma \ (O_i - E_i)^2 / E_i,$$

in which O_i is the *observed* cell count in cell i, and E_i is the *expected* cell
count in cell i for $i = 1$ to k cells. The observed values are the cell counts

found in Table 5.2. Expected counts for each cell are computed by calculating the following: Row total × Column total / Table total. Use of the chi-square requires expected cell counts of at least 5. The distributions of statistics used to perform significance testing have a characteristic form, in this case, the chi-square distribution. These distributions have a parameter known as the "degrees of freedom" (df) that will influence their shape and the resulting significance values associated with statistical tests. The degrees of freedom associated with the Chi-square statistic for analyzing crosstabulations is equal to (Number of rows − 1) × (Number of columns − 1). The mean of the Chi-square distribution, assuming no relationship between the variables, is expected to equal the degrees of freedom. The Pearson chi-square associated with Table 5.2 is 1,750.36. With only two degrees of freedom, this value of chi-square will occur with a probability of less than 0.001, indicating that the relationship between vote intention and most watched cable news network is statistically much larger than one would expect by chance. In other words, based on the distribution of scores we would expect for the chi-square statistic, a value this large is not very likely. Hence, there must be something accounting for the large value of the statistic, and this is assumed to be a relationship between the row and column variables.

Although the significant chi-square allows us to conclude that there is a relationship between the variables in the table, this analysis does not support a causal interpretation. It is not clear whether FOX viewers were more likely to support Bush than CNN and MSNBC viewers *prior to* viewing the channel or if viewing the news on FOX swayed their intentions. It is also possible that the relationship would disappear if we controlled for other variables. For example, variables such as party identification may cause both watching certain cable channels and vote intentions. That is, perhaps Democrats who are more likely to vote for Kerry may be more likely to be drawn to CNN and MSNBC. We will return to this possibility shortly.

Though the chi-square statistic is desirable for analyzing the relationship between two nominal variables, crosstabulations of ordinal variables can employ the *gamma statistic* in order to determine the presence and significance of a monotonic relationship. While the chi-square statistic does not assume any ordering of the categories, gamma assumes that the categories are ordered and evaluates monotonic relationships between the variables. One substantial advantage that the gamma statistic has over the chi-square statistic is that it provides a metric for the strength of the relationship between the variables. Gamma varies between +1 and −1, with +1 indicating a perfect positive monotonic relationship between the variables, and −1 indicating a perfect negative

TABLE 5.3. CROSSTABULATION OF VIEWING *THE DAY AFTER TOMORROW* AND
GLOBAL WARMING AS A PROBLEM (JUNE 1–10, 2004)

Global warming problem	Saw movie N (%)	Did not see movie N (%)	Total N (%)
Very or somewhat serious	119	1,403	1,522
	(87.5)	(77.8)	(78.5)
Not too serious or not serious at all	17	400	417
	(12.5)	(22.2)	(21.5)
Total	136	1,803	1,939
	(100.0)	(100.0)	(100.0)

Cell entries contain number and percent of cases in the column.

monotonic relationship between the variables. Consider Table 5.3, a
two-by-two crosstabulation between seeing the movie *The Day After Tomorrow* (cFE15) and how seriously respondents reported global warming to
be a problem (cCF09).

For a two-by-two crosstabulation, gamma (γ) is computed using the
following formula:[5]

$$\gamma = (a * d - c * b) / (a * d + c * b),$$

where *a* corresponds to the upper left cell (119), *b* to the upper right
cell (1,403), *c* to the lower left cell (17), and *d* to the lower right cell
(400). For Table 5.3, γ is 0.33 ($p < 0.01$).

Crosstabulations are not only important in understanding the relationship between two variables; they can be used to evaluate the influence of third variables. Consider the following two examples. Suppose
that we were interested in knowing whether there was any difference in
young people's (cWA02) knowledge of which candidate favored changing the Medicare prescription drug law to allow reimporting drugs from
Canada (cCC26).[6] As Table 5.4 shows, young people were less likely to
know that Kerry was the candidate who supported this change, $\chi^2 (1) =$
6.79, $p < 0.01$.

The relationship between this knowledge question and age shown in
Table 5.4, however, permits only limited conclusions. This crosstabulation, for example, does not allow one to conclude that the Kerry campaign was less effective in informing young people about Kerry's
position on importing drugs from Canada. As Rosenberg (1968)
explains,

whenever we find a relationship between two variables, we attempt to make
sense of it by suggesting how the independent variable exercises some influence
on the dependent variable. The danger always lurks, however, that we are being

TABLE 5.4. CROSSTABULATION OF AGE AND KNOWLEDGE OF CANDIDATE IN FAVOR OF PRESCRIPTION DRUG IMPORTATION FROM CANADA (AUGUST 11–NOVEMBER 3, 2004)

Knowledge question	18- to 25-year-olds N (%)	26-year-olds and older N (%)	Total N (%)
Incorrect	673	6,681	7,354
	(44.9)	(41.5)	(41.8)
Correct	825	9,435	10,260
	(55.1)	(58.5)	(58.2)
Total	1,498	16,116	17,614
	(100.0)	(100.0)	(100.0)

Cell entries contain number and percent of cases in the column.

Model 1: Causal Relationship

Model 2: Confounded Relationship

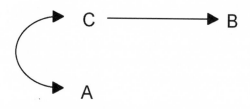

Figure 5.3. Two models of potential causal relationships between an independent A, a dependent B, and a third variable C.

misled. There may, in fact, be no "inherent link" between the two variables but simply a common association with a third variable. (32)

Figure 5.3 shows two possible causal models for two variables, A and B. In Model 1, A causes B directly. This interpretation would suggest that age (A) leads to more knowledge about Kerry's position on importing drugs (B). However, it is also possible that the tendency for more educated respondents to know more about the candidates' positions than less educated respondents explains the relation between age and knowledge. This possibility, shown in Figure 5.3 (Model 2), indicates that age is related to knowledge only because it is partly related to or *confounded* with education (C). The use of the term confounded implies that A and C are related, but the exact nature of the relationship is unclear. It might mean that some other set of variables cause both A and C or that A and C are causally related themselves. Nevertheless, if we control for education, the relation between age and knowledge may disappear. A significant chi-square statistic for a crosstabulation of A and B is consistent with both models. In addition to the models shown in Figure 5.3, there are other possible models accounting for the relationship between A and B. However, we can argue for eliminating some models on logical grounds; for example, we know from the meaning of the variables that it is unlikely for education to cause age. In this example, we can use the causal ordering inherent in the definitions of the variables to eliminate potential causal models. In order to evaluate whether C is a confounding variable, one can control for C and then examine whether the relationship between A and B remains. If C is a confounding variable, then the relationship between A and B should decline after controlling for C.

As shown in Table 5.5, controlling for education considerably reduces the relationship between the variables. This can be accomplished by computing separate chi-square statistics for the crosstabulations associated with three levels of education. The chi-square associated with those with less than a high school degree is 0.003, df $= 1$, $p = 0.96$. The chi-square associated with those with a high school degree to some college is 0.03, df $= 1$, $p = 0.85$. Finally, the chi-square associated with those with a college degree or more is 0.004, df $= 1$, $p = 0.95$. The relationship between age and political knowledge is completely eliminated when controlling for education. Hence, we could conclude that Model 2 is the correct interpretation of the significant relationship between age and knowledge.

For a second example, we can return to the relationship between most watched cable news network and vote intention for the two major party candidates in 2004 (Table 5.2). The question remains: is the observed relationship between the variables the result of exposure to particular news programs or of preferences that party members have for one or the other cable news stations?

In order to test this hypothesis, one can control for party identification and reevaluate the relationship between most watched cable news network and vote intention. If the observed relationship is due to party identification, then after controlling for party, we would expect the chi-square statistic to decline in size and statistical significance. Again, several possible models could be considered as described in Figure 5.3. According to Model 2 in Figure 5.3, it is possible that party identification and news preference are confounded, in the same way that age and edu-

TABLE 5.5.　CROSSTABULATION OF AGE AND KNOWLEDGE OF CANDIDATE IN FAVOR OF CANADIAN DRUG IMPORTATION, CONTROLLING FOR EDUCATION (AUGUST 11–NOVEMBER 3, 2004)

Knowledge question	18- to 25-year-olds N (%)	26-year-olds and older N (%)	Total N (%)
Less than a high school degree			
Incorrect	101	631	732
	(61.2)	(61.4)	(61.4)
Correct	64	396	460
	(38.8)	(38.6)	(38.6)
Total	165	1,027	1,192
	(100.0)	(100.0)	(100.0)
High school degree through some college			
Incorrect	471	3,877	4,348
	(46.0)	(46.3)	(46.3)
Correct	552	4,488	5,040
	(54.0)	(53.7)	(53.7)
Total	1,023	8,365	9,388
	(100.0)	(100.0)	(100.0)
College degree and above			
Incorrect	94	2,114	2,208
	(31.9)	(32.0)	(32.0)
Correct	201	4,484	4,685
	(68.1)	(68.0)	(68.0)
Total	295	6,598	6,893
	(100.0)	(100.0)	(100.0)

Cell entries contain number and percent of cases in the column.

cation were related in the previous example. It is also possible that party identification causes both vote intentions and news station preference. In either case, controlling for party identification would result in a non-significant chi-square value in the relation between cable news and vote intention.

The results of the crosstabulation between cable news network and vote intention controlling for party identification are shown in Table 5.6. The chi-square statistics associated with this table are Republican, $\chi^2(2) = 110.64$, $p < 0.001$; Democrat, $\chi^2(2) = 141.14$, $p < 0.001$; Independent, $\chi^2(2) = 341.94$, $p < 0.001$; and Other Party, $\chi^2(2) = 47.33$, $p < 0.001$. Since the associated chi-square statistics remain significant, we can conclude that even after controlling for party identification, there is still a relationship between vote intention and most watched cable news network. These tests indicate that the relation between vote and news

TABLE 5.6. CROSSTABULATION OF MOST WATCHED CABLE NETWORK AND TWO-PARTY VOTE INTENTION, CONTROLLING FOR PARTY IDENTIFICATION (SEPTEMBER 6 THROUGH NOVEMBER 1, 2004)

Vote intention by party ID	FOX N (%)	CNN N (%)	MSNBC N (%)	Total N (%)
Republican				
Bush	2,155 (97.7)	974 (89.6)	310 (89.3)	3,439 (94.5)
Kerry	51 (2.3)	113 (10.4)	37 (10.7)	201 (5.5)
Total	2,206 (100.0)	1,087 (100.0)	347 (100.0)	3,640 (100.0)
Democrat				
Bush	163 (25.0)	188 (8.5)	43 (7.9)	394 (11.6)
Kerry	490 (75.0)	2,016 (91.5)	499 (92.1)	3,005 (88.4)
Total	653 (100.0)	2,204 (100.0)	542 (100.0)	3,399 (100.0)
Independent				
Bush	631 (76.8)	455 (36.6)	151 (39.2)	1,237 (50.5)
Kerry	191 (23.2)	787 (63.4)	234 (60.8)	1,212 (49.5)
Total	822 (100.0)	1,242 (100.0)	385 (100.0)	2,449 (100.0)
Other				
Bush	131 (75.7)	112 (43.1)	26 (44.8)	269 (54.8)
Kerry	42 (24.3)	148 (56.9)	32 (55.2)	222 (45.2)
Total	173 (100.0)	260 (100.0)	58 (100.0)	491 (100.0)

Cell entries contain number and percent of cases in the column.

station preference is robust to challenge from controls for party identification. Nevertheless, we cannot rule out the possibility that other third variables are responsible for the relationship.

TESTS ON MEANS

Another approach to analyzing the relationship between two variables is to compare the means of the dependent variable as a function of the values of the independent variable. We illustrate this method in the simplest case of an independent variable with two values using the *independent sample t-test*. In this method, one calculates the difference in the

TABLE 5.7. MEANS AND STANDARD DEVIATIONS OF BUSH AND KERRY
FAVORABILITY BEFORE AND AFTER THE DEMOCRATIC AND REPUBLICAN
NATIONAL CONVENTIONS

	Democratic National Convention		Republican National Convention	
	Before (7/19–7/25/04) Mean (SD)	After (7/30–8/5/04) Mean (SD)	Before (8/23–8/29/04) Mean (SD)	After (9/3–9/9/04) Mean (SD)
Bush favorability	5.11 (3.62) $n = 1,820$	5.11 (3.72) $n = 1,981$	5.06 (3.72) $n = 2,082$	5.51 (3.76) $n = 1,978$
Kerry favorability	5.14 (3.07) $n = 1,747$	5.50 (3.31) $n = 1,944$	5.21 (3.29) $n = 2,050$	4.87 (3.32) $n = 1,946$

means of the dependent variable as defined by the two values of the
independent variable. The test is called an independent sample test
because the two means are based on separate samples corresponding to
the two values of the independent variable. The t-statistic is computed
using the formula:

$$t = (\bar{x}_1 - \bar{x}_2) / \sqrt{(s_1^2 / n_1 + s_2^2 / n_2)},$$

where n_1 and n_2 are the sample sizes for the two means. The associated
degrees of freedom are $n_1 + n_2 - 2$. For example, if one were interested
in whether the party conventions assisted their respective candidates,
independent sample t-tests could be performed to compare the means
of the national sample's favorability ratings of each candidate (cAA01
and cAB01) before and after each convention. Table 5.7 shows the favorability means and standard deviations. An analysis was performed using
the independent sample t-test function in SPSS.

The difference between Bush's favorability before and after the
Democratic National Convention is not significant, $t(3,799) = -0.06$,
$p = 0.95$. There is a significant increase, however, in Kerry's favorability
from before to after the convention, $t(3,689) = -3.32$, $p < 0.001$. Evaluating changes over time associated with the Republican National Convention, use of the independent t-test demonstrates that Bush's
favorability was significantly higher after the convention compared to
before the convention, $t(4,058) = -3.79$, $p < 0.001$, and Kerry's favorability was significantly lower after the convention compared to before
the convention, $t(3,994) = 3.21$, $p < 0.01$. Though the t-tests are significant, one must be cautious in attributing these changes to the
national conventions. It is always possible that other events occurring
during this period were responsible for these shifts. Nevertheless, one

can demonstrate with this test that there are significant differences between the means of a dependent variable for groups of scores defined by an independent variable.

SCATTERPLOTS OF RELATIONS BETWEEN VARIABLES

The *correlation coefficient* provides a measure of the relationship between two non-nominal variables (x and y). To see the relationship between two variables visually, one can use a scatterplot, which is a graph with one variable on each axis and each point representing a pair of data points (see Figure 5.4). The most popular measure of the relationship between two variables, the Pearson correlation coefficient, or r, measures the linear relationship between two variables. It is computed using the following formula:

$$r = \Sigma \left[((x_i - \bar{x}) / s_x) ((y_i - \bar{y}) / s_y) \right] / (N),$$

where the summation is carried out over the k pairs of values and s is defined as the standard deviation of each variable. Correlation coefficients vary from -1 to $+1$, with either $+1$ or -1 indicating a perfect linear relationship. From the scatterplots in Figure 5.4, it is clear that there is a stronger linear relationship as the correlation increases and gets closer to $+1$. Scatterplots may also reveal that the variables are non-linearly related. In these cases, steps can be taken to account for nonlinearities as will be discussed in later chapters.

The correlation coefficient is most sensitive to linear relationships when both variables have symmetric distributions. Unfortunately, this is not always the case. In cases when one or both variables are skewed, one can use can use *nonparametric statistics*, such as γ, to evaluate the relationship between two variables. These types of statistics make fewer assumptions about the properties of the measurement scales and can be used for ordinal and nominal data. As an example, let's say that you were interested in whether there was a relationship between listening to National Public Radio (cEA14) and accessing information about the campaign online. Both variables are skewed. Looking at the three days before the Iowa caucuses in 2004, for instance, the Pearson correlation between the variables is 0.07 ($p = .20$); however, γ is 0.26 ($p < 0.05$). Due to the skewed nature of the data, the γ statistic would be more sensitive to the relationship between the variables. In analyzing the NAES, one should consider using different analytic procedures (e.g., statistical techniques for ordinal and interval level data, parametric and nonparametric approaches) before concluding that a particular result holds. Through the use of appropriate techniques, one may uncover support

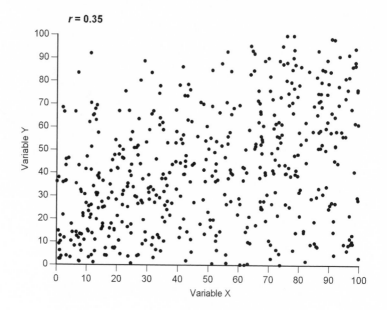

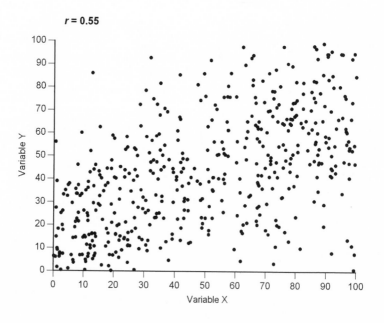

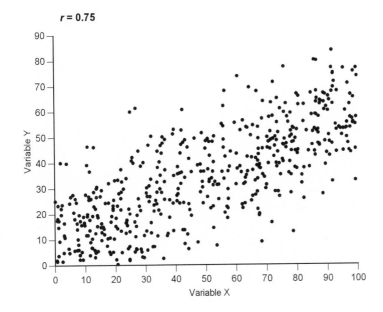

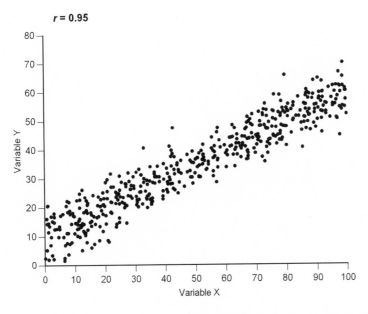

Figure 5.4. Scatter plots and correlations with increasing degrees of relationship.

for a relationship that is not apparent when using analytic approaches that are less appropriate for the data.

Conclusion

Inspection of a variable's distribution and consideration of scale type (e.g. nominal, ordinal, or interval) can help one to determine the most appropriate descriptive statistics. For example, while the mode is an appropriate measure of central tendency for nominal variables, the median can be used for ordinal measures and is less sensitive to skewed distributions than the mean. Before conducting statistical tests, researchers should conduct exploratory data analyses to understand each variable's distribution and relations with other variables. However, we do not recommend using scale type as a strict guide to the statistical technique that will be used. As Velleman and Wilkinson (1993) caution, "To restrict our investigation only to hypotheses and calculations permitted by an a priori assignment of scale type would be . . . irresponsible" (71).

To ensure that conclusions are justified, it is desirable to use multiple statistical methods and to evaluate the similarities in results. For example, when faced with evaluating the relationship between two variables, one may elect to use both a nonparametric and a parametric technique to evaluate whether they produce the same results. If the techniques agree, one may feel more comfortable presenting the parametric results. If they do not agree, one should consider whether one analysis is more appropriate than another based on the distributions of the data and their scale types. For example, for highly skewed data, the gamma statistic will produce a more sensitive description of the relationship between two variables than a Pearson correlation.

The data analytic techniques discussed in this chapter are important steps for investigating relationships in the data. One should not progress to the more advanced methods discussed in subsequent chapters without having an understanding of these techniques. Unless one has coded variables appropriately and taken note of skewed distributions, one will almost certainly have difficulty in applying the more complex methods that follow.

Notes

1. Though this is similar to a normal distribution, some restraint is used in labeling the distribution as "normal" because the formal characteristics of a normal distribution (e.g. appropriate levels of skewness and kurtosis) are not evaluated here.

2. Note that the "most" and "some" categories in the dataset have been combined in this chart.

3. It is possible distinguish interval level scales and ratio scales (ratio scales have an absolute zero while interval scales do not). We do not do so here because the analyses we discuss throughout the text require only interval data.

4. It is always important to carefully think about how one will treat responses of "don't know" or "refused." In the examples discussed in this chapter, these responses were not included in the computations (i.e., they were treated as missing data) unless otherwise noted.

5. For more details about computing gamma, see Siegel and Castellan (1988, 291–98).

6. Note that, in this example, "don't know" and "refused" responses to cCC26 are treated as incorrect.

References

Johnson, David R. and James C. Creech. 1983. Ordinal Measures in Multiple Indicator Models: A Simulation Study of Categorization Error. *American Sociological Review* 48: 398–407.

Lord, Frederic. 1953. On the Statistical Treatment of Football Numbers. *American Psychologist* 8: 750–51.

Moore, David S. and George P. McCabe. 1993. *Introduction to the Practice of Statistics.* 2nd ed. New York: W.H. Freeman.

Rosenberg, Morris. 1968. *The Logic of Survey Analysis.* New York: Basic Books.

Schutt, Russell K. 1996. *Investigating the Social World: The Process and Practice of Research.* Thousand Oaks, Calif.: Pine Forge Press.

Siegel, Sidney and N. John Castellan, Jr. 1988. *Nonparametric Statistics for the Behavioral Sciences.* 2nd ed. New York: McGraw-Hill.

Tukey, John W. 1977. *Exploratory Data Analysis.* Reading, Mass.: Addison-Wesley.

Velleman, Paul F. and Leland Wilkinson. 1993. Nominal, Ordinal, Interval, and Ratio Typologies Are Misleading. *American Statistician* 47, 1: 65–72.

Zumbo, Bruno D. and Donald W. Zimmerman. 1993. Is the Selection of Statistical Methods Governed by Level of Measure? *Canadian Psychology* 34, 4: 390–400.

Chapter 6
Visualizing Data Across the Campaign

KATE KENSKI

Charts and graphs can give insight into patterns and relationships that are not readily apparent when relying solely on statistical summaries. Cleveland (1993) argues that "Visualization is critical to data analysis. It provides a front line of attack, revealing intricate structure in data that cannot be absorbed in any other way. We discover unimagined effects, and we challenge imagined ones" (1). This chapter emphasizes the importance of graphing data when studying campaign dynamics. There are many ways in which researchers can use visual techniques to help them better understand their data and convey that understanding to others. This chapter suggests a couple of ways that information can be graphically displayed. We begin by discussing how researchers can be misled when they do not take a look at their data through visual techniques. Next, we turn our attention to the process of aggregating and smoothing data. And finally, we illustrate some of the advantages of using visual approaches with one's data.

Reasons for Visualizing Data

Visual techniques can uncover campaign dynamics in ways that statistical summaries of data often cannot. Charts and graphs can bring us closer to our data and help us explain our findings to others. Tufte (1983) argues that "Graphics *reveal* data. Indeed graphics can be more precise and revealing than conventional statistical computations. Consider Anscombe's quartet: all four of these data sets are described by exactly the same linear model (at least until the residuals are examined)" (13). Table 6.1 provides the data from Anscombe's quartet. The quartet refers to four datasets. Each dataset has eleven cases and two variables, X and Y. The individual values on each variable differ from dataset to dataset. Nevertheless, each has an X variable with a mean of 9 (SD = 3.32), and a Y variable with a mean of 7.5 (SD = 2.03). When a linear regression

TABLE 6.1. ANSCOMBE'S QUARTET

1		2		3		4	
X	Y	X	Y	X	Y	X	Y
10.0	8.04	10.0	9.14	10.0	7.46	8.0	6.58
8.0	6.95	8.0	8.14	8.0	6.77	8.0	5.76
13.0	7.58	13.0	8.74	13.0	12.74	8.0	7.71
9.0	8.81	9.0	8.77	9.0	7.11	8.0	8.84
11.0	8.33	11.0	9.26	11.0	7.81	8.0	8.47
14.0	9.96	14.0	8.10	14.0	8.84	8.0	7.04
6.0	7.24	6.0	6.13	6.0	6.08	8.0	5.25
4.0	4.26	4.0	3.10	4.0	5.39	19.0	12.50
12.0	10.84	12.0	9.13	12.0	8.15	8.0	5.56
7.0	4.82	7.0	7.26	7.0	6.42	8.0	7.91
5.0	5.68	5.0	4.74	5.0	5.73	8.0	6.89

equation is calculated for each dataset, the equation is the same: $Y = 3.0 + .5X$.[1]

Based on the means, standard deviations, and regression equations, it is tempting to assume that each dataset is essentially the same as the others. Visual techniques can highlight important aspects of the data that are not readily apparent by means, standard deviations, and other statistics. Figure 6.1 plots Anscombe's quartet and shows that the relationship between X and Y varies greatly from dataset to dataset. Each dataset looks quite different from the others. These plots show that a linear model does not suit some of these datasets. Dataset Two, for example, needs a curvilinear model to capture it more accurately.

Graphical displays of data can help us better understand phenomena. In his discussion of the Anscombe quartet, Diebold (2001) offers four reasons to look at graphics (53). First, "*Graphics helps us summarize and reveal patterns in data,* as, for example, with linear versus nonlinear functional form in the first and second Anscombe datasets." When we run correlations or ordinary least squares (OLS) regressions, we assume that the data have an underlying linear form. When we plot the data and see that nonlinear patterns are apparent, we must rethink our assumptions. Sometimes this means that we should transform the variables in some way, and other times it means that we need to rethink the types of statistical methods we are using.

Second, "Graphics helps us identify anomalies in data, as in the third Anscombe dataset." There is a single outlier in the top right corner of Dataset Three's graph. Such an outlier will pull the regression line toward it. When outliers appear, we should take steps to identify them. Outliers can often give us new insight into our theories. In the event that

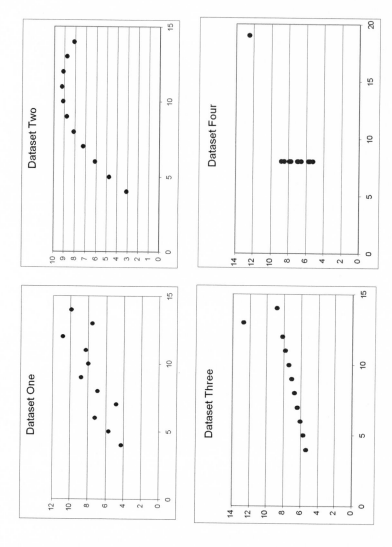

Figure 6.1. Scatter plots of Anscombe's quartet.

we decide to delete outliers from our analyses and re-run our models, we must make sure that we note the deletion in our reports.

Third, Diebold notes, "Less obvious, but most definitely relevant, is the fact that graphics facilitates and encourages comparison of different pieces of data." By plotting these datasets next to one another as we did in Figure 6.1, for example, we can compare them instantaneously. One immediately sees the datasets exemplify very different relationships. And finally, he explains that:

There is one more aspect of the power of statistical graphics. It comes into play in the analysis of large datasets, so it wasn't revealed in the analysis of the Anscombe datasets, which are not large, but it is nevertheless tremendously important. *Graphics enables us to present a huge amount of data in a small space, and it enables us to make huge datasets coherent.*

Aggregating Data

The NAES data files contain individual-level data. Each case in these data reflects the responses of an individual respondent. To look at variations in the data over time, the individual cases can be aggregated to a larger, temporal unit, such as day. Many statistical packages have commands that allow researchers to convert data into larger units. To aggregate data to day, a variable is selected from one of the RCS datasets, in which many individuals have responded. So that the date of interview variable can become the new unit of analysis, a mean of the individual responses on the variable of interest should be calculated for each day. A new dataset can be made, where each case is now the date of interview rather than individual respondent.

Figure 6.2 shows the average feeling thermometer evaluations of Republican Dick Cheney (cA48) and Democrat Joseph Lieberman (cA49), the 2000 vice-presidential candidates, from August 7, 2000 to January 19, 2001. Overall, the public gave relatively favorable ratings to the VP candidates. Neither candidate had evaluation averages that went below 50, the value given to candidates for whom respondents felt neither favorable nor unfavorable. How were these data aggregated? The feeling thermometer evaluations for each candidate were aggregated for each day. For example, on August 7, there were 233 respondents who gave substantive answers to the Cheney feeling thermometer question, meaning that the respondents received the question and did not refuse to answer it. Their answers ranged from 0 to 100. These responses were averaged together so that a single number, 57.79, represents responses for August 7. The same was done for the Lieberman evaluations.

As mentioned in Chapter 4, data on some dates are missing in the NAES datasets because we did not interview people on some holidays.

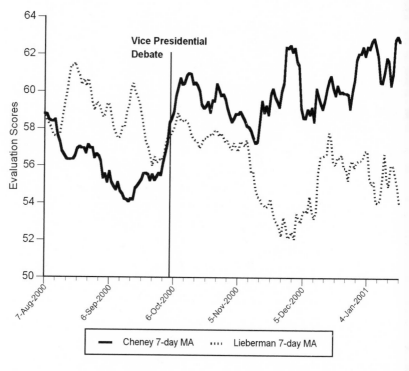

Figure 6.2. Cheney and Lieberman's feeling thermometer evaluations from August 7, 2000 to January 19, 2001 (MA, moving average).

There are different strategies for handling missing data. One could chart the data and simply leave the missing dates out of the continuum. One could also take an average of the days surrounding the missing date and insert the average to hold the date's place in the continuum. For example, since November 7 is missing, one could take an average from the responses made on November 6 and 8 and insert the average before charting the data. Whichever strategy is used, researchers should report how they have decided to handle these dates in their data analysis reports. In the dataset used to create Figure 6.2, missing data appeared on November 7, November 23, December 24–25, December 31, and January 1. We inserted averages for the dates on which data were missing.

Illustrating the Relationships Between Series

On October 5, 2000, the vice-presidential candidates had participated in a televised debate. Around this time, Cheney's evaluations rose, while

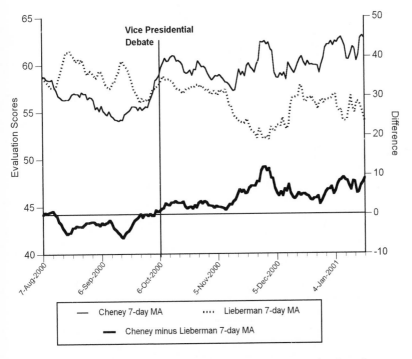

Figure 6.3. Cheney and Lieberman's feeling thermometer evaluations from
August 7, 2000 to January 19, 2001 (MA, moving average).

Lieberman's fell slightly, as shown in Figure 6.2. While one can see that
there is a relationship between these two series of evaluations, graphs
can be used to illustrate differences between series even more strikingly.
Figure 6.3 builds on the graph shown in Figure 6.2, adding a line that
shows the difference between the Cheney and Lieberman evaluations.
The thick black line at the bottom of the graph shows the difference
between Cheney and Lieberman's evaluations using the righthand side
axis of the graph. When this line is above zero, it means that Cheney's
evaluations were higher than Lieberman's. When it goes below zero, it
means that Lieberman was rated more highly than Cheney on average.

Smoothing Data Through Moving Averages

Daily cross-sections are subject to sampling variation. The underlying
patterns in data can be obscured by this variation, which decreases as
one's sample size increases. Consequently, pooling data across days
makes graphs more readable: "otherwise the real shifts would be

TABLE 6.2. HYPOTHETICAL EXAMPLE OF MOVING AVERAGES

Day	Original value	Five-day centered moving average	Five-day prior moving average
1	5		
2	4		
3	3	3.4	
4	3	3.2	
5	2	3.2	3.4
6	4	4.2	3.2
7	4	4.6	3.2
8	8		4.2
9	5		4.6

scarcely detectable through the uninteresting day-to-day fluctuation induced by sampling error" (Johnston et al. 1992, 26). By pooling data across days, some of the random sampling variation is smoothed out of the graph, giving us a better sense of where the true population percentages lie.

One way to smooth data is by using moving averages, which pool data across days. Two commonly used moving average techniques are the centered moving average and the prior moving average. The centered moving average for a particular day is that day's value averaged with specified values around it. A five-day centered moving average, for example, takes the value of a particular day plus the values on the two days before it and the values on the two days after it and averages them. In Table 6.2, the five-day center moving average for day 3 is the sum of the values for days 1–5 divided by 5: (5 + 4 + 3 + 3 +2) / 5. By performing similar calculations for the other days, a smoother pattern than the initial observations is revealed when the data are plotted.

The prior moving average for a particular day is that day's value averaged with a specified set of values before it. A five-day prior moving average, for example, takes the value of a particular day plus the values on the four days preceding it and averages them. Notice that the five-day moving average is the same as the centered moving average simply offset by two days.

There are no hard-and-fast rules about which type of moving average is preferable. It is important to note, however, that the centered moving average takes on the values of data following a given day. Since day 3 of a five-day centered moving average is influenced by the values that come after it, changes in the data may appear in the graph before they actually occurred. Let's suppose, for example, that some event occurred on day 8. This event increased the value of the variable. While the increase is

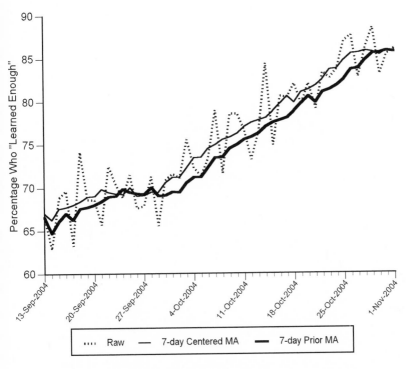

Figure 6.4. Percentage of citizens who said they had "learned enough" about the candidates and issues from September 13 to November 2, 2004 by raw aggregations, centered moving averages, and prior moving averages (MA, moving average).

not picked up in the prior moving average until day 8, it is picked up in the centered moving average on day 6. This does not make the centered moving average less useful. The dynamics will still be picked up in the data but at a slightly earlier point in time.

Figure 6.4 illustrates the difference between a centered moving average and a prior moving average. Beginning September 13, 2004, survey respondents were asked: "So far have you learned enough about the candidates and the issues to make an informed choice between the candidates, or have you found it difficult to choose because you feel you have not learned enough?" (cFF16).[2] Figure 6.4 tracks the percentage of citizens who had reported that they had "learned enough." The graph shows that the centered moving averages change before the prior moving averages.

The more days that are used to create the moving average, the

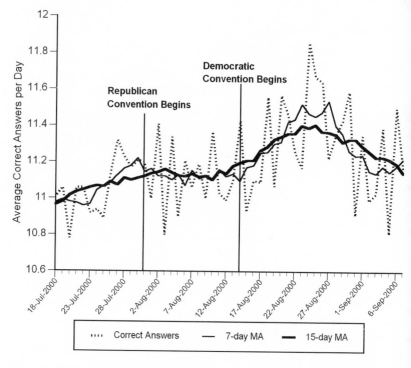

Figure 6.5. Knowledge index of major party candidate issue positions from July 18 to September 7, 2000 (MA, moving average).

smoother that the data become. Figure 6.5 contains a seven-day centered moving average and a fifteen-day one. From July 18 to September 7, 2000, NAES respondents were asked a total of eighteen candidate issue position questions—nine questions about George W. Bush and nine about Al Gore.[3] These questions were used to create a knowledge index. The sampling variation in the initial observations covers up some of the important patterns in the data. Using the centered moving averages, it becomes clear that knowledge increased as the Republican National Convention began. Knowledge about the candidates then leveled off until the beginning of the Democratic National Convention, when knowledge increased again. About a week after the Democratic convention ended, the gains in knowledge began to recede.

Across how many days should data be averaged? The answer depends in part on the daily sample sizes. If they are small, one may need to pool more days to smooth out the sampling variation. But once again, there are no hard-and-fast rules. If one uses too many days to create the moving average, one risks oversmoothing the data to the point where important variation is obscured. Johnston et al. (1992) observe that "pooling has a disadvantage: where the true percentage is shifting, mixing values together from different days can mask the shift" (26). If one smoothes across as many days as possible, the value will take on the mean of the variable. For those wanting to capture campaign dynamics, this smoothing approach is not useful. As a general rule, it is better to have graphs containing some sampling variation than risk oversmoothing the data to the point where dynamics are concealed. The goal is to find a balance between sampling variation obscuring the dynamics at one extreme and merely reflecting the overall mean of the variable at the other.

To see if the patterns of knowledge acquisition differed by candidate, the candidate knowledge index was broken down into two indices: one for knowledge about Bush's issue positions and one for Gore's. Figure 6.6 tracks these indices around the convention periods using seven-day and fifteen-day centered moving averages. While the lines using the seven-day moving average are not as smooth as they could be, the campaign dynamics are revealed. There are some changes in the respondents' understanding of Bush's issue positions, but the greater changes appear in their understanding of Gore's. Knowledge about Bush increased as the Republican convention approached but then leveled off. Knowledge about Gore, however, increased most dramatically after the Democratic convention began. In transmitting knowledge about issue positions, the Democratic convention was more successful than the Republican convention.

Advantages of the Visual Approach

There are two major advantages to engaging in the task of graphing data. First, graphs may reveal relationship structures that were not assumed previously. And second, graphs can communicate information to one's audience more easily and efficiently than information given in tabular form. To illustrate these advantages, we will use data from the NAES on absentee and early voting during the 2000 general election campaign.

As we saw with Anscombe's quartet, it is often not until data are graphed that we begin to understand their underlying structure. Cleveland (1993) explains that bivariate data in a scatterplot have two components of variation. "One component is a smooth underlying pattern . . . Fitting such bivariate data means determining a smooth curve that describes the underlying pattern. The second component is residual variation about this underlying pattern—the vertical deviations of the

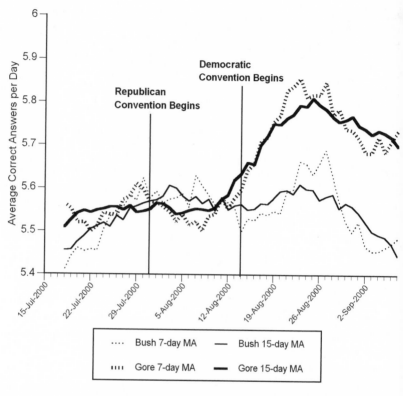

Figure 6.6. Knowledge of Bush and Gore's issue positions from July 18 to September 7, 2000 (MA, moving average).

points from the smooth curve" (8). Determining the underlying structure is important.

Election Day is thought to be the time when American citizens cast their votes for the political leaders of their choice. The notion that all American voters cast their ballots on a single day, however, is no longer accurate. In many states, citizens are given the opportunity to vote prior to Election Day by either balloting by mail or voting early at polling stations. Election Day is more accurately described as the last day when voting for candidates takes place. As this section will demonstrate through the graphing of responses from the NAES, campaign studies that fail to acknowledge that voting often takes place weeks before Election Day ignore an important campaign dynamic.

As explained in Chapter 2, a unique feature of the NAES preelection surveys was that rather than assuming that they had not voted before

Election Day, respondents were asked whether they had already voted at the time they were interviewed. This allows researchers to distinguish between voting intentions and behavior during the preelection period. Ajzen and Fishbein (1980) argue that intentions and behavior are not synonymous; a large body of social psychological research confirms this distinction. As absentee and early voting grows in popularity, the distinction between voting intentions and voting behavior during the preelection period becomes an increasingly important one.

How prevalent was voting before Election Day in the 2000 presidential campaign? The NAES 2000 weighted postelection survey data collected between November 8 and November 21, treated as a single cross section, show that 14 percent of those who voted in the general election cast their ballots before Election Day. The unweighted data put the estimate at 15 percent. Why should it matter to campaigns that one in seven U.S. voters cast their ballots early in 2000? If all absentee and early voting ballots were cast the day before the election, then absentee and early voting would not greatly affect how campaigns are conducted. If absentee and early voting takes place over the course of several weeks prior to Election Day, however, politicians would have to adopt different types of campaign strategies to ensure that they get their messages out before citizens have cast their ballots. The structure of absentee and early voting during the preelection period, therefore, becomes important for us to understand.

We can use the preelection national rolling cross section to trace the prevalence of absentee and early voting from October to Election Day in 2000. The unweighted dataset is used so that readers can replicate the results more easily.[4] What does a graph of absentee and early voting reveal? Figure 6.7 shows that over the course of October, the percentage of the electorate, defined as those who plan to vote (cR30) or have already voted (cR34) in the general election, that has already cast ballots increases as Election Day approaches. Because the daily samples are subject to sampling variation, a five-day centered moving average is used to approximate the underlying dynamics by pooling the data across five days. The five-day moving average reveals that by October 23, fifteen days before Election Day, about 5 percent of the electorate had already voted. Nine days before Election Day, on October 29, 10 percent of the electorate had cast their ballots. By November 4, around 15 percent of the electorate had balloted.

This example shows that plotting data can challenge our assumptions about campaign dynamics. Data from the NAES clearly show that voting does not take place on a single day. For a many voters, the act of voting takes place weeks before Election Day. Campaigns that fail to recognize that some will vote before Election Day may end up wasting their

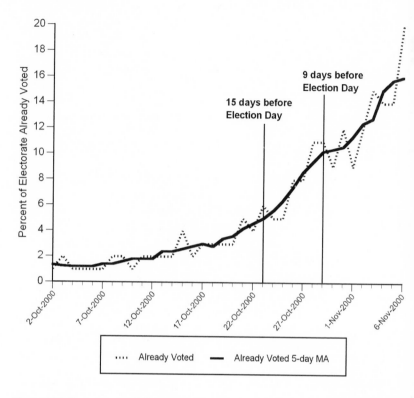

Figure 6.7. Percentage of electorate that voted prior to Election Day 2000 (MA, moving average).

resources on messages to people who have already cast their ballots. Political communication scholars who fail to recognize the prevalence of absentee and early voting miss out on understanding fundamental campaign dynamics.

In Figure 6.7, we used a five-day centered moving average to smooth the data in order to reveal an underlying pattern. While we can impose many types of structures on our data, Figure 6.7 reveals that the pattern underlying voting before Election Day was nonlinear. While the linear model is widely used, it does not always best reflect the true pattern underlying our observations.

Figure 6.8 shows two types of models that have been fit to the data: a linear trend and an exponential curve.[5] The jagged line represents our initial observations. Our visual inspection of the data suggests that the exponential curve fits over the observations better than the linear trend

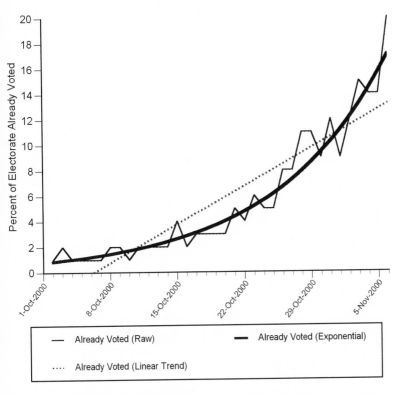

Figure 6.8. Percentage of electorate that voted prior to Election Day 2000 with linear and exponential fits to the data.

as there is less error between the initial observations and the exponential curve than there is between the initial observations and the linear trend.

Graphing data is an important component of the research process. Rather than just assuming that phenomena have a specific structure, data should be graphed to see whether the researcher's assumptions are valid. "Statistical graphs are central to effective data analysis, both in the early stages of an investigation and in statistical modeling" (Fox 1997, 35).

A second advantage of graphing data is that visual representations can capture dynamics in ways that are more striking than when dynamics are revealed in equations. The adage that "a picture is worth a thousand words" applies to data analysis. Pictures give us an intuitive understanding of data and allow us to better communicate our findings to others.

TABLE 6.3. PERCENTAGE OF THE TWO-PARTY VOTE FAVORING BUSH IN THE LAST
DAYS OF THE 2000 PRESIDENTIAL CAMPAIGN

Date	Voting intention for Bush	Already voted for Bush	Combined intention/ behavior for Bush
11/2/00	50%	52%	50%
	($N = 191$)	($N = 25$)	($N = 216$)
11/3/00	49%	60%	51%
	($N = 199$)	($N = 35$)	($N = 234$)
11/4/00	47%	56%	49%
	($N = 156$)	($N = 25$)	($N = 181$)
11/5/00	49%	43%	48%
	($N = 189$)	($N = 30$)	($N = 219$)
11/6/00	49%	63%	51%
	($N = 171$)	($N = 41$)	($N = 212$)

While tables are of great interest to researchers studying a topic, they hold less appeal for those who are less knowledgeable or initially less interested in it. Graphs can often convey a wealth of information more easily than tables.

For example, campaign researchers want to know: Where did the electorate stand at a given point during the campaign? Because of absentee and early voting, researchers should not rely solely on the voting intentions variable when using the NAES data to figure out which presidential candidate was ahead or behind in the general election campaign. In 2000, those who cast their ballots before Election Day were more likely to vote for Bush. In the unweighted postelection sample from November 8 to January 19, 58.2 percent of early voters said they voted for Bush compared to 51 percent of Election Day voters (chi-square $= 8.761$, df $= 1$, $p<.003$).[6]

Since those who voted before Election Day were more likely to cast their ballots for Bush, preelection analyses should take early voters into account. If one is interested in only those who are capable of being persuaded, then *voting intentions* may be the variable of interest. However, if one is interested in where the whole electorate stood at any given point in time, then one should combine the survey's voting intention and voting behavior variables.

Table 6.3 shows the daily percentages of the two-party vote favoring Bush in the last five days of the campaign. The voting intentions percentages tend to lean toward Gore (cR27). The early voting decisions tend to lean toward Bush (cR35). When combined, neither candidate is predominant.

Figure 6.9 tracks the percentages of the two-party vote choice for Bush from October 16 to November 6, 2000, using a seven-day centered mov-

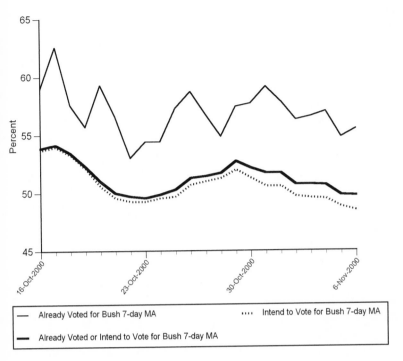

Figure 6.9. Percentage of two-party vote preference for Bush by intention, early ballot, and combined from October 16 to November 6, 2000 (MA, moving average).

ing average. This graph demonstrates that as Election Day approaches, it becomes important for researchers to combine the voting intention and voting behavior measures if they want to capture where the electorate stands in its vote preference. While looking solely at the voting intention variable would suggest that Gore was over a percent ahead of Bush the day before Election Day, the combined intention/behavior measure suggests a statistical dead heat between the candidates.

There are a few drawbacks to the visual approach. While graphing techniques can give us greater insight into our data, they are not a replacement for hypothesis testing. There is a bit of subjectivity used when constructing graphs. Potentially, researchers could tell a story around the data, rather than bringing a story to the data and testing it. The problem with telling stories around the data is that when data are collected via random sampling, there is a possibility that the results appear by chance.

Conclusion

There are many ways that data can be visually displayed. We have discussed only a few techniques in this chapter. One does not necessarily need to aggregate data to look at the relationship between time and other variables. Nevertheless, aggregating data to the daily level can allow researchers to look at campaign dynamics in compelling ways.

Graphical displays of data can challenge the assumptions that we make and effectively communicate findings. When used in conjunction with other methods, graphing data across the campaign helps researchers better understand and explain campaign dynamics.

Notes

1. The R^2 statistic tells us how much of the variation in the dependent variable that the model explains. The R^2 for each model is .67. The standard error of the regression for each dataset is 1.24.
2. Beginning September 23, 2004, the question was modified for those who had already cast their ballots (via early or absentee voting): "By the time you voted in the presidential election, did you learn enough about the candidates and the issues to make an informed choice between the candidates, or did you find it difficult to choose because you felt you had not learned enough?" (cFF17).
3. For Bush, these items were cBE18, cBF09, cBG08, cBE09, cBH04, cBG02, cBL02, cBD05, and cBC07. For Gore, these items were cBE19, cBF10, cBG09, cBE10, cBH05, cBG03, cBL03, cBD06, and cBC08.
4. The difference between the weighted and unweighted datasets on the early balloting estimates is small.
5. Trends will be discussed in more detail in Chapters 9 and 10.
6. The postelection absentee/early voting variable was cR36; the vote choice variable was cR35.

References

Ajzen, Icek and Martin Fishbein. 1980. *Understanding Attitudes and Predicting Social Behavior.* Englewood Cliffs, N.J.: Prentice-Hall.
Cleveland, William S. 1993. *Visualizing Data.* Summit, N.J.: Hobart Press.
Diebold, Francis X. 2001. *Elements of Forecasting.* 2nd ed. Cincinnati, Oh.: South-Western.
Fox, John. 1997. *Applied Regression Analysis, Linear Models, and Related Methods.* Thousand Oaks, Calif.: Sage.
Johnston, Richard, André Blais, Henry E. Brady, and Jean Crête. 1992. *Letting the People Decide: Dynamics of a Canadian Election.* Stanford, Calif.: Stanford University Press.
Tufte, Edward R. 1983. *The Visual Display of Quantitative Information.* Cheshire, Conn.: Graphics Press.

Chapter 7

Linear and Logistic Regression Models for Cross-Sectional Analyses

DANIEL ROMER

In this chapter we outline the major strategies for analyzing the NAES using cross-sectional designs. In addition, we review the ways in which linear and logistic regression can be used to analyze these data.

The NAES opens four avenues of analysis using different designs: (1) the panel design involving respondents who were interviewed more than once during the study period; (2) the cross-sectional design involving respondents at only one time period; (3) the repeated cross-sectional design that is the same as the cross-sectional design but conducted at successive time periods or in waves; and (4) the rolling cross-sectional design that permits time series analysis with respondents aggregated potentially at each day of the year.

Although the panel study has many advantages, it is limited in its ability to assess changes as they occur in time. Furthermore, repeated assessment in the panel design can introduce biases that are less likely when respondents have not been previously interviewed. One solution to the bias and limits of the panel study is to conduct a separate study using different cross-sectional samples to allow estimates of changes during the election and to avoid the problems of repeated assessment. This design has different individuals at each wave in the data table. It can be conducted as a stand-alone survey or as a complement to the panel design.

The Repeated Cross-Sectional Design

Table 7.1 contains the data matrix for a cross-sectional analysis in a hypothetical four-wave design. For purposes of illustration, we only show one dependent variable Y_{ti} and two independent variables X_{1ti}, X_{2ti} at each wave as an example of the data layout. There could be any number of both dependent and independent variables in each cell of the design.

TABLE 7.1. DATA MATRIX IN A REPEATED CROSS-SECTIONAL DESIGN WITH FOUR WAVES

Case (i)	Wave (t)			
	1	2	3	4
1	Y_{11}, X_{111}, X_{211}	Y_{21}, X_{121}, X_{221}	Y_{31}, X_{131}, X_{231}	Y_{41}, X_{141}, X_{241}
2	Y_{12}, X_{112}, X_{212}	Y_{22}, X_{121}, X_{222}	Y_{32}, X_{132}, X_{232}	Y_{42}, X_{142}, X_{242}
i	Y_{1i}, X_{11i}, X_{21i}	Y_{2i}, X_{12i}, X_{22i}	Y_{3i}, X_{13i}, X_{23i}	Y_{4i}, X_{14i}, X_{24i}
N − 1	$Y_{1N-1}, X_{11N-1},$ X_{2N-1}	$Y_{2N-1}, X_{12N-1}, X_{22N-1}$	$Y_{3N-1}, X_{13N-1},$ X_{23N-1}	$Y_{4N-1}, X_{13N-1},$ X_{24N-1}
N	Y_{1N}, X_{11N}, X_{21N}	Y_{2N}, X_{12N}, X_{22N}	Y_{3N}, X_{13N}, X_{23N}	Y_{3N}, X_{13N}, X_{23}

Y is the dependent variable; X_{1ti} and X_{2ti} are independent variables at wave t and case i.

The data points are identified by both cases (i) and waves representing successive time periods (t). Each case refers to a set of scores obtained from one respondent at one wave of data collection. Unlike the panel design, the cross-sectional design only includes observations on unique individuals at a single wave. There is no requirement that the number of cases at each wave be the same, although it is desirable to aggregate time periods with roughly similar numbers of cases. In this example, there are a total of NT unique cases in the design distributed over the T waves of data collection.

The rolling cross-sectional design of the NAES makes it possible to analyze changes on a daily basis. However, for this purpose, we recommend using the time series analyses described in Chapter 9. In this chapter, we assume more interest either in general relationships between responses in the survey at one time period (e.g., a month during the election cycle) or in more global changes assessed across time periods (e.g., successive weeks or months of the election cycle) than in daily trends. We will illustrate analysis strategies for both types of questions. First, because it is the model we will use most often to analyze cross-sectional data, we will review some basics of linear regression analysis.

The Linear Regression Model

To estimate models with time and other predictors, we use the most popular model in the social sciences, *linear regression*. The model is easy to estimate, and there is a unique solution for almost all data sets. In addition, it is easy to test the significance of the parameters. The analysis uses an equation that relates a dependent variable to one or more of k independent and nonredundant variables:

$$Y_i = b_0 + b_1 X_{1i} + \ldots + b_k X_{ki} + e_i.$$

here are $i = 1$ to N observations of each variable in the equation. As ong as there are more observations than variables, one can solve the quation. The more observations one has, the more certain one can be bout the range of values of the parameters (the values of b_k). Indeed, he standard error surrounding the estimates of the parameters is an nverse function of N. The last term in the model (e_i) is a random component that is assumed to have a mean of 0 and a standard deviation hat is constant across predicted values of Y. This term is called the error or residual in the equation because it is not predicted by any of the X variables in the model. The major aim of the regression model is to predict values of Y. The random component is simply the residual that emains after the predicted score Y_i is subtracted from the observed score Y_i:

$$e_i = Y_i - Y_i.$$

Causal Model Representation of Linear Regression

Another way to represent a regression model is to use a causal diagram (Figure 7.1) The diagram tells us that the independent variables lead to the dependent variable with weights from b_0 to b_k. A regression model does not imply causation, but we often use it to estimate "effects" that are assumed to represent causal relations between the independent variables and dependent variable. Even if we do not interpret the relations as causal, we often try to rule out reverse causal directions from Y to any of the Xs.

The curved arrows between the independent variables tell us that the variables may be related to each other. But these relations only indicate that the variables are potentially correlated with each other and do not specify a causal connection. The b weights represent the relation between each independent variable and the dependent variable holding constant correlations with other variables. One consequence of possible correlation between variables is that estimates of the weights depend on the variables in the model. If a variable that is related to a predictor is left out of the model, the predictor's effect may be misrepresented.

The potential for unknown predictors is shown in Figure 7.1 by the presence of U_y. In causal model diagrams, unobserved variables are enclosed by circles while observed variables are in boxes. If U_y were correlated with any of the Xs, the weights could change. The model assumes that the effect of unknown components is represented by the constant term in the model (b_0). There is often no way to know whether the constant term contains variables that are correlated with the Xs, but researchers tend to include as many relevant variables as possible in

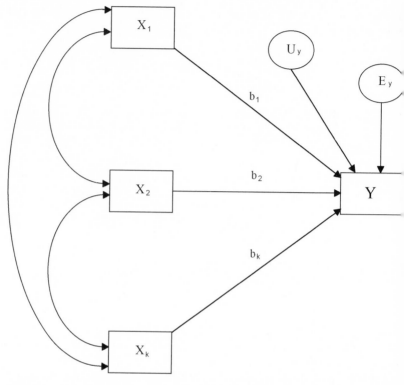

Figure 7.1. Causal diagram of relations between independent (X) and dependent variables (Y), including the contribution of unknown causes (U_y) and measurement error (E_y).

their models to reduce the chances that an important variable has been neglected. Short of this strategy, one must assume that any unknown predictors are uncorrelated with the Xs (as the diagram indicates). The diagram also tells us that the measurement error in Y is uncorrelated with the predictors. This is also an assumption in the model. *The analysis always produces an error term that is uncorrelated with the predictors, so one cannot test this assumption directly.* But if the assumption is incorrect, then the model will misrepresent the effects of one or more predictors.

Ordinary Least Squares Estimation of the Linear Regression Model

We usually use a procedure called *ordinary least squares* (OLS) to estimate the regression model. This procedure estimates the parameters in the model such that the resulting error variation is minimized (i.e., the error variance). The error variance around the predicted scores is defined as

$$V_E = \Sigma \, (Y_i - Y_i)^2 \, / \, N.$$

The simplest OLS estimate of any variable is the mean. The mean serves as the best predictor of a score if no other information is available. It is also the estimate with the smallest error variance. The variance around the mean defines the total variance in the dependent variable, V_T. This variance is equal to the error variance plus whatever variance is predicted by the model (V_P):

$$V_T = V_P + V_E.$$

One measure of the ability of an OLS solution to fit the data is the ratio of the predicted variance divided by the total variance,

$$R^2 = V_P \, / \, V_T.$$

This measure is called R^2 because it equals the square of the correlation between the predicted score and the dependent variable.

Even if a model has a good fit, it is not necessarily useful. When two or more independent variables are so highly related that there is nothing unique about them (they are essentially redundant), we have a situation known as collinearity. In this case, the model may fit the data quite well, but the parameters will also be uninterpretable. We usually see this happen when the parameters and their standard errors are extremely large. Another sign of possible collinearity is dramatic change in the direction of the parameters when collinear variables are added to the equation. If parameters exhibit dramatic sign changes or become extremely large as variables are added to the equation, then it is a good idea to see if some of the predictors are so highly related that they cancel each other in the prediction equation.

When we use OLS to estimate the parameters of the linear regression model, we make at least three assumptions.

1. Variance in the error is constant across predicted values of Y, a condition known as *homoskedasticity*. If the errors vary systematically in size with predicted values of Y (*heteroskedasticity*), then the model cannot produce a single set of estimates of the standard errors.
2. The errors are uncorrelated with each other. That is, the error for

one case is not related to the error of another case. This is the assumption of zero autocorrelation.

3. The analysis also assumes that the errors have a normal distribution. This permits us to use standard statistical tests for the parameters (e.g., t tests).

CODING OF PREDICTORS

One of the more important considerations in setting up a regression model is the coding of the independent variables. There are three basic types of independent variables in a regression model.

1. *Quantitative* variables represent ordered variation in a predictor (see Chapter 5 for a discussion of different types of variables). Some examples include political ideology, age, education, and ratings of candidate personality. We also can rescale any of these variables so that they have a mean of zero, in which case they are called *contrasts*.

The benefit of this rescaling is that it permits an interpretation of the b weight as a value relative to the average of the predictor. So, a score above zero adds to the dependent variable and a score below zero detracts from the dependent variable. Although rescaling is helpful in interpreting the b weights, it does not change the statistical significance of a predictor. Some examples of quantitative variables include

- 1, -1 for a two-level variable, where 1 represents high values and -1 low values;
- 1, 0, -1 for a three-level variable where 0 represents an intermediate value;
- -1, 2, -1 for a three-level variable that peaks in the middle;
- 1, 2, 3, 4 for increasing levels of a variable, such as attention to news about an election.

2. *Dummy* variables are indicators that represent a distinction between a category and everything else. Some examples include the following:

- male gender as $+1$ and female gender as 0;
- Democrats as $+1$ and everyone else as 0;
- persons who saw a debate as $+1$ and everyone else as 0.

This procedure can be used to make $J - 1$ predictions for any variable with J distinctions. For gender, there is only one possible dummy variable because it only takes one variable to distinguish between two categories. For political party there can be more dummy variables. Typically, one makes at least three distinctions among party types in the United States (i.e., Democrat, Republican, and independent).

Each predictor adds the value of the *b* weight for the category when it is equal to 1 and adds nothing for the category when it has a score of zero. Categories that are always assigned a value of zero (e.g., females in the example above) are termed *reference* categories because all the other dummy variables are contrasted with the reference.

3. *Interaction* variables are products of either of the aforementioned variables. For example, we can multiply gender by political ideology to ask whether either variable predicts the dependent variable differently across values of the other variable. Some analysts call this a *moderator* effect.

For example, if one wanted to know whether the effect of party identification depended on gender, one could construct an interaction between the two variables. If gender were coded 1, 0 (male, female) and party were coded 1, 0, -1 (Republican, Independent, Democrat), then the interaction of gender X party would be 1, 0, -1 for men and 0 for all women.

CODING OF DEPENDENT VARIABLES

When we analyze a dependent variable, it is sometimes helpful to rescale the response or to combine responses across dependent variables. One combination takes differences between candidates as indicators of differential response to the candidates. For example, if we were interested in differential reactions to Bush and Gore in the 2000 election on the favorability thermometer scale, we could take the difference between them as a measure of this reaction: Bush-Gore. A positive score would reflect a more favorable reaction to Bush than to Gore. A negative score would reflect the reverse.

Difference scores remove idiosyncratic uses of the thermometer scale by different respondents. Some respondents may use the lower end of the scale for all candidates, while others may use the upper end. But when we take differences, we measure the relative standing of one candidate versus the other.

If we want to remove this kind of idiosyncratic use of the response scale for all candidates, we can take all the thermometer ratings a respondent provides and calculate the mean of these ratings. We can then take each rating (X_i) and subtract the mean (M) from it. In this case, the scores reflect each candidate's standing relative to the mean of all candidates:

$$x_i = (X_i - M).$$

Another strategy that removes not only the mean but also the tendency to use a wider range of the scale standardizes all the ratings that a respondent makes on a common scale with a mean of zero and a standard deviation of 1. This removes both the average level of response and the dispersion of response. This is the familiar standard score,

$$Z_i = (X_i - M) / SD (X_i),$$

where SD represents the standard deviation or square root of the variance.

Examples of Cross-Sectional Analyses

EFFECTS OF BACKGROUND VARIABLES ON POLITICAL OUTCOMES

One of the simpler uses of cross-sectional data examines the relation between stable background variables, such as demographic variables or party affiliation, and attitudes toward candidates or issues. For example, how do respondent party affiliation and political ideology influence attitudes toward candidates? To illustrate the use of an interaction term in a regression model, we will analyze thermometer ratings in the 2000 election of Bush's favorability (cAOl) using the respondent's party affiliation (cVOl) and political ideology (cVO4) as predictors.

Based on theories of social identity (e.g., Turner 1987), we would expect that party members would be less inclined to evaluate a candidate on the basis of their own political ideology and more inclined to evaluate the candidate on the basis of membership in their party. On the other hand, we would expect Independents to evaluate either candidate of the major parties more on the basis of their own ideology than on party identification. This prediction involves an interaction between party affiliation and ideology such that the effect of ideology is stronger among Independents than among Democrats or Republicans.

We select for analysis a time range in the survey when the parties have made their choices of presidential nominee, namely, a four-week span beginning in early September. We can see if the predictors interact by examining the means of the dependent variable as a function of the predictors. Figure 7.2 shows that Bush is rated most favorably by both conservatives and Republicans, as we would expect. In addition, Bush's ratings decline as respondents' ideology becomes more liberal. However, we are interested in the prediction that political ideology has less impact on Bush's rating among Republicans and Democrats than among Independents[1]. These interactions are understandable if party affiliation increases loyalty to the party's nominee.

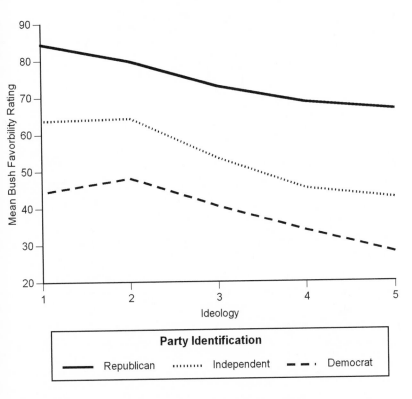

Figure 7.2. Bush's favorability rating as a function of respondent party and political ideology (1 = Very Conservative, 5 = Very Liberal).

To test these interactions, we can create dummy variables for the two parties, Republicans and Democrats, with Independents as the reference category. We can also transform ideology into a contrast that ranges from −2 (very conservative) to +2 (very liberal). This coding further defines the reference category as only including those Independents who label themselves at the midpoint of the ideology scale. We can also create interactions between the two parties and ideology to represent the possible moderating effect of party on ideology. The interactions are simply the products of the respective component variables (i.e., party X political ideology).

The results of the regression analysis in Table 7.2 show that indeed both party affiliation and political ideology influence ratings of Bush. For example, for every unit increase in liberal political ideology, there is an approximate 7.9 unit decrease in rating (see the unstandardized coefficients or B weights). Similarly, for every unit change in conserva-

TABLE 7.2. REGRESSION ANALYSIS OF BUSH FAVORABILITY RATING
(THERMOMETER) AS A FUNCTION OF RESPONDENT POLITICAL IDEOLOGY,
PARTY, AND INTERACTIONS BETWEEN PARTIES AND IDEOLOGY

	Unstandardized coefficients		Standardized coefficients		
	B	Std. error	Beta	t	Prob.
Constant	54.19	.53		102.48	.00
Ideology (PI)	− 7.88	.61	− .23	− 12.96	.00
Republicans (RP)	19.50	.89	.29	21.80	.00
Democrats (DP)	− 13.89	.76	− .21	− 18.29	.00
RP × PI	2.26	.92	.04	2.46	.01
DP × PI	1.89	.86	.03	2.20	.03

tive ideology (values of − 1 and − 2), there is the same *increase* in Bush's favorability.

The constant in the model is the reference point for all the other variables. In this case, it represents the rating of Independents with neutral ideology. As one moves from being an Independent to a Democrat, there is a drop of about fourteen units in Bush's rating. However, the interactions between each party and political ideology also contribute to the prediction of Bush's rating. In particular, for Republicans, each unit deviation toward liberal ideology results in a little over a two-unit increase in rating, reflecting the less severe effect of ideology among Republicans compared to Independents. A similar effect appears for Democrats who also show a less severe effect of ideology.

The t tests in the table are the ratios of the B weights to their standard errors. When t ratios are greater than 2.00 in absolute value in samples of at least moderate size ($N > 60$), they are significant at the .05 level. Most analyses using the NAES will easily exceed this sample size (as does this one, $N = 7,376$).

The standardized coefficients (Betas) in the table represent the regression weights for the variables when they are transformed into standard scores (Z scores) that have the same standard deviation (1). Betas permit an interpretation of differences in the sizes of the coefficients. In this analysis, Republican party is the strongest predictor, followed by ideology.

This analysis shows that Independents treat the candidates differently from the way party affiliates do. However, we have only examined half of the ideological spectrum. What would happen if we also looked at how respondents evaluate Gore?

To do so, we code a new dependent variable that assesses respondents' reactions to both candidates simultaneously, namely, by taking the dif-

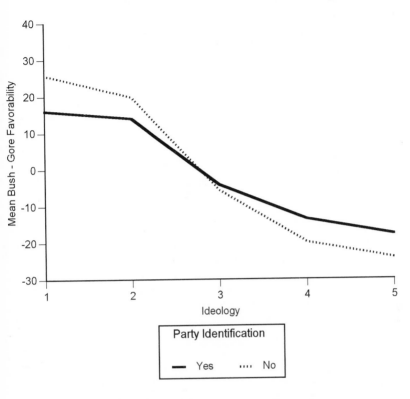

Figure 7.3. Bush minus Gore's favorability rating as a function of respondent party identification (Democrat and Republican = Yes; Independent = No) and political ideology (1 = Very Conservative and 5 = Very Liberal).

ference between Bush (cAOl) and Gore (cAll) on the same thermometer scale. This coding not only removes individual differences in scale usage but also allows us to examine the influence of party identification independent of the ideology of the candidate. When we combine the mean ratings of the two parties and compare them against Independents, we find a symmetric pattern of evaluation for the difference between the two candidates (see Figure 7.3). Liberals who identify with a party see less of a difference between the candidates than Independents. At the same time, conservatives belonging to a party also see less of a difference between the candidates than Independents.

We can test this interaction by combining the two parties and creating an interaction between this variable and ideology. The analysis shown in Table 7.3 reveals that party affiliation reduces the influence of ideology, with Independents relying on ideology more than members of either

TABLE 7.3. REGRESSION ANALYSIS OF BUSH-GORE FAVORABILITY RATING (THERMOMETER) AS A FUNCTION OF RESPONDENT POLITICAL IDEOLOGY, PARTY, AND INTERACTION BETWEEN HAVING A PARTY IDENTIFICATION AND IDEOLOGY

	Unstandardized coefficients		Standardized coefficients		
	B	Std. error	Beta	t	Prob.
Constant	−2.49	.86		−2.90	.00
Ideology (PI)	−17.89	.99	−.29	−17.41	.00
Republicans	36.12	1.34	.30	26.90	.00
Democrats	−32.54	1.23	−.28	26.53	.00
Party × PI	4.55	1.23	.06	3.69	.00

major party when assessing the difference between major party candidates. In comparing effects across the two analyses (Table 7.2 versus 7.3), we also see that the t ratios for party and ideology are larger in the difference score analysis, a result indicating that the dependent variable is now more sensitively measured than it was when we only analyzed Bush's rating. Hence, using difference scores allows us to examine the influence of ideology and party apart from candidate ideology and increases the power of the regression model.

EFFECTS OF BEHAVIOR ON POLITICAL OUTCOMES

Cross-sectional data can also be used to examine the relation between self-reported behavior, such as news use, debate watching, and other forms of political participation, and political outcomes, such as learning about the candidates, attitudes toward the candidates, and vote intentions. For example, how does exposure to news about the election influence learning about the candidates? To illustrate an analysis of this question in the 2000 election, we use the survey question that asks whether respondents feel they have learned enough about the candidates to make a choice in the election (cLlO). We would expect that the more in the past week a respondent has used a major news source, such as a daily newspaper (cEl3), the more opportunity the respondent would have to learn about candidates for office. In addition, we would expect that the more respondents reported exposure in the past week to election news in the newspaper (cEl4), the more likely they would be to say that they had learned something about the candidates.

Figure 7.4 shows the relation between use of newspapers in the past week and reports of learning about the candidates for president for the same September period we analyzed earlier. In addition, the figure shows the effect of exposure to election news in the newspapers. To

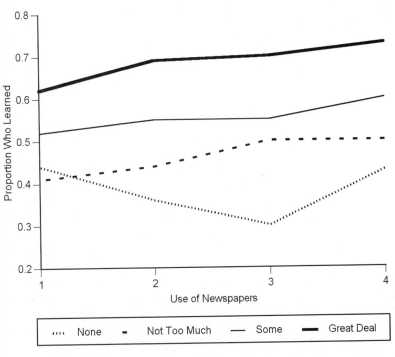

Figure 7.4. Proportion of respondents who claimed to have learned enough to make a choice among the presidential candidates as a function of newspaper use in the past week and exposure to election news in newspapers.

make the figure easier to comprehend, use of newspapers was recoded into a four-point scale (0, 1 days = 1; 2, 3 days = 2; 4, 5 days = 3; 6, 7 days = 4). The pattern of curves suggests that use of newspapers increases learning about candidates. However, this is not true when respondents have not been exposed to news about the election (the lowest curve). As a result, one would expect a regression model to require the inclusion of an interaction term for the two exposure measures.

To test this hypothesis, we set up a regression model of learning as a function of newspaper use (NU), exposure to election news in newspapers (EN), and the interaction of the two newspaper variables (NU × EN). Exposure to election news was reverse coded so that its value increased with exposure.

The results of this analysis, shown in Table 7.4, indicate that use of newspapers does not add much to predicting the learning outcome. However, exposure to election news and the interaction with use of

TABLE 7.4. REGRESSION ANALYSIS OF REPORTED LEARNING ABOUT CANDIDATES AS A FUNCTION OF USE OF NEWSPAPERS, EXPOSURE TO RECENT ELECTION NEWS IN THE NEWSPAPERS, AND THE INTERACTION OF THE VARIABLES

Predictor	Unstandardized coefficients		Standardized coefficients		
	B	Std. error	Beta	t	Prob.
Constant	.327	.066		4.99	.000
Use of newspaper (UN)	−.015	.022	−.032	−.68	.500
Exposure to election news in newspapers (EN)	.051	.028	.097	1.85	.064
UN × EN	.015	.008	.143	1.82	.068

newspapers does appear to increase learning, albeit at weak levels of statistical significance.

In addition to the weak results, one might question the validity of the analysis because exposure to election news and use of newspapers may be related to other background variables that are actually responsible for the relations we observe. For example, more educated persons or older persons may use newspapers more and the findings might have more to do with demographic differences than with actual use of newspapers.

To evaluate this alternative explanation, we test the same model holding constant demographic variables in the equation. In particular, we add quantitative variables for age (cWO2) and education (cWO6). In addition, we add dummy variables for gender (cWOl), Hispanic ethnicity (cWO5), and various distinctions (black, Asian, and others not classified by white, black, or Asian categories) obtained from the question on racial identity (cWO3). As Table 7.5 indicates, the effects observed in the first analysis largely remain. The unstandardized coefficients in each analysis are about the same. Nevertheless, the probability levels are not statistically significant by usual standards ($p < .05$), suggesting that the estimates of the coefficients are not very reliable. This analysis also shows that age, education, and gender are related to reported learning about candidates. In particular, older, more educated, and male respondents were more likely to report having learned about the candidates at this time in the election period than were their younger, less educated, and female counterparts.

Both of these analyses used the linear regression model. This model assumes that the error variance is constant across all predicted values of Y and that the error is drawn from a normal distribution. However, these assumptions are not very plausible when the outcome is a two-valued (dichotomous) variable, such as "learned enough" or "did not learn

TABLE 7.5. REGRESSION ANALYSIS OF REPORTED LEARNING ABOUT CANDIDATES, INCLUDING DEMOGRAPHIC VARIABLES IN THE ANALYSIS

Predictor	Unstandardized coefficients		Standardized coefficients		
	B	Std. Error	Beta	t	Prob.
Constant	.298	.076		3.921	.000
Use of newspaper (UN)	−.028	.022	−.061	−1.295	.196
Exposure to election news in newspapers (EN)	.048	.027	.092	1.779	.075
UN × EN	.013	.008	.125	1.607	.108
Gender	−.084	.017	−.084	−4.980	.000
Age	.028	.005	.094	5.145	.000
Hispanic ethnicity	−.053	.039	−.025	−1.369	.171
Black	.043	.032	.023	1.333	.183
Asian	−.125	.072	−.029	−1.724	.085
Other race	−.028	.037	−.014	−.753	.451
Education	.021	.004	.093	5.439	.000

enough" about the candidates. As the predicted score approaches either 1 or 0, the error variance tends to depart significantly from normal. Hence, it is best to analyze data with a dichotomous outcome using a different analysis model called logistic regression. Before we illustrate a logistic regression solution with the present example, let's look briefly at how this model works.

THE LOGISTIC REGRESSION MODEL

A more recent addition to the analysis arsenal, the logistic regression model is more difficult to estimate than OLS. However, with the advent of computers and maximum likelihood estimation procedures, these difficulties no longer pose a significant problem.

The logistic regression model is used to analyze dichotomous outcomes. When one analyzes such data, one expects the predicted scores to range between 0 and 1, the equivalent of a probability scale. The problem with doing this analysis using OLS is that the predicted scores need not stay within the 0–1 range. Indeed, OLS assumes that the relation between the predicted score and the dependent variable is linear. However, with a probability scale, the relation will look more like the curve in Figure 7.5. Because this relation is nonlinear, the linear regression model will fail to capture the relationship, especially as the probability of the outcome departs from 0.5.

Tests for interactions using OLS can be very misleading when the relationship actually conforms to the nonlinear pattern shown in Figure 7.5.

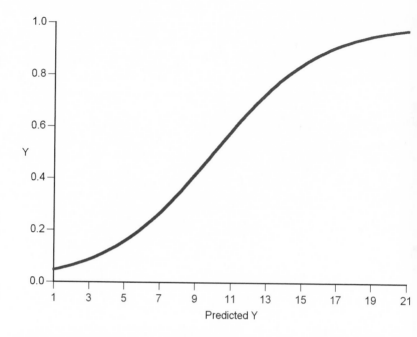

Figure 7.5. Relation between predicted score and actual probability of outcome with a dichotomous outcome variable (Y).

To see this, consider the effect when one goes from 1 to 5 on the X-axis. The change along the probability scale is only about .1 units. However, when one goes from 5 to 9 along X, the change in probability is about .3 units even though the change along X is the same in the two cases. As a result of the nonlinear relation between Y and X, apparent interactions between variables will occur that are the result of differential change along the probability scale.

The apparent interaction effect is illustrated in Figure 7.6. The effects of one independent variable X_1 are shown with a change of 4 units along the X-axis. The effect of similar change in a second variable X_2 is shown for the two separate curves. The greater effect of X_1 when X_2 is larger is entirely attributable to the greater rise in probability that occurs as X_2 is added to X_1. Hence, the apparent interaction is purely the result of the nonlinear increase in Y as X increases (as illustrated in Figure 7.5).

Despite the nonlinearity of the relationship between X and Y, problems with using OLS are often not very serious, especially if the average predicted score is in the middle of the 0 to 1 scale. However, even if one does not report the use of a logistic regression analysis, one usually tries

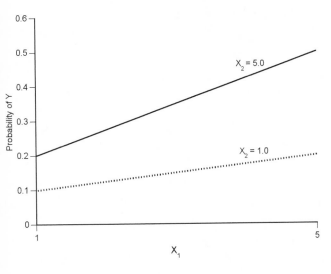

Figure 7.6. Example of apparent interaction between two predictors that results from nonlinear increase in probability as a function of two predictors, X_1 and X_2.

the analysis to make sure the findings are comparable. This caution is especially important when one is testing interaction predictions.

INTERPRETING LOGISTIC REGRESSION WEIGHTS

Many of the interpretations of logistic regression are the same as for OLS. The weights associated with the predictors represent the magnitude of the relationship with the dependent variable. When important predictors are left out of the model, the weights for the remaining predictors may be misspecified. Coding of the predictors is done the same way as in OLS. However, the meaning of the coefficients in the model is different. In logistic regression, the dependent variable is a function of the odds of the outcome:

$$\text{Odds} = P / (1 - P).$$

For example, if the probability of winning a lottery is .01, then the odds of winning are 1 to 99, or $.01/(1 - .01)$. Odds have the desirable property of ranging from zero to infinity. One benefit of the odds scale is that one can say that the odds are twice as great that something will happen no matter what the odds are. This is not possible with probabilities because they are bounded by 0 and 1.

A further transformation of the odds ratio allows the scale to be unbounded for scores less than zero. The log of the odds is zero when $P = .5$ because the log of 1 $(.5/.5)$ is zero. For values less than .5, the log of the odds is negative. Hence, the log odds can range from minus to plus infinity. Although the probability outcome looks like an S-shaped curve when plotted against a predictor, the log odds are linear with predictors.

The log odds, or logit, are the actual outcome that logistic regression estimates. Remember that the log of x equals the exponent to which the base of the log is raised in order to equal x.

$$\text{If } \log x = m, \text{ then } x = \text{base}^m.$$

As a result, the log of any base raised to a power m is simply m.

The base is arbitrary. Some people like to use 10. In statistical applications, the base is usually e, which is approximately 2.72. In addition, the log to the base e is usually written as ln. Any product can be represented as the sum of two logs: If $Y = X(Z)$, then $\ln Y = \ln X + \ln Z$.

The log of e raised to a power is simply the exponent. For example, $\ln e^{b_0} = b_0$. The coefficients in a logistic regression are part of an exponential expression of the form

$$P / (1 - P) = e^{b_0}\, e^{b_1 X_1} \cdots e^{b_k X_k},$$

Or in log odds form:

$$\ln [P / (1 - P)] = b_0 + b_1 X_1 + \cdots + b_k X_k.$$

The coefficients in the above version of the logistic regression model can be translated into an odds ratio. For example, if X_1 takes on the value 1 when the respondent is a Republican and 0 otherwise, and b_1 is 1.30, then $e^{1.3} = 3.67$ for Republicans and $e^0 = 1$ for everyone else. This means that odds of the response are more than three times greater for Republicans than for people in other parties.

When a coefficient is zero, then the exponential function is 1. In this case, the odds are no different for the relevant group than for the others.

If the independent variable is coded as a continuous variable, such as age or political ideology, then the coefficient is typically small and represents the increase in odds for a unit change in the variable. However, a simpler interpretation uses the following formula:

TABLE 7.6. LOGISTIC REGRESSION ANALYSIS OF LEARNING ABOUT THE
PRESIDENTIAL CANDIDATES

Predictor	B	S.E.	Wald	df	Prob.	Exp(B)
Use of newspapers (UN)	−.021	.043	.232	1	.630	.979
Exposure to election stories in newspaper (EN)	.283	.116	6.002	1	.014	1.328
UN × EN	.031	.035	.761	1	.383	1.031
Gender	−.361	.073	24.175	1	.000	.697
Age	.118	.023	25.347	1	.000	1.125
Hispanic ethnicity	−.229	.168	1.844	1	.175	.796
Black	.192	.139	1.915	1	.166	1.212
Asian	−.541	.312	2.996	1	.083	.582
Other race	−.124	.161	.592	1	.442	.883
Education	.089	.016	29.404	1	.000	1.093
Constant	−1.109	.270	16.910	1	.000	.330

$$100(e^b − 1) = \% \text{ change for a unit increase in } X.$$

For example, if $e^b = 1.1$, then a unit change in X produces a 10% change
in the odds of the outcome.

AN EXAMPLE OF LOGISTIC REGRESSION

We can now conduct a regression analysis using logistic regression and
compare it with the results of linear regression. Let's look at the example we just presented predicting learning about the presidential candidates based on demographic variables and use of newspapers. The
results of this analysis, shown in Table 7.6, indicate that only exposure
to election stories in the newspapers is related to learning about the candidates. The B weight of .283 translates into an odds ratio of 1.33 (Exp.
(B) in the table), which means that an increase of one unit on the exposure scale increases the odds of learning about the candidates by 33%
[100(1.33 − 1.0)]. The Wald test for each coefficient in the analysis is
similar to the t test in OLS in that it represents the ratio of the unstandardized coefficient divided by its standard error. However, it is the
square of this ratio, and it uses the chi-square distribution to evaluate
statistical significance. As a result, values greater than 3.84 are significant
at the .05 probability level for a single degree of freedom test.

Another difference between the logistic and linear regression models
is the measure of goodness of fit. In logistic regression analysis programs, the estimation procedure does not minimize the error variance.
Rather, it attempts to maximize the likelihood that the model matches
the data. A measure of this maximization is usually given in computer
outputs as

$-2 \times$ the log likelihood, or $- 2LL$ for short.

This value should get smaller the better the fit of the model.

As one adds variables to a logistic regression model, $-2LL$ gets smaller. One can assess the significance of the added prediction by subtracting the value of the smaller absolute score from the larger one. This value can be tested using a chi-square test with k degrees of freedom representing the number of predictors that have been added to the equation. By this procedure, adding a single predictor to a logistic regression equation should reduce the $-2LL$ by at least 3.84 if the variable is to be regarded as adding significant ($p < .05$) prediction to the model. In the Statistical Package for the Social Sciences (SPSS), this test is called the omnibus test of model coefficients.

The logistic regression analysis does not find much evidence of interaction between use of newspapers and exposure to election stories. It seems to indicate that the only variable with importance is actual exposure to election stories in the press. That is, it does not seem to matter whether respondents read newspapers a lot or a little; their confidence that they have learned enough about the candidates only increases as exposure to election stories increases. The analysis does confirm the findings from OLS with regard to the other predictors. Male, older, and more educated respondents were more likely to report confidence that they had learned enough to make a decision about the candidates.

Time as a Predictor in Repeated Cross-Sectional Datasets

Our examples of analyses using cross-sectional data have focused on the use of a time slice (e.g., September) in the national rolling cross-sectional database. However, the NAES also has the potential for repeated cross-sectional analyses with time as a predictor. One potential model for analyzing the data in this design is

$$Y_i = b_1 + b_2\text{TIME} + BX + e_i,$$

where Y_i is the measure of the critical outcome at different points in time (TIME = 1 to T). We can use this model to predict changes that occur as an election campaign progresses. For example, TIME might predict changes in awareness of a candidate or of the candidate's issue positions (see Figure 7.7).

In this model, X is a matrix of demographic and other variables that we want to control in assessing changes that occur over time. B is a matrix of coefficients that weights the variables in X to predict Y. Including the X matrix is the best we can do to control for other variables that

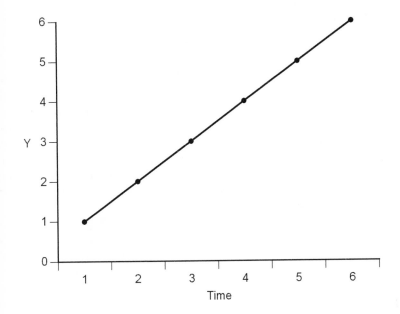

Figure 7.7. Example of change in *Y* as a function of time.

might be related to initial levels of *Y* at the individual level. It also can control for variables that might change with time but that are unrelated to the hypothesized causal process that occurs over TIME. For example, we might be interested in changes in support for a candidate over time controlling for the demographic characteristics of respondents.

Fortunately, in the NAES, we do not expect major changes in demographic variables as a function of time because the sampling plan is designed to hold these differences relatively constant. Nevertheless, holding constant *X* increases confidence that TIME is the causal factor and not other changes that might have occurred as well. In trying to understand changes that can occur during a campaign, the ability to study variables related to change is a major benefit of this design over the panel design.

Another feature of the repeated cross-sectional design is the ability to study causal factors that might interact with time. For example, one might be interested in the effects of exposure to news about the election. As time passes, heavy exposure to election news should produce greater learning about the candidates and their positions. The effect of news exposure should build over time and produce more learning among those who pay a lot of attention to news about the election than

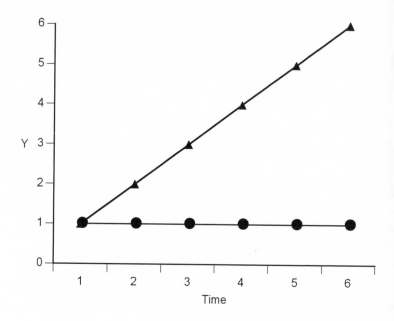

Figure 7.8. Example of interaction between time and attention to election news in affecting *Y* (*triangles* represent high exposure; *circles* represent low exposure).

among those whose attention is minimal. Those who pay less attention to the news should display a weaker effect of time, since they will not benefit as much from their exposure to news. The cross-sectional design should allow one to observe these different trends.

An example of an interaction between time and a causal factor that should interact with time is shown in Figure 7.8. In this example, time is coded into 1, 2, 3, 4, 5 successive periods, and attention to news about the election is coded as high = 1 versus low = 0. In this example, the interaction predicts that time will increase *Y* for people who pay attention to news about the election but that time will make no difference for those who pay no attention to election news.

ANALYZING TIME IN A REPEATED CROSS SECTION

To illustrate the use of a repeated cross-sectional design, we will use the 2000 Super Tuesday file that contains data for the Super Tuesday states from January 4 to March 6, 2000, the last day before the primary on March 7. We can convert our rolling cross section into a repeated cross section by aggregating time periods. Our objective is reducing the number of time periods so that changes over time are sufficiently stable to

TABLE 7.7. NUMBER OF CASES IN THE 2000 SUPER TUESDAY FILE AGGREGATED
BY WEEKS

Time	Frequency	Percent	Valid percent	Cumulative percent
1.00	165	2.5	2.5	2.5
2.00	424	6.4	6.4	8.9
3.00	546	8.2	8.2	17.1
4.00	587	8.9	8.9	26.0
5.00	723	10.9	10.9	36.9
6.00	604	9.1	9.1	46.0
7.00	1031	15.6	15.6	61.6
8.00	1232	18.6	18.6	80.2
9.00	1315	19.8	19.8	100.0
Total	6627	100.0	100.0	

enable an analysis of trends. If we choose time periods that are too large, we will minimize our ability to see change. On the other hand, if we choose periods that are too small, we will allow unsystematic changes to dominate the trend lines. We can begin by examining trends in weekly data points. Let's code each seven days into a single time point and create a variable called "TIME" for this new predictor.

The frequency distribution of TIME will tell us how many cases we have per time period. The data in Table 7.7 indicate that we have an increasing number of cases as time increases and that no time period has fewer than one hundred cases. This distribution should be adequate for analyzing change. However, we should withhold judgment until we have examined an outcome in which we are interested.

We will continue to pursue our example of learning about candidates. In addition, we will examine the influence of exposure to news about the election to see if it predicts change over TIME in learning about the candidates. Means of these variables as a function of TIME are shown in Table 7.8.

The first thing we note is that attention to election news was not assessed until the fourth week of the survey period. Nevertheless, we will be able to study the influence of news exposure for a period of six weeks. In addition, the question about learning was not asked of the entire sample. However, there are sufficient numbers of respondents at each time period to permit an analysis of this dependent variable. Our preliminary analysis indicates that we can proceed with the analysis of learning during the primary.

To determine whether the time periods we have created are sufficiently stable to permit identification of trends, we can plot the data by time period. This plot in Figure 7.9 indicates that the time trend is quite stable and is linear, especially from weeks 4–9.

TABLE 7.8. MEANS AND NUMBER OF CASES FOR THREE VARIABLES ASSESSED IN THE 2000 SUPER TUESDAY FILE

Time		Learned enough to make a choice	Attention to national television news	Attention to newspapers
1.00	Mean	.174		
	N	46		
2.00	Mean	.202		
	N	109		
3.00	Mean	.271		
	N	144		
4.00	Mean	.234	2.394	2.135
	N	137	348	348
5.00	Mean	.249	2.477	2.213
	N	193	723	723
6.00	Mean	.295	2.492	2.247
	N	156	604	604
7.00	Mean	.313	2.467	2.263
	N	243	1031	1031
8.00	Mean	.335	2.517	2.252
	N	296	1232	1232
9.00	Mean	.356	2.503	2.289
	N	315	1315	1315
Total	Mean	.294	2.487	2.250
	N	1639	5253	5253

Although the data are suggestive, we are still examining the entire universe of respondents, including those who have no intention of voting in the primary. By restricting our analysis to those who report an interest in voting in the primary (cR07), we isolate a still smaller universe ($N = 998$ versus 1,639). Fortunately, there are still sufficient respondents to observe time trends even if we restrict the analysis to those who report an intention to vote in the primary (see Table 7.9). Furthermore, the time trend for this group of respondents (Figure 7.10) is stronger than the trend for the entire sample (Figure 7.9), which is not surprising in view of our selection of respondents who have expressed an interest in voting.

We can now examine the relation between time and learning about candidates controlling for attention to news about the primary election. The plot in Figure 7.11 indicates that learning increased primarily for those who devoted a "great deal" of attention to news on network and cable television about the election. TIME had little or no impact on those who devoted less attention to news.

To assess this prediction, we create a new variable to represent the interaction between attention and time. We create a dummy variable

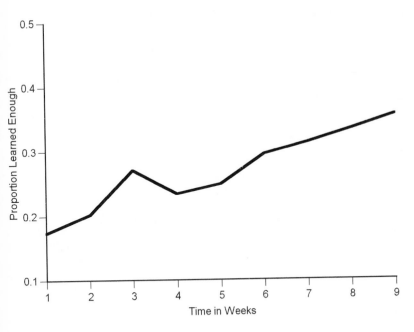

Figure 7.9. Growth in learning about the candidates for the primary in the Super Tuesday states.

that has the value of 1 when attention is the highest (a great deal) and zero otherwise. We can also create dummy variables for two other levels of attention to news: some and not too much. We then multiply the dummy variable for high attention by TIME. This interaction essentially says that when attention is highest, there is an added effect of TIME over and above that produced by TIME alone. We can also test the other interactions between lower levels of attention to news and TIME to see if they contribute to the model.

The results of this logistic regression, shown in Table 7.10, indicate that the best prediction of learning is the joint influence of time and intense attention to the news. Neither time nor attention alone is sufficient to increase learning. In addition, neither medium or low levels of attention to national television news in interaction with time affected learning to an appreciable degree.

We can add other predictors to the model to challenge the finding, but in this case demographic changes are less likely to account for the effect of time or attention to news. The results of this analysis, shown in Table 7.11 indicate that the interaction between time and news exposure remains significant despite the inclusion of demographic variables.

TABLE 7.9. MEANS AND NUMBER OF CASES FOR THREE VARIABLES ASSESSED IN THE 2000 SUPER TUESDAY FILE AMONG THOSE WHO PLANNED TO VOTE IN THE PRIMARY

Time		Learned enough to make a choice	Attention to national television news	Attention to newspapers
1.00	Mean	.172		
	N	29		
2.00	Mean	.250		
	N	72		
3.00	Mean	.280		
	N	75		
4.00	Mean	.212	2.524	2.262
	N	85	233	233
5.00	Mean	.288	2.665	2.377
	N	125	475	475
6.00	Mean	.324	2.655	2.419
	N	105	377	377
7.00	Mean	.378	2.595	2.399
	N	156	671	671
8.00	Mean	.387	2.678	2.396
	N	173	772	772
9.00	Mean	.416	2.676	2.464
	N	178	756	756
Total	Mean	.333	2.645	2.403
	N	998	3284	3284

Summary

The major use of the simple cross-sectional design is to assess the relation between background variables and political outcomes, such as perceptions of the candidates. A more dynamic picture of the influence of behavior, such as exposure to election news or other political activity, can be obtained using the repeated cross-sectional design. OLS regression is a valuable technique for assessing the relation between predictors and outcomes. However, logistic regression is also valuable when the outcome is measured dichotomously at the individual level. Logistic regression is particularly valuable for assessing interaction effects with a probabilistic response scale.

Exercises

- Analyze news exposure during the month of October 2000 to see if it behaves the same as during September.
- Analyze the effect of news exposure to newspapers rather than tele-

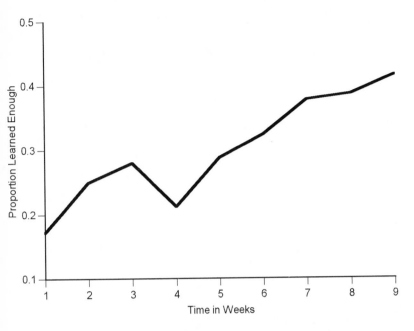

Figure 7.10. Relation between time and learning about the candidates in the Super Tuesday primary states.

vision to see if the same pattern appears during the 2000 Super Tuesday primary period.

- Analyze the effect of news exposure on vote choice during the 2000 Super Tuesday primary period.

Note

1. For this analysis, we removed those respondents who did not know their party identification or political ideology. Respondents who reported that they were classified in some other way than as Democrats, Republicans, or Independents were also removed from the analysis. However, coding them as Independents would not have changed the findings of this analysis.

Reference

Turner, John. T. 1987. *Rediscovering the Social Group: A Social Categorization Theory of Group Behavior.* New York: Blackwell.

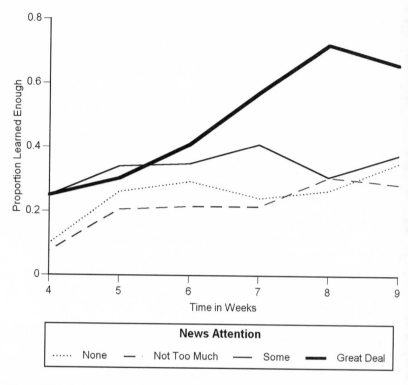

Figure 7.11. Relation between attention to network and cable television news and reports of learning enough about the candidates in the Super Tuesday primary election (time is in weeks leading up to March 7).

TABLE 7.10. LOGISTIC REGRESSION ANALYSIS OF LEARNING ABOUT CANDIDATES

Variable	B	S.E.	Wald	df	Prob.	Exp(B)
Time	.052	.047	1.230	1	.267	1.05
High attention to news (AH)	−1.500	.832	3.251	1	.071	.223
Medium attention to news (AM)	.317	.604	.276	1	.599	1.374
Low attention to news (AL)	−1.182	.888	1.772	1	.183	.307
AH × Time	.365	.120	9.299	1	.002	1.441
AM × Time	−.005	.090	.003	1	.953	.995
AL × Time	.131	.125	1.099	1	.295	1.139
Constant	−1.277	.246	26.957	1	.000	.279

TABLE 7.11. Logistic Regression of Learning About Candidates with Demographic Variables Included

Variable	B	S.E.	Wald	df	Prob.	Exp(B)
Time	.056	.048	1.401	1	.237	1.058
High attention to news (AH)	−1.840	.85	4.685	1	.030	.159
Medium attention to news (AM)	.387	.617	.394	1	.530	1.473
Low attention to news (AL)	−1.137	.907	1.572	1	.210	.321
AH × Time	.395	.122	10.471	1	.001	1.484
AM × Time	−.012	.092	.017	1	.897	.988
AL × Time	.141	.128	1.217	1	.270	1.151
Gender	−.514	.143	12.890	1	.000	.598
Age	.113	.045	6.369	1	.012	1.120
Hispanic	−.251	.314	.640	1	.424	.778
Black	.167	.234	.513	1	.474	1.182
Asian	−.199	.493	.163	1	.686	.819
Other race	.198	.334	.352	1	.553	1.220
Education	.083	.032	6.634	1	.010	1.086
Constant	−1.457	.432	11.389	1	.001	.233

Chapter 8
Analysis of Panel Data

KATE KENSKI AND DANIEL ROMER

In the last chapter, we described the use of cross-sectional data to analyze change during an election period. This chapter approaches the same problem using another analysis strategy, the panel design. The NAES contains several panel datasets to permit analysis of the same individuals before and after major election events such as the conventions and presidential debates. In this chapter, we will illustrate panel data analysis using the 2000 NAES first presidential debate panel to shed light on changes in individuals' political talk and their opinions about the debate performances of George W. Bush and Al Gore.

The layout of data in a panel design is similar to that of the repeated cross-section. As seen in Table 8.1, the major difference is that the same individuals ($i = 1$ to N) are interviewed at each wave of data collection (t). One dependent variable (Y) and two independent variables (X_1, X_2) are shown for purposes of illustration, with subscripts for respondents (i) and waves of data collection (t). Scores for the dependent variable are represented as Y_{ti}, while scores for the first independent variable are represented as X_{1ti}.

The time window between waves is selected to allow the effects of important events during the election period to be assessed. In the 1980 NES, for example, a panel was created and interviewed at four time points during the election year: January, June, September, and November. This structure made possible analyses of changes that occurred as the election year unfolded.

Analysis of panel data uses the following equation for a two-wave design (omitting the respondent's subscript):

$$Y_2 = b_0 + b_1 Y_1 + b_2 X_{11} + b_3 X_{12} + e_2.$$

The initial status of Y is entered into the model along with the prior status of a variable X_{11} that is predicted to cause change in Y_2 over the

TABLE 8.1. DATA LAYOUT IN A PANEL DESIGN WITH FOUR WAVES

Individuals (i)	Wave (t)			
	1	2	3	4
1	Y_{11}, X_{111}, X_{211}	Y_{21}, X_{121}, X_{212}	Y_{31}, X_{131}, X_{231}	Y_{41}, X_{141}, X_{241}
2	Y_{12}, X_{112}, X_{212}	Y_{22}, X_{122}, X_{222}	Y_{32}, X_{132}, X_{232}	Y_{42}, X_{142}, X_{242}
i	Y_{1i}, X_{11i}, X_{21i}	Y_{2i}, X_{12i}, X_{22i}	Y_{3i}, X_{13i}, X_{23i}	Y_{4i}, X_{14i}, X_{24i}
$N-1$	$Y_{1(N\text{-}1)}, X_{11(N\text{-}1)},$ $X_{21(N\text{-}1)}$	$Y_{2(N\text{-}1)}, X_{12(N\text{-}1)},$ $X_{22(N\text{-}1)}$	$Y_{3(N\text{-}1)}, X_{13(N\text{-}1)},$ $X_{23(N\text{-}1)}$	$Y_{4(N\text{-}1)}, X_{14(N\text{-}1)},$ $X_{24(N\text{-}1)}$
N	Y_{1N}, X_{11N}, X_{21N}	Y_{2N}, X_{12N}, X_{22N}	Y_{3N}, X_{13N}, X_{23N}	Y_{4N}, X_{14N}, X_{24N}

time interval between waves of the survey. The final status of X is also included in the model to control for any changes that might have occurred to the presumed causal variable subsequent to its assessment at time 1.

The coefficient b_1 represents stability from time 1 to 2 in the status of Y; b_2 represents the causal effect of X_1 on change in Y; b_3 represents any contemporaneous relation between X and Y at time 2 that is unrelated to the causal effect of X at time 1; and e_2 represents a random component in Y at time 2 that is unrelated to any of the X predictors. The constant b_0 represents all of the influences on Y that are not captured by the other components of the model. Writing the equation in a slightly different way emphasizes that it is change in Y that is being predicted in this model:

$$Y_2 - b_1 Y_1 = b_0 + b_2 X_{11} + b_3 X_{12} + e_{i2}.$$

The difference score ($Y_2 - b_1 Y_1$) represents the part of Y that remains after the initial status of Y has been removed. Because b_1 is typically less than 1, the model only removes that part of Y_1 that is reliably related to Y_2. If we were simply to use the raw difference score ($Y_2 - Y_1$), we would assume that b_1 were exactly 1, which is unlikely. Since we can estimate b_1, there is no reason to make this assumption.

A similar situation exists in the representation of X at both time periods. It might be tempting to use the difference score between X at both time periods ($X_{12} - X_{11}$) to assess its effect on change in Y. This, however, also forces the stability coefficient for X to be 1. The best model is one that allows both stability coefficients to be estimated from the data.

A major benefit of the panel design is the ability to assess change at the level of individual respondents. This is not possible in the cross-sectional design where we can only assess change at the group level. In the rolling cross-sectional design, we have the benefit of knowing that demographic differences are held constant across waves of the study.

TABLE 8.2. OPINIONS ABOUT SOCIAL SECURITY IN THE STOCK MARKET FROM THE NATIONAL RCS AND FROM THE FIRST PRESIDENTIAL DEBATE PANEL STUDY IN 2000

	Repeated cross-sections	
	Before first debate (Sept. 21–Oct. 2)	After first debate (Oct. 4–10)
Favor	55.1	58.5
Oppose	34.7	33.5
Don't know	9.1	7.6
Refused	1.0	0.4
N	1,785	1,022

	First presidential debate panel				
		Wave 1: before first debate (Sept. 21–Oct. 2)			
		Favor	Oppose	Don't know	Refused	Total
Wave 2:	Favor	82.2	18.7	33.8	44.4	55.0
after first	Oppose	14.1	75.6	33.8	22.2	37.4
debate	Don't know	3.4	5.7	32.4	33.3	7.4
(Oct. 4–10)	Refused	0.2	—	—	—	0.1
N		411	262	74	9	756

Nevertheless, we can only examine changes as a function of such group characteristics as demographics or behavior (see Chapter 7 for examples of these analyses). While aggregates can reveal dynamic patterns, they can also conceal fluctuations that occur within individuals. Table 8.2 shows how an aggregation of opinion at the group level does not reflect the changes that occurred within individuals. In 2000, respondents were asked: "Do you personally favor or oppose allowing workers to invest some of their Social Security contributions in the stock market?" (cBC05, rBC05). The top half of Table 8.2 shows that in aggregate, public opinion about contributions to the stock market was stable. Between September 21 and October 2, 55.1 percent of respondents said they favored the position, while 58.5 percent favored the position after the debate—a difference of 3.4 percent. The bottom half of the table presents results of the panel study. While individual opinions were relatively stable, as 82.2 percent who favored the position at time 1 also favored it at time 2 and 75.6 percent who opposed it at time 1 also opposed it at time 2, the panel results show more change than was evident from just looking at the repeated cross-sections.

Assessing change at the individual level also permits more sensitive measurement of change, because all of the reliable individual variation in Y at time 1 is controlled. This situation results in smaller standard errors of prediction for analyses that attempt to predict change in Y. For example, consider the hypothetical data in Table 8.3. If the cases in this

TABLE 8.3. HYPOTHETICAL DATA FOR CHANGE IN Y AT TWO TIME POINTS

Case	Y_1	Y_2	$Y_2 - Y_1$
1	1	3	2
2	2	4	2
3	3	4	1
4	4	4	0
5	5	5	0
Mean	3	4	1

data table represented different individuals at each time period, then we would have to measure change by comparing the means of Y_1 and Y_2, which in this example indicates a change of one unit. The standard error for this analysis depends on the standard deviations of the scores at each time period.[1] If the cases represented the same individuals at each time period, however, change could be estimated for each individual. Notice that although this estimate of change is the same as for the difference between means at each time point, the variation surrounding the individual difference scores is smaller than the total variation in the two measure of Y. In practice, the variation in difference scores will be smaller than the variation in the scores at each time point. As a result, change can be estimated with less error if the same individuals are assessed at each time period.

A second benefit of the panel design is that it allows us to analyze potential causes of change at the individual level. For example, if X at time 1 can predict change in Y_2, this is strong evidence for a possible causal role of X. This feature is not available in the cross-sectional design.

Despite the benefits of the panel design, there are some drawbacks to its use. First, selecting the time period between waves is an important decision because the ability to observe change and potential predictors of that change will depend on the choice of the time lag. If the lag is too long, then the causal effect of a variable may no longer be evident. If it is too short, then the time window may not be long enough to permit enough measurable change to occur. Furthermore, once a time lag is selected, then all of the variables in the dataset will be subject to analysis with that lag. If some variables have short causal lags while others have longer lags, it will not be possible to conduct useful analyses with all of the variables in the dataset.

A second possible drawback is the potential for sensitization to the survey questions. The cross-sectional study always interviews respondents who have not been exposed to the survey. By contrast, panel respondents are interviewed at two or more times. There is considerable evi-

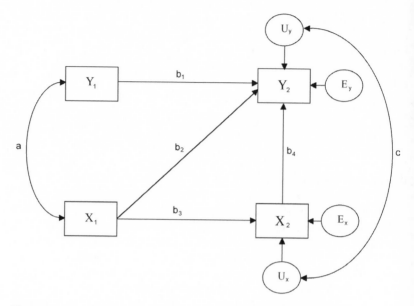

Figure 8.1. Causal diagram showing relations between variables in a panel design.

dence, however, that respondents can respond differently to the same questions depending on the content of prior questions (Sudman, Bradburn, and Schwarz 1996). This factor can make the interpretation of changes in survey responses somewhat problematic. Was the change produced by the events that occurred between waves, or is it the result of repeated questioning of survey respondents? We will discuss some strategies for controlling survey sensitization in the analysis of individual change. There may not be a good control for effects that influence the entire sample other than pairing the subsequent waves of a panel with separate cross-sectional samples.

Causal Interpretation of Panel Data

To appreciate the factors that enter into a causal interpretation of panel data, it is helpful to use a causal diagram to consider the relation between the variables (see also Finkel 1995 for a discussion of the causal relations underlying panel data).

The causal diagram in Figure 8.1 is revealing because it shows that both Y and X at time 2 are influenced by errors of measurement (e_x, e_y) as well by unknown components, U_x and U_y. We do not get estimates of these separate components when we conduct regression analyses.

Their influence is represented in the constant term and the random component of the model. Nevertheless, they may affect the outcomes of the analysis. The correlation between X_1 and Y_1 (a) reflects the fact that the variables including their unknown components may initially be related. However, we are able to estimate paths from time 1 to time 2 holding constant those interrelations at time 1. Indeed, X_1 may directly influence Y_2. Although we assume that the unknown components are not related to each other or to the other predictors in the model, this is merely an assumption. If they are related to the prior status of X or Y, then we will get incorrect estimates of the effects of those variables. For this reason, one should control as many as possible of the variables that might be related to X and Y.

The major challenge to analyzing the panel model is to rule out alternative interpretations for any observed relation between X_1 and Y_2. There are at least two ways that X_1 may appear to predict Y_2: (1) if X_2 directly affects Y_2 or (2) if the unknown components are related to each other $(c \neq 0)$ and X_1 is related to X_2. In the latter case, the path from X_1 to Y_2 will include the correlation between the unknown components. One possible source of correlation between the variables at time 2 in the panel design is sensitization of the respondents to the content of the variables. For example, if asking about party affiliation and evaluation of the candidates prompts respondents to think more about being consistent with their party, this increased attention to the relation between the variables might encourage them to synchronize their evaluation of candidates with their party. As a result, party affiliation at time 1 would predict candidate evaluation at time 2. The source of this relation, however, would be the result of sensitization to the questions and not of increasing congruence with party affiliation over time. If this was the case, a cross-sectional survey would not find increasing correlation between party and candidate evaluation over time because respondents would not have been previously exposed to the items.

Errors of measurement may also be correlated in the panel design, but this source of relation between variables is also present in the cross-sectional design. The only way to identify this source of misspecification would be to use different types of measures for each variable in the survey. Unfortunately, we seldom have the luxury of including more than one type of measure of any variable in a large survey such as the NAES. Hence, we make the assumption that even if the errors of measurement are correlated, this source of error is not so large that it will account for significant relations between variables.

One way to handle the problem of correlation between unknown components in the variables at time 2 is to hold constant X_2 in the regression model. Doing this will control for the relation between X_2

and Y_2 that is unrelated to the direct effect of X_1 on Y_2. This strategy will work as long as X_1 and X_2 are not so highly related that they are indistinguishable from each other. If the correlation between them is very high (because they have not changed much), then this strategy may introduce collinearity and defeat the purpose of the analysis.

Another strategy to demonstrate that changes over time are not the result of sensitization is to show that the effect does not occur for everyone in the survey. For example, if prior party affiliation is hypothesized to predict changes in candidate evaluations after an event (such as a debate), then the effect should only occur for those who have been exposed to the debate. In this case, one would predict that the causal effect of X_1 would only occur for those who reported exposure to the debate. One could then create a dummy variable for debate exposure and use the product of this variable and X_1 to predict Y_2. If the hypothesis is correct, then party identification should predict subsequent candidate evaluation better for those who were exposed to the debate than for those who missed the event. Another approach illustrated in the next section is to use debate exposure itself to predict changes in an outcome.

NAES Presidential Debate Panel Examples

To illustrate some of the ways in which panels can be analyzed, we will take a look at the NAES October 3, 2000, presidential debate panel ($N = 1,514$). In wave 1, predebate interviews took place between September 21 and October 2. The postdebate followup, wave 2, occurred between October 4 and October 10.

Debates give members of the electorate the opportunity to compare candidates and issue positions. Do debates stimulate individuals' levels of political engagement? One way in which people engage in politics is by talking about politics with others. For a deliberative democracy to work effectively, political discussion within the citizenry is essential. In 2000, NAES respondents were asked how many days they had talked about politics with friends and family (cK05) and how many days they talked with coworkers or online in the past week (cK09). A random half of panel respondents were asked these questions before and after the debate (rK05, rK09). Paired sample t-tests were conducted to see whether there was change in the amount of time that people talked about politics. While respondents reported talking about politics with friends and family 2.36 days in the past week on average, after the debate this increased to 2.63 days. The difference between the pre- and postdebate amounts of political discussion in our panel was statistically significant ($t = -4.34$, df $= 779$, $p < .001$). The reported amounts of political discussion with coworkers or online, however, did not change significantly. On average, respondents said they had talked with coworkers or online 0.87 days per week before the debate compared to .91 days per week after the debate ($t = -0.76$, df $= 778$, $p = .446$).

While we observed differences in the amounts of political discussion with friends and family when comparing the pre- and postdebate responses, it is unclear that watching the debate contributed to the differences in these individuals. One way that we can test the impact of debate-watching on political discussion is by constructing a model that uses debate-watching to predict talking about politics with friends and family. After the first presidential debate in 2000, NAES respondents were asked: "Did you happen to watch the presidential debate October 3 between George W. Bush and Al Gore? (If yes) Did you watch all, most, or just some of it?". These responses were recoded so that those who did not watch the debate could be compared to individuals who watched some, most, or all of it.

Using the postdebate variable on political talk with friends and family as the dependent variable, we can determine whether watching the debate had an impact. Other variables should be taken into account as well. NAES respondents were asked about their interest in politics:

Some people seem to follow what is going on in government and public affairs most of the time, whether there is an election or not. Others are not that interested. Would you say you follow what is going on in government and public affairs most of the time, some of the time, only now and then, or hardly at all? (rK01)

This response was recoded into a dichotomous variable so that those who said they were interested in politics most of the time could be compared to those less interested in politics. To test whether debate watching (rF35) produced an increase in talking about politics with friends and family (rK05), a multivariate model was created allowing us to control for political interest (cK01, rK01) and predebate responses to the political talk question (cK05).

Let's return to our initial equation for a two-wave design:

$$Y_2 = b_0 + b_1 Y_1 + b_2 X_{11} + b_3 X_{12} + e_2.$$

In this example, Y_2 represents postdebate political talk with friends and family and Y_1 represents predebate political talk. X_{11} stands for political interest before the debate interview and X_{12} stands for political interest after the debate. To this equation, we add another independent variable (X_{21}), having watched the debate. Our new equation can be expressed as follows:

$$Y_2 = b_0 + b_1 Y_1 + b_2 X_{11} + b_3 X_{12} + b_4 X_{21} + e_2.$$

Table 8.4 shows the results of regression analyses using this model and some modified versions of it. Model 1 is a simple regression using predebate political talk to predict postdebate political talk. Not surprisingly, predebate political talk is statistically significant, capturing 50 percent of the variation in postdebate political talk as demonstrated by the R^2.[2] Model 2 includes predebate political interest. Model 3 adds our primary variable of concern, debate watching. All three independent variables in this model are statistically significant. Model 4 best represents the equation just given. Even when controlling for pre-debate political talk, predebate political interest, and postdebate political interest, having watched the first presidential debate is a significant predictor of talking about politics with friends and family (postdebate). This model explains 55 percent of the variation in postdebate political talk.

As already mentioned, collinearity between variables can be a problem if the independent variables are highly correlated. One might expect collinearity problems, for example, when different versions of the same variable are put into a model, as is the case with political interest at time 1 and time 2. In this example, however, collinearity did not pose a problem in the analysis.

The debate panels can be used to answer other questions as well. Rather than focusing on the change in a particular variable, we may be interested in predicting a variable at time 2 based on an experience at time 1. For example, did watching the debate affect which candidate, Bush or Gore, respondents thought performed better in the debate? Individuals who watched the debate and individuals who had not but had heard about the debate were asked: "(From what you have heard or read,) who do you think performed best in this debate, George W. Bush or Al Gore?" (rF55). Around 42.6 percent of respondents said that Gore had performed better in the October 3 debate, 37.0 percent said that Bush had performed better, and 20.4 percent said that there was no difference between them.[3] This variable was recoded into a dichotomy where those who said that Bush had performed better were compared to those who either thought that Gore had performed better or saw no difference between them.

Table 8.5 presents the results of a logistic regression predicting the opinion that Bush had performed better. Since party identification frequently influences people's opinions about candidates, the predebate party identifications were put into the model. Controlling for education (cW06) and party identification (cV01), those who watched the debate (rF35) were more likely to say that Bush had performed better in the

TABLE 8.4. REGRESSION MODELS PREDICTING POSTDEBATE POLITICAL DISCUSSION WITH FRIENDS AND FAMILY IN THE PAST WEEK IN 2000 USING FIRST DEBATE PANEL

	Model 1		Model 2		Model 3		Model 4	
	B (SE)	Beta	B (SE)	Beta	B (SE)	Beta	B (SE)	Beta
Constant	.919*** (.085)		.755*** (.091)		.368*** (.108)		.350** (.107)	
Predebate political talk with friends and family (0–7 days)	.728*** (.026)	.709	.673*** (.028)	.655	.635*** (0.28)	.619	.606*** (.028)	.591
Predebate political interest (Interested most of the time = 1; Not interested, interested now and then, or only some of the time = 0)			.663*** (.128)	.140	.549*** (.126)	.116	.275# (.144)	.058
Watched October 3 debate (Yes = 1, No = 0)					.815*** (.127)	.165	.785*** (.126)	.159
Postdebate political interest (coding same as predebate)							.577*** (.150)	.120
R^2	.502		.518		.541		.550	
Adjusted R^2	.502		.517		.539		.548	
N	780		776		774		773	

# $p < .10$; * $p < .05$; ** $p < .01$; *** $p < .001$.

TABLE 8.5. BINARY LOGISTIC REGRESSION PREDICTING THE OPINION THAT BUSH PERFORMED BETTER THAN GORE IN THE OCTOBER 3 PRESIDENTIAL DEBATE IN 2000 USING FIRST DEBATE PANEL

	B	SE	Wald	Exp (B)
Constant	.069	.443	.024	1.071
Education (in years)	-.066*	.029	5.240	.936
Republican (Yes = 1, Else = 0)	1.160***	.149	60.903	3.191
Democrat (Yes = 1, Else = 0)	-1.554***	.201	59.697	.211
Watched October 3 Debate (Yes = 1, No = 0)	.388*	.169	5.286	1.473
Cox & Snell R^{2a}	.196			
Nagelkerke R^2	.268			
N	1,157			

$*p < .05$; $**p < .01$; $***p < .001$.

[a] These measures of R^2 are designed to provide comparable information to estimates from OLS regression. They are based on the likelihood function rather than squared residuals and thus should not be interpreted as variance explained. The Nagelkerke measure has an upper bound of 1 which makes it more comparable to R^2 from OLS regression (see Allison 1999 for a discussion of these statistics).

debate (rF37). Watching the debate was a statistically significant predictor of opinion about Bush's debate performance.

As mentioned previously, sensitization can make effects appear significant because of repeated questioning. One way to show that changes over time are not the result of sensitization is by demonstrating that the effect does not occur for everyone in the survey. We can test this hypothesis by seeing if there is an interaction between the party identification variables and debate watching. If the interaction is significant, then our concerns about sensitization from repeated testing are somewhat allayed. We elaborated on the model in Table 8.5 by including party identification and debate watching interactions. These interactions, however, were not significant. Does this mean that there is a testing effect that is producing sensitization? Not necessarily. A null result neither proves or disproves that sensitization is occurring.

How might we demonstrate that results from Table 8.5 are not due to sensitization? One way is to run the model on a cross-section of respondents who have not previously been surveyed. Using the NAES national RCS, we can take respondents interviewed during the same time period that the postdebate panel respondents were interviewed (October 4 to October 10) and see if similar patterns appear in these data. We know that sensitization to party affiliation is less likely to have affected responses to the debate evaluation question in the cross-section because party identification is asked at the end of the survey.

Table 8.6 reveals that party identification and debate-watching (cF35) were significant predictors of respondents' opinions about debate performance in the October 3 debate (cF37). Indeed, the effect of watching the debate was slightly stronger in the cross-sectional sample (0.477 versus 0.388). In addition, the effects of party identification were comparable in the two surveys. These findings suggest that predebate sensitization was not responsible for the effects of party identification or reports of debate watching. Independent of party identification, respondents who had watched the debate were more likely to say that Bush had won the debate.

One difference between the panel and RCS respondents was that education was not a significant predictor for the RCS respondents. This is not particularly surprising considering that the effect was only significant at the .05 level for panel respondents. Another difference to note is that the RCS respondents were slightly different from those in the panel in a few key characteristics. While the panel and RCS respondents were not statistically different in their gender composition or strength of partisanship, the panel respondents were slightly more interested in politics and more educated than their RCS counterparts.

TABLE 8.6. BINARY LOGISTIC REGRESSION PREDICTING THE OPINION THAT BUSH PERFORMED BETTER THAN GORE IN THE OCTOBER 3 PRESIDENTIAL DEBATE USING NATIONAL RCS DATA, OCTOBER 4–10, 2000

	B	SE	$Wald$	$Exp (B)$
Constant	-.840*	.389	4.663	.432
Education (years)	-.027	.025	1.188	.973
Republican (Yes = 1, Else = 0)	1.404***	.132	112.748	4.071
Democrat (Yes = 1, Else = 0)	-1.180***	.168	49.325	.307
Watched October 3 Debate (Yes = 1, No = 0)	.477***	.143	11.196	1.611
Cox & Snell R^2	.178			
Nagelkerke R^2	.247			
N	1,571			

*p < .05; **p < .01; ***p < .001.

Additional Uses for the Panels in RCS Analyses

Johnston and Brady (2002) argue that the RCS design "necessitates an estimation strategy that distinguishes time-series from cross-sectional effects" (283). They make the case for a method in which a post-election panel can be used as a control so that one can differentiate between time series and cross-sectional variation. Researchers interested in this approach should read Johnston and Brady's important article on the rolling cross-section design.

Conclusion

Unlike the repeated cross-section design, which can only track changes at the group level, panel data allow us to track changes in individuals. Using panel data, we can control the variation from responses at prior points in time. There are two risks in the panel design. First, researchers must anticipate the time points when they think significant events will occur. They must also decide how much time should pass before subsequent waves of data are collected. If these two judgments are not sound, the panel design will be costly and unproductive. Second, when respondents answer questions repeatedly, they may become sensitized to the questions and act differently than they would have if they had not answered an initial round of questions. Despite the drawbacks, researchers who want to make inferences about the causes of variables on individual-level processes must use data collected on the same individuals at more than one point in time.

Notes

1. The standard error of the difference between means is $\sqrt{[(s_1)^2/n_1 + (s_2)^2/n_2]}$, where $(s_t)^2$ is the estimate of the variance for time t and n_t is the sample size at time t. The corresponding standard error for the difference scores is $\sqrt{[s_1^2/n]}$, where s^2 is the variance estimate of the differences and n is the sample size. Inserting the values for our example in Table 8.3 produces a standard error of 0.77 for the difference between independent samples versus a value of 0.45 for the differences in matched scores. The standard error is over 70 percent larger in the independent samples compared to the matched sample.

2. The R^2 statistic tells us how much of the variation in the dependent variable the model explains. It is important to note that "a sizable R^2 does not necessarily mean we have a *causal* explanation for the dependent variable; instead, we may merely have provided a *statistical* explanation" (Lewis-Beck 1980, 24).

3. This dataset was not weighted.

References

Allison, Paul D. 1999. *Logistic Regression: Using the SAS System.* Cary, N.C.: SAS Institute.

Finkel, Steven. E. 1995. *Causal Analysis of Panel Data.* Thousand Oaks, Calif.: Sage.

Johnston, Richard and Henry E. Brady. 2002. The Rolling Cross-Section Design. *Electoral Studies* 21: 283–95.

Lewis-Beck, Michael S. 1980. *Applied Regression: An Introduction.* Newbury Park, Calif.: Sage.

Sudman, Seymour, Norman M. Bradburn, and Norbert Schwarz. 1996. *Thinking About Answers: The Application of Cognitive Processes to Survey Methodology.* San Francisco: Jossey-Bass.

Chapter 9
Time Series Models

Daniel Romer

In this chapter we introduce methods for analyzing the data from the NAES that take advantage of the information contained in the daily observations made throughout the period of the survey. This analysis relies primarily on the quantitative methods introduced by economists for the study of time series data (see Chatfield 1999; Diebold 2001; Enders 1995; Harvey 1993 for overviews of these methods). Because these techniques are less well known, our discussion is lengthier than that devoted to the methods in previous chapters.

In this chapter, we will review methods for uncovering cycles in the daily behavior of the U.S. electorate. We will also examine ways to study the influence of events that occurred during the election year using the daily reactions of the public. Finally, we will examine how the public's daily reactions to a candidate (e.g., learning the candidate's likelihood of victory) might affect their evaluation of the candidate.

What Is a Time Series?

A time series is a set of observations, Y_t, measured at regular intervals of time, $t = 1, 2, 3, \ldots, T$. In this chapter, we analyze such series by looking at relations between values of Y at time t and at k prior time periods or lags, $t - k$, of Y. For example, we can calculate the average interest in the election on any given day and determine if that interest is related to the public's interest one day or two days earlier. Ordinarily when we correlate variables, we examine the relation between ordered pairs of values for two variables measured at the same time. In time series analysis, we examine relations between variables that are paired at different lags. As seen in Table 9.1, a series with T periods of observations is paired with values of the same series one lag (Y_{t-1}) and two lags (Y_{t-2}) back in time. Note that each time the series is paired with a lag of itself, initial observations in the original series are no longer paired with the lagged

TABLE 9.1. EXAMPLE OF TWO LAGS OF A TIME SERIES WITH T TIME PERIODS

	Term in the series				
Lag	First	Second	Third	Fourth	Last
Y_t	Y_1	Y_2	Y_3	Y_4	Y_T
Y_{t-1}		Y_1	Y_2	Y_3	Y_{T-1}
Y_{t-2}			Y_1	Y_2	Y_{T-2}

versions. A series that is lagged k times will have k fewer observations paired with the original series.

Approaches that analyze time series as a function of lags of the original series focus on the time domain of a series. Another approach to analyzing time series involves the frequency domain, in which a series is analyzed in terms of recurring waves represented by trigonometric functions. Either approach can be applied to time series data, but we will restrict our analysis to the time domain because this approach is of more interest to the disciplines that study politics, such as political science, communication, economics, and sociology. For a discussion of time series analysis in the frequency domain, see Chatfield (1996).

The Purely Random Time Series

Before considering how to analyze a series in the time domain, it will be helpful to consider the simplest of all series, the purely random series. No matter what time series we examine, it will almost certainly have a random component that is uncorrelated between lags. In time series terminology, this series is known as white noise. A series composed of white noise has values that are uncorrelated with any other lags in the series, a mean of 0, and a constant standard deviation. In such a series, the observations at each time period are drawn at random from the same distribution of potential scores. These scores can be written as

$$Y_t = e_t,$$

where e_t is the randomly drawn score at time t. If the distribution from which e_t is drawn is normal, then the series is completely described by its mean and standard deviation. Each value is statistically independent of other values in the series. In the NAES, we can aggregate the scores from each day's interviews to obtain a set of means. According to the central limit theorem for means, these means will tend to be normally distributed as the sample size increases. So, we can also be relatively confident that the white noise in our series approximates a normal distribution.

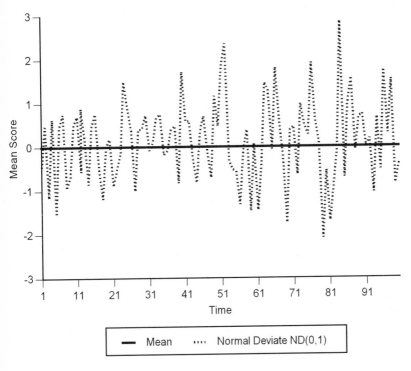

Figure 9.1. Simulated series of white noise with mean = 0 and standard deviation = 1.

Figure 9.1 shows a randomly generated series for one hundred time periods drawn from a normal distribution that was simulated using the random number generator in SPSS with a mean of zero and a standard deviation of 1 or ND(0, 1). The series fluctuates around the mean, and the fluctuations are relatively unsystematic. This series has no systematic relations between time periods because it was designed that way. Scores at one time period t are unrelated to scores at other time periods $t - k$.

These scores exhibit another important feature of time series data: covariance stationarity. A white noise series will have the same mean and standard deviation across all possible time periods. As a result, it also will have the same *covariance* between lags, which will be $C(Y_t, Y_{t-k}) = 0$ for any value of k. Although the covariance is theoretically zero, in practice as sampling error enters into the estimates, it will vary around zero.

Quite often in time series data, a series will have a constant mean and variance, but the scores at one time period will be systematically related to those of other time periods. These dependencies can take at least two forms, described by autoregressive (AR) and moving average (MA) models. Both models suppose that observations at time t are related to observations at different lags. But the form of the relation is different.

The Autoregressive Model

In the simplest autoregressive model, the score at time t is based only on the immediately previous score:

$$Y_t - m = a_1(Y_{t-1} - m) + e_t,$$

where a_1 is a regression coefficient that is assumed to have a value between -1 and $+1$, m is the mean of the series, and e_t is a random variable representing white noise. The coefficient a_1 transfers the effect of Y at time $t - 1$ to Y at time t. If we remove the mean from the series, then the model simplifies to

$$Y_t = a_1 Y_{t-1} + e_t.$$

The restriction that the value of a_1 lies between -1 and $+1$ is important because the series would not be stationary unless this condition were met. You can see this by inserting the value of $a_1 Y$ repeatedly into each succeeding value of the series. Unless a_1 is less than 1 in absolute value, the series will change its mean dramatically and no longer be stationary. Later we will see what happens when the value of a_1 is exactly 1. In this case, the series is also not stationary because the variation around the mean may be unstable.

The autoregressive model is essentially a multiple regression model with the dependent variable predicted by a lagged value of itself, hence the term autoregressive process. It is called an AR(1) model because only one lag is involved in influencing the values of the series. The general model is an AR(p) process with up to p lags influencing the scores at any time period.

Although the AR model is akin to OLS regression, the values of the independent and dependent variables are the same sets of scores. The only difference is that the ordering has been shifted by one time period for each lag of Y that is used to predict Y.

WHY ARE TIME LAGS RELATED?

There are at least two reasons for the presence of lagged relations in time series data. The relation can be causal, in which case the observations at one time period influence the observations at a later time period. An example would be an imitative effect in which publicly observable events at time t lead to similar events at time $t + k$. For example, it is believed that some crimes lead to copycat behavior by others. If this is true, then crimes at one time period will produce similar behavior at a subsequent time period.

Highly publicized suicide is discussed as subject to imitation. In the business world, the daily closing values of the stock market are well known to market participants and can influence trading on the succeeding day. Housing starts and other conspicuous forms of consumption may also lead to imitative effects such that a spurt in buying at one time period can lead to imitative effects at later time periods.

In addition to imitative effects, relations between lags may represent underlying changes that take time to unfold. Observations at nearby time periods may be related because people's feelings or perceptions at one time point carry over to succeeding ones. The relations may or may not be causal, but the effect at the level of observations is the same. Whether they are causally related or not, the autoregressive model assumes that characteristics of observations at previous time periods carry over to succeeding periods.

In political campaigns, an AR(1) model might mean that respondents at any point in time have the same reactions they had one period earlier in time. For example, people's feelings toward a candidate might be influenced by how they felt yesterday as well as by new, unrelated influences today. On the next day, their feelings from today will carry over to tomorrow along with tomorrow's new influences. If we assume that the mean of the observations stays the same over time and that the variability does as well, then these processes will tend to cycle. These cycles are important because we need to model them if we want to understand how people's feelings, knowledge, and perceptions change over time and possibly affect each other.

In addition to continuous cycles in an election time series, alterations in a campaign can introduce change that systematically shifts the mean of the series. But such influences are different from the cycles we are describing in an AR(p) process. An AR process will characterize a series for a relatively long period of time that is independent of sudden changes in the direction of a campaign (a new election strategy by a candidate) or of outside events that change the standing of the candidates in an election (economic or other events).

Figure 9.2 illustrates two AR(1) time series using the same set of random deviates as were shown in Figure 9.1. Notice that the two series are nearly identical and only vary in their dispersion around the mean of the series. The variance of an AR(1) process is

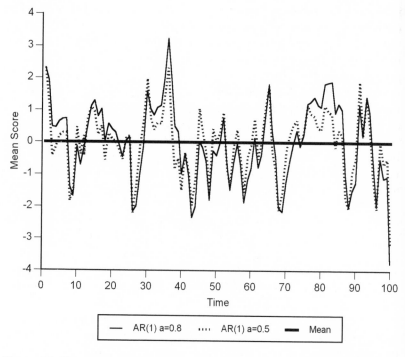

Figure 9.2. Two autoregressive models that differ in the regression parameter, a_1.

$$\sigma^2 \, / \, (1 - a_1{}^2),$$

in which σ^2 represents the variance of the white noise contained in the series. This equation indicates that the variance of the AR series grows larger as a_1 increases.

THE MOVING AVERAGE MODEL

A second model that has been widely studied is the moving average model. This series is different from an AR process in that the carryover from previous days is restricted to the random process rather than to the entire previous observed score. For example, in an MA(1) model, the equation looks like this:

$$Y_t = e_t + b_1 e_{t-1},$$

where the random process at the previous time point, e_{t-1}, carries over to the next time period, with a coefficient of b_1. The new score at time t

is also influenced by the random process for that time period, e_t. The coefficient b_1 is also restricted to a value no greater than 1 in absolute value. In the MA model, the restriction in values of b_1 does not function to ensure stationarity. The MA series will be stationary even if b_1 is greater than 1. However, the restriction is maintained so that the MA model can be approximated by an AR model. Just like the AR model, the general MA process can also have any number of lags represented as an MA(q) model.

Unlike the AR model, the MA model is not based on observed scores because neither of the random processes is directly observed. In the AR (1) model, the random process can be estimated by subtracting the predicted score from the observed score:

$$e_t = Y_t - a_i Y_{t-1}.$$

In the MA (1) model, the random process can be written as

$$e_t = Y_t - b e_{t-1},$$

This equation says that the current random score is a function of the present score and the immediately previous random score. But that random score can be written as

$$e_{t-1} = Y_{t-1} - b e_{t-2}.$$

If you keep going with this line of reasoning, you will not get to an observed score until you arrive at the first score in the series. Despite this problem, we can see a pattern in the relations between different time lags in an MA(1) process. If we substitute equations for each prior value of e_t, we get the following result:

$$Y_t = e_t + b Y_{t-1} - b^2 Y_{t-2} + b^3 Y_{t-1} + \cdots - (-b)^j Y_{t-j},$$

where j equals different lagged values of the series. This result tells us that the relation between lags in an MA(1) process is positive for odd-numbered lags and negative for even-numbered lags. In addition, if b is less than 1 in absolute value, the coefficients decline in absolute size as lag size increases. This feature of the MA model allows us to approximate the series using observed scores; but we cannot reduce the series to observed scores as we can with the AR model.

Diagnosing Model Type: The Correlogram

A very important way of diagnosing the characteristics of a time series is to examine the correlations between lags. The correlation coefficient is a standard measure of linear relationship that is equal to

$$r_{xy} = C(x,y) \: / \: [S(x)\,S(y)],$$

where C stands for the covariance of two variables (x, y) and $S(x)$ and $S(y)$ stand for their respective standard deviations. The covariance measures the extent to which the two variables are linearly related. The more two variables are related, the greater the absolute size of the covariance. However, the covariance has no upper or lower bounds. Dividing the covariance by the product of the standard deviations produces a score that varies from -1 to $+1$. If x and y are perfectly correlated, then their covariance equals the product of their standard deviations. If they are positively related, then r will equal 1. If they are negatively related, r will equal -1.

When different lags of a time series are correlated with each other, we can observe systematic relations between lags. The *autocorrelation function* (ACF) is the name for the relation between the correlation coefficient at different lags (k) and the value of the lag. It is defined as

$$r_k = C(x_t - m, \: x_{t-k} - m) \: / \: V_x,$$

where V_x represents the variance of the series.

One major difference between the AC coefficient and the regular correlation coefficient is that one assumes that the series is stationary when analyzing the ACF. Instead of using the mean of the series at each lag to calculate the difference scores, the mean (m) is fixed at the value of the entire series. In addition, the variance of the series is assumed to be constant. This allows the ACF to detect systematic patterns in the lag structure.

When the series has an AR structure and a is positive, it tends to produce an ACF that gradually dampens. The AC is always 1 at zero lag (the series correlated with itself). However, as the number of lags increases, the AC declines as the square of a. The resulting graph of the ACF is called the correlogram of the series (see Figure 9.3).

When a series has an MA structure and b is positive, it tends to produce an abrupt drop at the number of lags that carry over in the process. In the example in Figure 9.4, there is only one lag in the MA process, and so the ACF drops dramatically after one lag.

This difference in the pattern of the ACF makes sense, since the AR

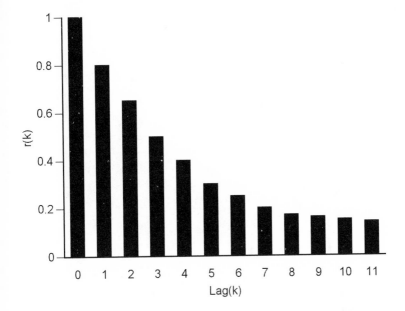

Figure 9.3. Autocorrelation function for an AR(1) process.

process brings with it the effects of previous lags at each time period. The MA process only carries information from the lags that influence the present time period. In this sense, the AR process is said to have a longer *memory* than the MA process.

For example, consider what happens when you have an AR(1) process with a positive coefficient. In this case, the first three values of the series are

$$Y_1 = e_1,$$
$$Y_2 = a_1 Y_1 + e_2,$$
$$Y_3 = a_1 Y_2 + e_3.$$

If one inserts the equation for Y_2 into Y_3, one obtains

$$Y_3 = (a_1)^2 Y_1 + a_1 e_2 + e_3.$$

As is evident, time 3 is related to time 1 as the square of a_1, while time 2 is related to time 1 as a_1. So, time 3 is related to time 1, although at a weaker level than time 2 is related to time 1. If one continued this process for successive lags, the AC between Y_t and other lags would decline

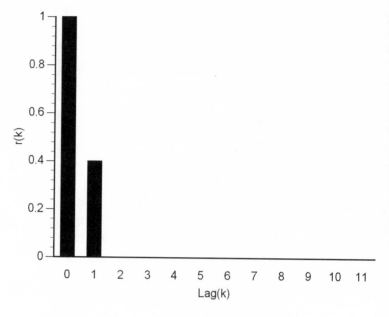

Figure 9.4. Autocorrelation function for an MA(1) process.

until it effectively reached zero. If a_1 is negative, then the relation would be negative for odd lags and positive for even lags.

Compare the AR(1) process with an MA(1) process. In the MA(1) case, we have the following relations across three successive time periods:

$$Y_1 = e_1,$$
$$Y_2 = e_2 + b_1 e_1,$$
$$Y_3 = e_3 + b_1 e_2,$$

Even if we recognize Y_1 in Y_2, there is still no carryover from Y_1 to Y_3. This produces a basic difference between the two series that can be observed in the ACF.

THE PARTIAL AUTOCORRELATION FUNCTION

Another diagnostic tool for interpreting time series data is the partial autocorrelation at different lags. If we predict the series at lag 0 using successive lags in a stepwise multiple regression model, then the partial AC is the standardized regression coefficient for the series at lag p with

$p - 1$ prior lags in the model. For the first lag, the partial AC is always equal to the AC at the first lag. As more lags are added to the model, earlier lags are held constant and the coefficient for the pth lag represents the additional prediction afforded by that lag once all earlier lags are held constant.

The partial ACF (PACF) is the relation between the coefficients and their respective lag values. For an AR(p) process, the partial ACF will drop to zero after the pth lag. For an AR(1) process, the partial for the second lag should be zero, since the second lag produces no autocorrelation beyond that produced by the first lag.

For an MA(1) process, the PACF tends to oscillate around and to gradually approach zero. For larger orders ($q > 1$), the PACF can either oscillate or dampen gradually depending on the characteristics of the lag parameters. So, the characteristics of the PACF are the opposite of the ACF for the two types of series.

Analysis of Time Series

Some Artificial Examples

Let's create an MA(1) series using $Y_t = .5(Z_{t-1}) + Z_t$, where Z is drawn from a normal distribution with a mean 0 and standard deviation 1 (ND(0,1)). First we can examine the ACF and partial ACF for the white noise series Z. We use the autocorrelation procedure in SPSS to produce the output shown in Table 9.2. Because we created the series from white noise, we expect the ACF to show no significant values for any lag. There are two ways to assess this prediction.

Correlations lying outside the confidence bands defined by 2 times $1/\sqrt{N}$ are regarded as significant at the .05 level. This is a helpful tool for quickly identifying significant relations between lags. The first several coefficients representing the nearest lags are usually the critical ones because we would expect them to be most related to the series at lag 0.

Another helpful tool for diagnosing the results of the ACF is the *Box-Ljung* test for independence across lags. If the time series has no serial dependence, the Box-Ljung statistic will be nonsignificant except for the occasional type I error. The Box-Ljung is a chi-square test of the hypothesis that the first P lags in a time series have correlations equal to 0. It has P degrees of freedom and is calculated as

$$T(T + 2) \sum r_k^2 / (T - k),$$

TABLE 9.2. AUTOCORRELATION OUTPUT FROM SPSS FOR A SIMULATED WHITE
NOISE SERIES (Z)

```
Autocorrelations:   Z   random variable drawn from ND(0,1)

       Auto- Stand.
Lag    Corr.  Err.  -1  -.75  -.5 -.25   0   .25  .5  .75   1  Box-Ljung  Prob.
                    ├───┼───┼───┼───┼───┼───┼───┼───┤

  1    .053  .099                         .  *  .                 .292   .589
  2   -.122  .098                         . **  .                1.841   .398
  3   -.141  .098                         .***  .                3.933   .269
  4    .016  .097                         .  *  .                3.962   .411
  5    .069  .097                         .  |* .                4.471   .484
  6    .045  .096                         .  |* .                4.687   .585
  7   -.261  .095                       *.***|  .               12.177   .095
  8    .008  .095                         .  *  .               12.184   .143
  9   -.084  .094                         . **|  .              12.975   .164
 10    .004  .094                         .  *  .               12.976   .225
 11    .025  .093                         .  *  .               13.046   .290
 12   -.007  .093                         .  *  .               13.051   .365
 13   -.027  .092                         . *|  .               13.137   .437
 14    .029  .092                         .  |* .               13.238   .508
 15    .093  .091                         .  |** .              14.269   .505
 16    .103  .091                         .  |** .              15.561   .484

Plot Symbols:      Autocorrelations *     Two Standard Error Limits .

Total cases:  100     Computable first lags:  99

Partial Autocorrelations:   Z   random variable drawn from ND(0,1)

       Pr-Aut- Stand.
Lag    Corr.   Err.  -1  -.75  -.5 -.25   0   .25  .5  .75   1
                     ├───┼───┼───┼───┼───┼───┼───┼───┤

  1    .053   .100                        .  |* .
  2   -.125   .100                        .***|  .
  3   -.129   .100                        .***|  .
  4    .016   .100                        .  *  .
  5    .036   .100                        .  |* .
  6    .026   .100                        .  |* .
  7   -.258   .100                      *.***|  .
  8    .059   .100                        .  |* .
  9   -.150   .100                        .***|  .
 10   -.047   .100                        .  *|  .
 11    .008   .100                        .  |* .
 12   -.028   .100                        .  *|  .
 13   -.012   .100                        .  *  .
 14   -.038   .100                        .  *|  .
 15    .131   .100                        .  |***.
 16    .025   .100                        .  |* .

Plot Symbols:      Autocorrelations *     Two Standard Error Limits .

Total cases:  100     Computable first lags:  99
```

where k runs from 1 to P. T is the number of time periods in the series, and r_k is the autocorrelation at lag k.

Its value at each lag tests whether any correlations are significant up to and including that lag. The test is usually significant at early lags if some degree of autocorrelation is present. However, as the number of lags increases, the test tends to become nonsignificant because later lags are usually not as highly correlated as earlier ones.

We see that the Box-Ljung statistic is not significant at any lag. However, it approaches significance at lag 7. This lag also has an AC that lies outside the 95% confidence interval. This pattern illustrates that even a randomly generated series can have some dependencies by chance. If one encountered such a result for a series in the NAES dataset one would have to consider the possibility that the significant value at lag 7 merely represents a type I error. That is, something that happens by chance once every twenty times when one uses the .05 level of significance. However, another possibility is that behavior is dependent on the calendar, such that people's responses are similar on the same day of the week. Later we will discuss how to test for such a possibility.

We also see that the partial AC at lag 7 is significant, a result that again supports the possible presence of a relation between days one week apart. The graph of the MA(1) series along with the random series Z is shown in Figure 9.5. The MA(1) series has a mean of 0 and a variance of $1 + b^2$, which is somewhat larger than the white noise series (1.25 versus 1.0). As one would expect given the nature of an MA series, there is also evidence of greater carryover from one time period to the next.

The ACF and PACF for the MA(1) are shown in Table 9.3. The significant AC for the first lag is consistent with the way we defined the series. Recall that the succeeding lags should drop off dramatically and should alternate in sign. As you can see, the second lag has a negative value. In addition, we see the spuriously significant coefficient at lag 7. The partials show a significant coefficient at lag 1 and a significant negative coefficient for lag 2. The second coefficient is also spurious. It represents the characteristic pattern of the ACF for an MA process. Succeeding PACs will oscillate until they dampen to zero. The spurious coefficient at lag 7 introduces a relatively large coefficient that also oscillates from that point onward.

We now turn to an artificially created AR(1) series using the same random series Z as the basis for the series. In this case, the series is defined by $Y_t = .5(Y_{t-1}) + Z_t$. As the plot in Figure 9.6 indicates, the series looks very similar to the MA(1). It is only by comparing the correlograms that one can see the characteristic differences associated with an AR and MA series. Although the first coefficient in each ACF is significant, succeeding AR coefficients are more positive than those in the MA series. The

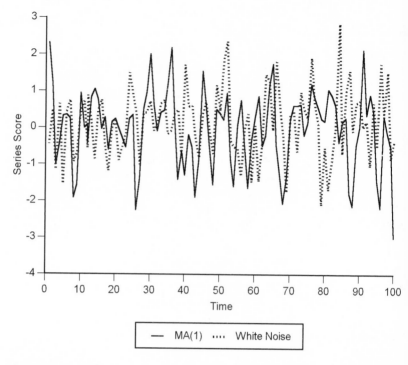

Figure 9.5. A plot of the MA(1) series defined by $Y_t = .5 \, (Z_{t-1}) + Z_t$ and white noise defined by Z_t.

PACF for the MA also appears to oscillate more than in the AR series. It is also noteworthy that the seventh coefficient is significant, which is the same spurious lag we observed in the original random series. Unless one had a good reason to suppose that there was a seven-day lag, one would treat this coefficient with skepticism (see Table 9.4).

Actual Data from the NAES

Let's now look at an actual data series from the 2000 NAES. In Figure 9.7, we plot the average favorability rating of Al Gore (cAll), using the thermometer scale during the months of January through April 2000. The series looks relatively stationary. There is no apparent change in the mean of the series or in the dispersion of values during this period. One important factor that could affect the dispersion of the series is the number of interviews done per day. However, during this period in the national sample, the number of interviews remained relatively stable at approximately eighty-five per day.

TABLE 9.3. CORRELOGRAM ANALYSIS OF SIMULATED MA(1) SERIES

Autocorrelations for series defined as: $Y = Z_t + .5Z_{t-1}$

```
     Auto- Stand.
Lag  Corr.  Err. -1  -.75  -.5 -.25   0   .25  .5   .75   1   Box-Ljung  Prob.
                   ├──┼──┼──┼──┼──┼──┼──┼──┼──┤
  1  .356   .099                    .    ***.***             13.083    .000
  2 -.160   .098                  .***    .                  15.750    .000
  3 -.181   .098                 ****     .                  19.193    .000
  4 -.008   .097                    .*    .                  19.200    .001
  5  .063   .097                    . |*  .                  19.621    .001
  6 -.051   .096                    . *|  .                  19.899    .003
  7 -.229   .095                 *.***    .                  25.673    .001
  8 -.116   .095                    .**|  .                  27.159    .001
  9 -.073   .094                    . *|  .                  27.758    .001
 10  .009   .094                    .  |* .                  27.766    .002
 11  .023   .093                    .  |* .                  27.828    .003
 12 -.014   .093                    .  *| .                  27.850    .006
 13 -.046   .092                    . *|  .                  28.093    .009
 14  .030   .092                    .  |* .                  28.203    .013
 15  .146   .091                    .  |***.                 30.755    .009
 16  .112   .091                    .  |** .                 32.279    .009
```

Plot Symbols: Autocorrelations *   Two Standard Error Limits .

Total cases: 100   Computable first lags: 99

Partial Autocorrelations for series defined as: $Y = Z_t + .5Z_{t-1}$

```
     Pr-Aut- Stand.
Lag   Corr.  Err. -1  -.75  -.5 -.25   0   .25  .5   .75   1
                    ├──┼──┼──┼──┼──┼──┼──┼──┼──┤
  1   .356   .100                    .   ***.***
  2  -.329   .100                 ***.***  .
  3   .015   .100                    . *|  .
  4   .025   .100                    . |*  .
  5  -.002   .100                    .  *  .
  6  -.100   .100                    . **| .
  7  -.186   .100                 ****     .
  8   .047   .100                    .  |* .
  9  -.189   .100                 ****     .
 10   .062   .100                    .  |* .
 11  -.055   .100                    . *|  .
 12  -.024   .100                    .  *| .
 13  -.060   .100                    . *|  .
 14   .025   .100                    .  *  .
 15   .119   .100                    .  |**.
 16  -.064   .100                    . *|  .
```

Plot Symbols: Autocorrelations *   Two Standard Error Limits .

Total cases: 100   Computable first lags: 99

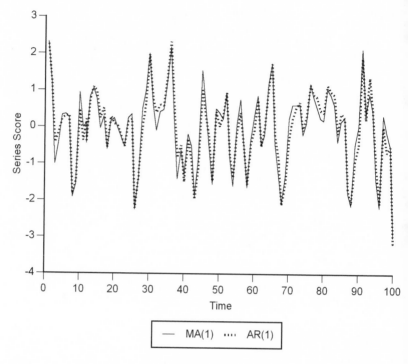

Figure 9.6. Comparison of autoregressive (AR) and moving average (MA) models.

We can test the hypothesis that the series mean remained stable by subjecting the series to a curve-fitting analysis. SPSS allows one to test various trends with its curve-fitting program. The results of this analysis shown in Table 9.5 indicate that neither linear nor quadratic trend terms are significant. Hence, we can be relatively confident that the series is stationary.

If we examine the ACF for this series, we find that there is no evidence of autocorrelation in the series. This suggests that people's ratings of Gore during this period displayed no evidence of carryover from one day to the next. Each day's ratings by the interview sample represented an independent sample from the distribution of feelings that people had toward Gore during this time period (see Table 9.6).

THE EFFECT OF SAMPLE SIZE ON THE STANDARD ERROR OF THE MEAN

As we noted earlier, mean scores for interview data for each day will approximate a normal distribution. As a result, two parameters will com-

TABLE 9.4. CORRELOGRAM ANALYSIS OF SIMULATED AR(1) SERIES

Autocorrelations for series defined as: $Y_t = .5(Y_{t-1}) + Z_t$.

Lag	Auto- Corr.	Stand. Err.	-1 -.75 -.5 -.25 0 .25 .5 .75 1	Box-Ljung	Prob.
1	.422	.099	***.****	18.374	.000
2	.055	.098	*	18.686	.000
3	-.085	.098	**	19.441	.000
4	-.019	.097	*	19.480	.001
5	-.022	.097	*	19.533	.002
6	-.103	.096	**	20.678	.002
7	-.267	.095	*.***	28.489	.000
8	-.138	.095	.***	30.587	.000
9	-.126	.094	.***	32.378	.000
10	-.021	.094	*	32.430	.000
11	.003	.093	*	32.431	.001
12	-.009	.093	*	32.441	.001
13	-.020	.092	*	32.487	.002
14	.039	.092	*	32.667	.003
15	.124	.091	**	34.515	.003
16	.121	.091	**	36.291	.003

Plot Symbols: Autocorrelations *   Two Standard Error Limits .

Total cases: 100   Computable first lags: 99

Partial Autocorrelations for series defined as: $Y_t = .5(Y_{t-1}) + Z_t$.

Lag	Pr-Aut- Corr.	Stand. Err.	-1 -.75 -.5 -.25 0 .25 .5 .75 1
1	.422	.100	***.****
2	-.150	.100	.***
3	-.059	.100	*
4	.066	.100	*
5	-.057	.100	*
6	-.105	.100	**
7	-.217	.100	****
8	.082	.100	**
9	-.160	.100	.***
10	.051	.100	*
11	-.010	.100	*
12	-.053	.100	*
13	-.024	.100	*
14	-.001	.100	*
15	.119	.100	**
16	-.052	.100	*

Plot Symbols: Autocorrelations *   Two Standard Error Limits .

Total cases: 100   Computable first lags: 99

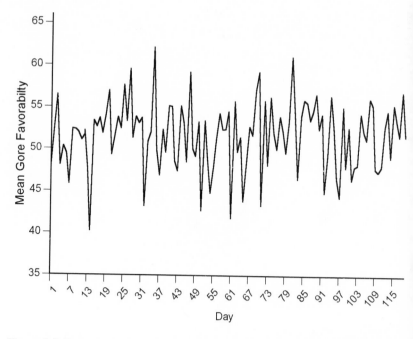

Figure 9.7. Ratings of Gore's favorability using the thermometer scale, January 3 to April 30.

TABLE 9.5. REGRESSION ANALYSIS OF GORE'S THERMOMETER RATING USING LINEAR AND QUADRATIC TRENDS AS PREDICTORS

Predictor	R^2	df	t	Prob.
Linear	.001	117	.36	.714
Quadratic	.002	116	.30	.913

pletely specify the distribution of scores for a series defined on means: the mean and the standard deviation. However, the size of the sample that is observed each day will determine the size of the standard error. In general, the standard error of the mean is proportional to the standard deviation of the individual interview scores σ divided by the square root of the size of the sample N:

$$\sigma / \sqrt{N}.$$

If we assume that σ stays the same despite changes in sample size, then the standard error will decrease as the inverse of the square root of the

TABLE 9.6. CORRELOGRAM ANALYSIS OF GORE'S FAVORABILITY THERMOMETER

Rating from January 3 to April 30

Autocorrelations: cAll   (Gore Favorability Rating)

Lag	Auto- Corr.	Stand. Err.	-1	-.75	-.5	-.25	0	.25	.5	.75	1	Box-Ljung	Prob.
1	-.017	.091					.	*	.			.035	.851
2	-.034	.090					.	*|	.			.180	.914
3	-.014	.090					.	*	.			.206	.977
4	.020	.089					.	*	.			.257	.992
5	.086	.089					.	|**	.			1.190	.946
6	-.002	.089					.	*	.			1.191	.977
7	.034	.088					.	|*	.			1.339	.987
8	.006	.088					.	*	.			1.344	.995
9	-.028	.087					.	*	.			1.447	.998
10	.161	.087					.	|***	.			4.857	.901
11	-.144	.087					***		.			7.608	.748
12	.086	.086					.	|**.				8.609	.736
13	-.054	.086					.	*|	.			9.005	.773
14	-.034	.085					.	*|	.			9.164	.820
15	-.091	.085					.	** |	.			10.317	.799
16	-.212	.085					* . **	|	.			16.576	.414

Plot Symbols: Autocorrelations *   Two Standard Error Limits .

Total cases: 119   Computable first lags: 118

Partial Autocorrelations: cAll   (Gore Favorability Rating)

Lag	Pr-Aut- Corr.	Stand. Err.	-1	-.75	-.5	-.25	0	.25	.5	.75	1
1	-.017	.092					.	*	.		
2	-.035	.092					.	*|	.		
3	-.016	.092					.	*	.		
4	.019	.092					.	*	.		
5	.086	.092					.	|**	.		
6	.002	.092					.	*	.		
7	.041	.092					.	|*	.		
8	.009	.092					.	*	.		
9	-.029	.092					.	*|	.		
10	.155	.092					.	|***.			
11	-.147	.092					. ***	|	.		
12	.094	.092					.	|**	.		
13	-.067	.092					.	*|	.		
14	-.034	.092					.	*|	.		
15	-.120	.092					.	** |	.		
16	-.211	.092					****	|	.		

Plot Symbols: Autocorrelations *   Two Standard Error Limits .

Total cases: 119   Computable first lags: 118

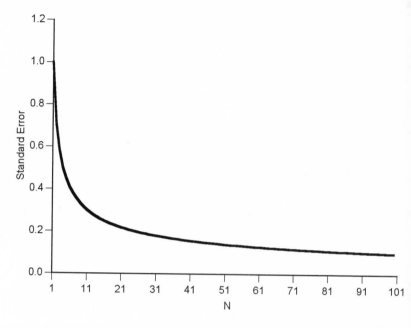

Figure 9.8. The effect of sample size on the standard error of the mean with a value of 1 for σ.

sample size. The relation between the standard error and sample size is shown in Figure 9.8. The largest decrease occurs in the range from one to thirty. After sample size of thirty, the standard error changes relatively little. Nevertheless, differences in daily sample size will have an effect on the variability of a series.

The effect of sample size can be seen by comparing daily samples from the national survey from January 3 to April 30, 2000. Figure 9.9 shows the sample size for each day for the full sample and for a randomly selected half of the sample. One can see that the daily sample size increased heading into the March primaries and then declined during April (Days 92–120). Nevertheless, the sample size remained at thirty or higher in the smaller of the two series at least until April, so we would expect the variation to be greater in the half sample but not dramatically so.

Figure 9.10 compares daily thermometer ratings of Gore for the full sample and the random half. It is evident that the variation is larger in the half sample. Nevertheless, the two series are remarkably similar. They are expected to have the same mean and only slightly different standard deviations. Differences in variability are most evident in April when the sample size of the half sample dipped below thirty per day.

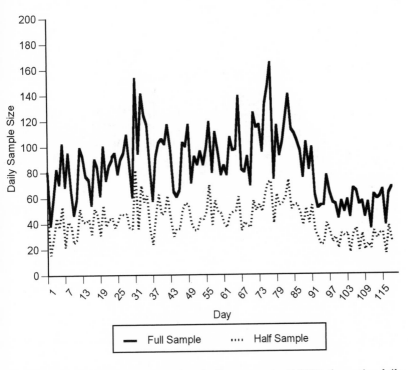

Figure 9.9. Comparison of sample sizes for January to April 2000, the entire daily national sample and a random half of the national sample.

DESCRIBING A TIME SERIES: GOING BEYOND RANDOM VARIATION

In order to examine some of the basic characteristics of time series data, we first explored the simplest component of any time series, the random variation that enters at each time point. When this variation displays no relation to other time points, it is known as white noise. A second source of potential variation in a time series is the systematic cycles that are described by $AR(p)$ and $MA(q)$ processes. We now consider two other components that have not been discussed, namely, trends and seasonal or calendar effects. In total, we will see that there are four potential components of any time series:

1. Trends, such as linear, curvilinear, or exponential changes in the level of the series.
2. Seasonal or calendar-related components, such as stable variation coinciding with days of the week or months of the year.

186   Daniel Romer

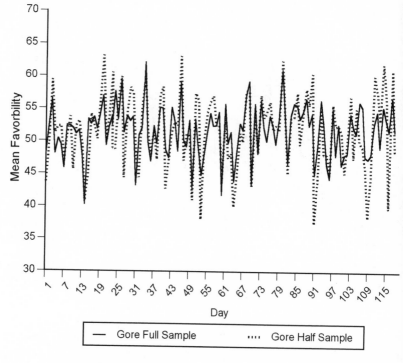

Figure 9.10. Comparison of mean thermometer rating of Gore for the entire national sample and for a random half of the sample from January to April 2000.

3. AR(p) or MA(q) processes.
4. White noise.

Trends and seasonal changes can also introduce correlations between lags. To use the correlogram to detect AR or MA components, it is important to first remove all other trends in the series that introduce systematic departures from the mean and standard deviation over time. This strategy is an attempt to achieve covariance stationarity. For normally distributed data, covariance stationarity is achieved when a series has a constant mean and standard deviation. We can reduce considerable variation in the standard deviation by making sure that the number of interviews per day is relatively constant across days of the survey. If not, then a minimal condition is that the number of interviews is greater than thirty per day. Unless there is a true change in the variability of the time series over time, holding constant the number of interviews should achieve stationarity in the standard deviation.

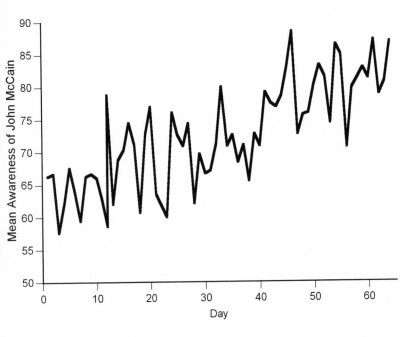

Figure 9.11. Awareness of John McCain (% aware) in the national sample, January 3 to March 6, 2000.

If the series undergoes change in its mean, these changes are attributable either to trends or to seasonal variation. Furthermore, systematic changes in mean will introduce correlations between time periods, and these correlations will obscure our ability to identify AR or MA processes.

We have already seen covariance stationarity in examples of MA(1) and AR(1) models and in people's feelings toward Gore during the primary season. We will now use graphing and regression techniques to achieve stationarity in a series that has a trend component so that we can identify potential MA and AR processes.

Let's look at a time trend in the 2000 NAES. Voter awareness of John McCain grew steadily early in 2000 (Figure 9.11). Awareness of candidates can be assessed using responses to the favorability thermometer questions (which for McCain is cA21). When respondents were asked to rate their overall favorability toward candidates (on a 0 to 100 scale), they were given the option of saying that they did not know the candidate well enough to provide a rating (response 102). This measure of awareness was used to create the series plotted in Figure 9.11. We should

TABLE 9.7. REGRESSION ANALYSIS OF MCCAIN'S AWARENESS AS A
FUNCTION OF DAY

Predictor	Unstandardized coefficients		Standardized coefficients		
	B	Std. error	Beta	t	Prob
Constant	61.889	1.253		49.41	.000
Day	.334	.034	.784	9.96	.000

be able to detect the linear trend in awareness and remove it from the awareness series. The remaining or residual variation should then be stationary.

A regression analysis using Day as the predictor indicates a significant linear component (see Table 9.7). The regression analysis indicates that each day, a little over three tenths of a percentage point (.334) of Americans became aware of McCain. Although this rate of increase would eventually slow down as the total approached 100%, the pattern is relatively linear during this time period.

Once we remove the linear increase from McCain's series, we are left with the pattern shown in Figure 9.12. This plot shows the residuals (saved by the SPSS regression program). This series appears to be quite stationary. Indeed, we could attempt to fit other time trends to the series, but they would not add significant predictive power to the model.

We can now examine the correlogram for the residuals in McCain's awareness series (i.e., the awareness series after we have removed the linear trend component). The correlogram shows no systematic correlation across waves. It appears that aside from the dramatic increase in awareness in the national sample, the daily cycles in awareness are serially uncorrelated. There is no carryover in awareness from day to day other than the linear rise that is apparent in the daily trend (see Table 9.8).

With a linear trend, each additional time period t increases (or decreases) the outcome by a constant amount: $Y_t = Y_{t-1} + A$. This implies that increases will be a function of time and the starting value of the series: $Y_t = At + Y_0$. (Note that we now use t to indicate a single value in a series rather than an entire series at a particular lag.)

As an exercise, find the ACF for the original series of McCain's awareness. You will see a dramatic difference compared with the residuals we just analyzed. The very dominant pattern of recurrent positive correlations across lags is indicative of a nonstationary series.

DIFFERENCING AS A TREND REMOVAL STRATEGY

Another strategy for removing trends is to transform the series by taking differences between lags. The first order difference can be written as: Y

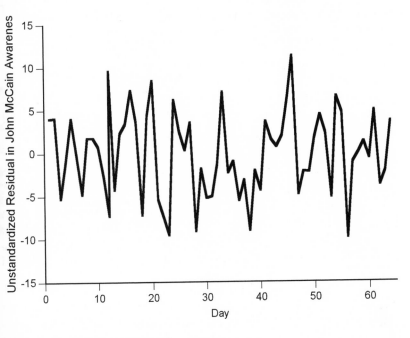

Figure 9.12. Residuals in McCain's awareness.

$-L(Y)$, where $L(Y)$ represents the first lag of the series. Every score in the lag of Y is subtracted from its corresponding score in Y. Since each lagged score has a value that is A less than the next score on average, this operation removes the linear trend.

Differencing works especially well if the series is a *random walk*. A random walk is so named because each step in the series is completely random with regard to the previous step. A random walk is the limiting case of an AR(1) when a_1 is 1,

$$Y_t = Y_{t-1} + e_t.$$

In this case, taking the difference score leaves only the random component in Y at each time point as the residual. This can be seen by examining three time periods in a random walk:

$$Y_3 = Y_2 + e_3 = e_1 + e_2 + e_3,$$
$$Y_2 = Y_1 + e_2 = e_1 + e_2,$$
$$Y_1 = e_1.$$

TABLE 9.8. CORRELOGRAM ANALYSIS OF RESIDUALS IN McCAIN AWARENESS
AFTER REMOVING LINEAR TREND

Autocorrelations: Residuals in McCain Awareness: Jan 3 to Mar 6

Lag	Auto- Corr.	Stand. Err.	Plot	Box-Ljung	Prob
1	-.067	.122	*	.300	.58
2	-.028	.121	*	.354	.83
3	-.021	.120	*	.386	.94
4	-.082	.119	**	.863	.93
5	.059	.118	*	1.109	.95
6	-.021	.117	*	1.141	.98
7	-.052	.116	*	1.340	.98
8	-.042	.115	*	1.475	.99
9	.116	.114	**	2.512	.98
10	-.015	.113	*	2.530	.99
11	-.029	.112	*	2.597	.99
12	-.160	.111	***	4.687	.96
13	-.014	.110	*	4.704	.98
14	-.157	.109	***	6.783	.94
15	-.053	.108	*	7.028	.95
16	-.118	.107	**	8.252	.94

Plot Symbols: Autocorrelations *   Two Standard Error Limits .

Total cases: 64   Computable first lags: 63

Partial Autocorrelations: Residuals in McCain Awareness: Jan 3 to Mar 6

Lag	Pr-Aut- Corr.	Stand. Err.	Plot
1	-.067	.125	*
2	-.033	.125	*
3	-.026	.125	*
4	-.087	.125	**
5	.046	.125	*
6	-.020	.125	*
7	-.056	.125	*
8	-.056	.125	*
9	.116	.125	**
10	-.012	.125	*
11	-.035	.125	*
12	-.168	.125	***
13	-.016	.125	*
14	-.202	.125	****
15	-.102	.125	**
16	-.187	.125	****

Plot Symbols: Autocorrelations *   Two Standard Error Limits .

Total cases: 64   Computable first lags: 63

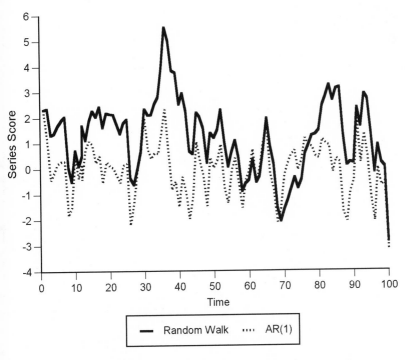

Figure 9.13. Comparison of a random walk with an AR(1) series using the same randomly generated white noise.

Each time period adds a random component to the previous random components. When successive time periods are differenced, one is left with only the random component from each time period, $Y_t - Y_{t-1} = e_t$.

It may seem strange that so subtle a change in the AR model should lead to such dramatic differences in the behavior of a series. However, one must keep in mind that in a random walk the entire score from the previous day is carried over to the next day ($a_1 = 1$). Furthermore, a random walk is not stationary. It can exhibit widely varying variation over time.

The erratic behavior of a random walk in comparison to a stationary series is illustrated in Figure 9.13. In this example, we use the same simulated random series to construct an AR(1) with a coefficient of .5 and a random walk with a coefficient of 1. The random walk has the same expected value of zero, but it meanders widely from this value. The AR series tends to oscillate around its expected value with the same variability over time.

If a series is not a random walk, then differencing leaves a more com plex pattern. For example, if we examine three time periods that con tain a linear trend, we see that each time period acquires the trend plus a random component:

$$Y_3 = 2A + e_3,$$
$$Y_2 = A + e_2$$
$$Y_1 = e_1,$$

When the series is differenced, the residual contains the average trend and the difference in random components for the present and previous time period:

$$Y_t - Y_{t-1} = A + e_t - e_{t-1}.$$

This differencing introduces an MA(1) process with a coefficient of -1. Let's examine this outcome with McCain's awareness growth using the previously analyzed first sixty-four days of 2000. We have seen that the residual of the awareness series after removing the linear trend is essentially white noise. If instead we detrend the series using difference scores, we find that the correlogram for this series exhibits a large negative autocorrelation at lag 1. In addition, the partial correlations exhibit gradual decay. These patterns are characteristic of an MA(1) (see Table 9.9).

If we calculate the mean of the differenced series we see that it is about .3 units. This implies that the average increase per day is .3 percentage units (very similar to what we found in our earlier regression analysis). However, the correlogram tells us that the random components are now correlated.

In essence, by applying the difference operation, we have introduced an MA(1) into the series. Later we will see how we can remove the MA(1) introduced by first order differencing. However, you can see that removing the trend using the residuals from regression analysis takes care of the problem of nonstationarity without introducing MA processes into the detrended series. Because we do not expect to find evidence of random walks in the NAES, we will opt to remove trends using regression techniques rather than differencing.

Nonlinear Trend

In addition to linear trend, there is also the possibility of nonlinear trend. A commonly encountered set of nonlinear trends can be mod-

TABLE 9.9. CORRELOGRAM ANALYSIS OF MCCAIN'S DIFFERENCED AWARENESS

Variable: Difference Score Missing cases: 1   Valid cases: 63

Autocorrelations: Difference Scores for McCain Awareness

```
      Auto- Stand.
Lag   Corr.  Err. -1 -.75 -.5 -.25  0  .25  .5  .75  1   Box-Ljung  Prob.

  1  -.516  .123          ***** .****    .              17.614     .000
  2   .029  .122                 .   |*  .              17.669     .000
  3   .017  .121                 .   |*  .              17.688     .001
  4  -.095  .120                 .  **|  .              18.321     .001
  5   .107  .119                 .   |** .              19.135     .002
  6  -.016  .118                 .   *|  .              19.153     .004
  7  -.026  .117                 .   *|  .              19.202     .008
  8  -.061  .116                 .   *|  .              19.476     .013
  9   .122  .115                 .   |** .              20.601     .015
 10  -.053  .114                 .   *|  .              20.819     .022
 11   .074  .113                 .   |*  .              21.255     .031
 12  -.144  .112                 . ***|  .              22.911     .028
 13   .126  .110                 .   |***.              24.213     .029
 14  -.115  .109                 .  **|  .              25.315     .032
 15   .079  .108                 .   |** .              25.848     .040
 16  -.087  .107                 .  **|  .              26.512     .047
```

Plot Symbols: Autocorrelations *   Two Standard Error Limits .

Total cases: 64   Computable first lags: 62

Partial Autocorrelations: Difference Scores for McCain Awareness

```
      Pr-Aut- Stand.
Lag   Corr.   Err. -1 -.75 -.5 -.25  0  .25  .5  .75  1

  1  -.516  .126          ***** .****    .
  2  -.325  .126            * .****      .
  3  -.200  .126              . ****     .
  4  -.274  .126            *****        .
  5  -.154  .126              . ***      .
  6  -.082  .126              .  **      .
  7  -.081  .126              .  **      .
  8  -.201  .126              .****      .
  9  -.048  .126              .   *|     .
 10  -.027  .126              .   *|     .
 11   .104  .126              .   |**    .
 12  -.061  .126              .   *|     .
 13   .086  .126              .   |**    .
 14  -.053  .126              .   *|     .
 15  -.005  .126              .   *|     .
 16  -.174  .126              . ***|     .
```

Plot Symbols: Autocorrelations *   Two Standard Error Limits .

Total cases: 64   Computable first lags: 62

eled using the exponential function. In this case, change is dependent on the previous value of Y. For example,

$$Y_t = Y_{t-1} + AY_{t-1}.$$

Here, changes in Y are proportional to previous values of Y:

$$Y_t - Y_{t-1} = AY_{t-1}.$$

One can also write this model in terms of the first value in the series:

$$Y_t = Y_0(1 + A)^t,$$

where each succeeding value is the product of $(1 + A) \times$ the preceding value. This trend implies the following equation:

$$Y_t = Y_0 e^{A't},$$

where A' is $1 + A$. Hence, the term *exponential growth*. Nevertheless, one can write this model as a linear function of the log of Y_t:

$$\ln(Y_t) = \ln(Y_0) + A't.$$

One can easily transform data that appear to exhibit exponential growth by taking the log of Y and doing a linear regression with time as the predictor. Then one is predicting constant percentage changes at each time point. It can be noted that an exponential growth trend may also produce nonstationary standard deviations. If the standard deviation is proportional to the value of the series, then taking the log of the series will reduce this source of nonstationarity as well.

If one wanted to stay in the same metric, then one could calculate predicted scores using the conversion $Y = ke^{A't}$ or by estimating this equation from the beginning. In Chapter 10, we provide some examples of how to fit an exponential model to data from the NAES.

Another exponential trend is the inverse of exponential growth, known as exponential decay. In this case, the coefficient (A) is negative and reflects a constant percentage decline (Figure 9.15).

A milder form of exponential change that is likely in public opinion contexts is shown in Figure 9.16. This curve is a typical media diffusion model in which a constant proportion of previously unexposed people is exposed to a message at each time point (Mahajan and Peterson 1985). As the media message reaches more and more people, the proportion of people still available to learn the message at each time point declines.

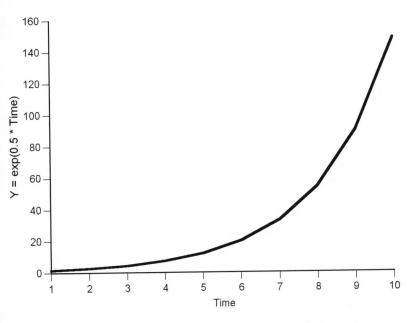

Figure 9.14. Example of exponential growth in which change at each time period is proportional to the value of the previous time period; the formula for y represents the exponential function (exp), using e as the base.

One can estimate the parameters of this model using nonlinear regression and then predicting the trend. As an exercise, try fitting this model to McCain's awareness using the first four months of data in the NAES. We also provide an example of how to fit such a model in Chapter 10.

Figure 9.17 shows a decay function in which the growth is subtracted from a starting point. Compare this with the first model and you will see that the decline is simply the inverse of exponential growth: slow at first, but then faster with time. This model can also be estimated using nonlinear regression.

MODELS WITH POWERS OF TIME

Despite the beauty of exponential functions for modeling trend, a useful trend analysis tool is to fit a curve that uses powers of time as predictors of trend. The model for this analysis is

$$Y_t = a_0 + a_1 t + a_2 t^2 + a_3 t^3 + \cdots + a_n t^n.$$

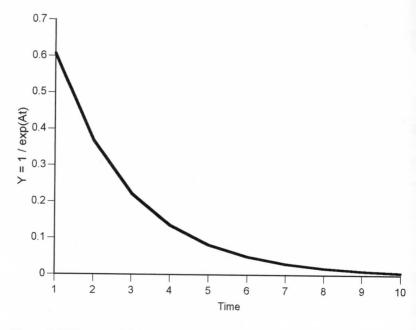

Figure 9.15 Exponential decay function

For example, a curve that has a quadratic component will look like the graph in Figure 9.18. This curve represents a trend that increases, reaches a peak, and then declines. This is a possible trend for support of a candidate or for interest in a news event. One can fit such a model using the curve-fitting program in SPSS or by writing an OLS regression model with increasing powers of time as predictors.

We can illustrate the power of this curve-fitting technique by examining media use during the primary season of the 2000 election. Starting on day 26, the survey asked respondents if they were attending to news about the primaries on various news media. Figure 9.19 shows the average rating of attention to news about the primaries on national television news in the past week (cE03).

The series was subjected to a trend analysis that tested the linear, quadratic, and cubic components of the series. The results of this analysis showing the effect of each additional trend is in Table 9.10. All three components of the curve were significant predictors in the analysis. This is evident in the significant t values for each predictor that was added to the model. The increments in R^2 also indicate that the additional variation was substantial.

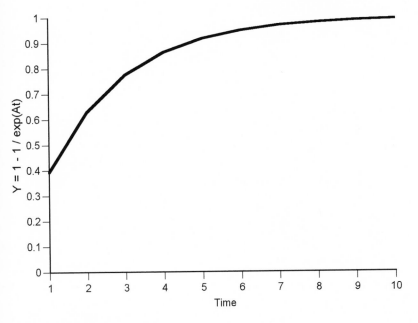

Figure 9.16 A diffusion model.

The fitted curve indicates that interest in the primaries peaked around day 50. It then gradually declined before leveling off and beginning to rise again around day 120. The series did not begin prior to day 26, so we cannot identify the trend prior to that day. Nevertheless, we can interpret this pattern as reflecting the effects of events during the primary period. The South Carolina and Michigan primaries occurred around day 50, and the American public was undoubtedly interested in the outcomes of these races.

Once the trend has been identified, we can examine the residuals in the series. The residuals of this detrended series are shown in Figure 9.20.

Examination of the correlogram (Table 9.11) indicates little evidence of systematic variation in the residuals. This finding suggests that once the cubic trend was removed, reports of weekly viewing of national television news for political information were relatively independent of reports on previous days. Nevertheless, this analysis tells us that attention to news exhibits rather dramatic changes as a function of events in the primary period.

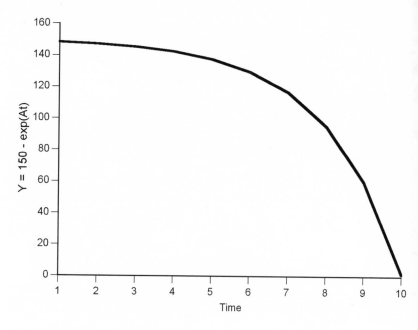

Figure 9.17. Inverse exponential decay.

Seasonal Influences

Another type of systematic trend is covariation attributable to seasonality or to the calendar. For example, one might hypothesize that respondents behave differently on weekends from the way they do on weekdays. If this were true, one would see a pattern in the time series such that weekend days looked different from other days. In addition, the correlogram would show systematic correlation at lag 7 reflecting the fact that the series was similar to itself every week.

Figure 9.21 shows an example of a series that was constructed to be high on weekends and low on other days. The series begins on a Sunday and proceeds through five weeks. It is evident that weekends tend to have higher scores than weekdays.

The correlogram shows a significant lag at seven days (Table 9.12). There is also a significant lag at fourteen days, reflecting the fact that this is a weekly pattern. There is some evidence of negative correlations at lags 3 to 5, reflecting the fact that high scores on weekends are inversely related to scores on weekdays. This effect is also evident in the partial correlations where there is a significant partial at lag 5 as well as at lag 7.

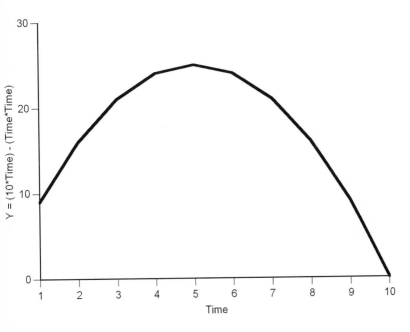

Figure 9.18. A trend that is a quadratic function of time.

To remove these weekend effects, one can regress the series on two dummy variables representing Saturday (D7) and Sunday (Dl). The results of this analysis are shown in Table 9.13. With these predictors held constant, the residual series looks more stationary. The detrended series shown in Figure 9.22 is much less influenced by the weekend effect, and the correlogram no longer shows a significant pattern (see Table 9.14).

Maximum Likelihood Estimation of ARMA Models

We have shown that it is possible to remove trends and seasonal components from time series using OLS regression. One of the cautions that has been emphasized in many treatments of time series data is the potential for violation of the assumptions of OLS regression. In particular, time series data can violate the assumption of independence between residuals, also known as the assumption of zero autocorrelation. The result is that estimates of the parameters in the equation may be inaccurate and the standard errors of the parameters may be underestimated.

Despite these cautions, the effects of violating the autocorrelation

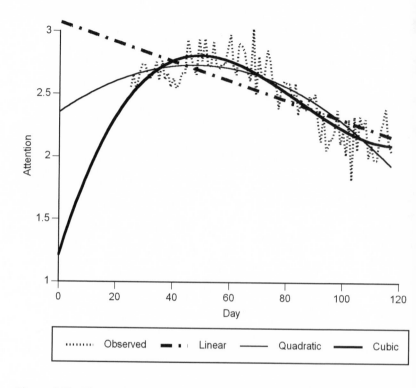

Figure 9.19. Observed and predicted time series of national television news exposure to stories about the presidential primaries (attention to news scored on a scale from 1 = None, 2 = Not Too Much, 3 = Some, and 4 = A Great Deal).

assumption are complex but may be quite minimal in large samples ($T > 100$). In addition, when we use polynomial predictors of time trends and other error-free variables, such as dummy variables for seasonal components, OLS produces accurate estimates of parameters and standard errors. As a result, the caution against conducting OLS regression with time series is often not as serious as might be expected (Harvey 1993).

Even though OLS regression is often satisfactory for estimating time series models, it is generally recommended that one test for the presence of both AR and MA components in time series data. We know from our discussion of the MA process that it can be represented as an AR model if one is willing to estimate an infinite series of terms. Since this is not possible using OLS, we need to employ maximum likelihood estimation techniques.

TABLE 9.10. THREE-STEP REGRESSION ANALYSIS OF ATTENTION TO ELECTION NEWS ON NATIONAL TELEVISION

	Step 1			Step 2			Step 3		
Predictor	B	t	Prob	B	t	Prob	B	t	Prob.
Day (linear)	−.00687	−11.92	0.00	.00916	2.98	0.004	.06473	5.56	0.000
Day² (quad.)				−.00011	−5.29	0.000	−.00095	−5.53	0.000
Day³ (cubic)							.00000	4.91	0.000
R²	.607			.699			.763		

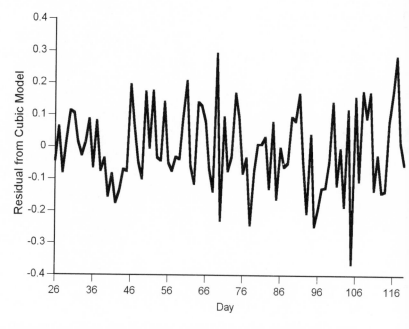

Figure 9.20. Residuals in television news interest during the primaries.

These techniques are available in programs used to estimate ARMA models that allow for the presence of both AR and MA components. In SPSS, this program is part of the trends package that can be added to the advanced statistics core.

The procedure for conducting an analysis of time series data is as follows:

1. Plot the series to identify potential trends or calendar effects.
2. Detrend the series with time or calendar predictors using OLS regression.
3. Conduct a correlogram analysis of the detrended series.
4. Test plausible models for AR and MA components in the detrended series.
5. Use goodness of fit statistics to evaluate the best model.
6. Combine the error-free trends and the best fitting ARMA processes into a single model.

GOODNESS OF FIT MEASURES

Building a model using the ARMA program often involves trying different combinations of AR and MA processes for the same model. Any data-

TABLE 9.11. CORRELOGRAM ANALYSIS OF RESIDUALS IN NATIONAL TV NEWS

Attention to News About the Primary

Variable: Residuals Cubic Model Missing cases: 25   Valid cases: 94

Autocorrelations: Residuals Cubic Model

```
     Auto- Stand.
Lag  Corr.  Err. -1  -.75  -.5 -.25   0   .25  .5  .75  1   Box-Ljung  Prob.
                   |---+---+---+---+---+---+---+---+---|
  1   .093  .102                     .  |** .                .837    .360
  2   .161  .101                     .  |***.               3.384    .184
  3   .048  .100                     .  |*  .               3.615    .306
  4   .073  .100                     .  |*  .               4.151    .386
  5   .009  .099                     .  *   .               4.159    .527
  6   .000  .099                     .  *   .               4.159    .655
  7  -.017  .098                     .  *   .               4.188    .758
  8  -.006  .098                     .  *   .               4.192    .839
  9  -.033  .097                     .  *|  .               4.305    .890
 10  -.013  .096                     .  *   .               4.324    .932
 11  -.076  .096                     . **   .               4.959    .933
 12  -.177  .095                     ****   .               8.425    .751
 13  -.097  .095                     . **   .               9.476    .736
 14   .001  .094                     .  *   .               9.476    .799
 15   .036  .094                     .  |*  .               9.626    .843
 16  -.067  .093                     .  *|  .              10.151    .859
```

Plot Symbols: Autocorrelations *   Two Standard Error Limits .

Total cases: 119   Computable first lags: 93

Partial Autocorrelations: ERR_3   Error for NATTV with DAY from CURVEFIT,

```
     Pr-Aut- Stand.
Lag  Corr.   Err. -1  -.75  -.5 -.25   0   .25  .5  .75  1
                    |---+---+---+---+---+---+---+---+---|
  1   .093   .103                     .  |** .
  2   .154   .103                     .  |***.
  3   .022   .103                     .  *  .
  4   .044   .103                     .  |* .
  5  -.011   .103                     .  *  .
  6  -.020   .103                     .  *  .
  7  -.019   .103                     .  *  .
  8  -.004   .103                     .  *  .
  9  -.026   .103                     .  *| .
 10  -.005   .103                     .  *  .
 11  -.066   .103                     .  *  .
 12  -.169   .103                     .***  .
 13  -.053   .103                     .  *  .
 14   .070   .103                     .  |* .
 15   .078   .103                     .  |**.
 16  -.065   .103                     .  *| .
```

Plot Symbols: Autocorrelations *   Two Standard Error Limits .

Total cases: 119   Computable first lags: 93

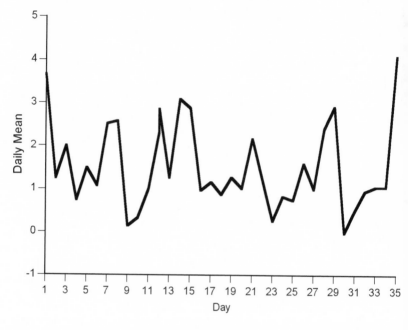

Figure 9.21. Example of a series with weekend effects.

set can be fit if you have enough parameters in a model. All else being equal, the best models are the simplest because they involve the fewest assumptions and are least likely to capitalize on chance or unique characteristics of a dataset. To do this, one needs a measure of goodness of fit. To help diagnose model fit, one can use two descriptive statistics that are sensitive to both the closeness of fit and the number of parameters that have been used to fit the data.

One of the best known (but no longer considered adequate) is the adjusted R^2. This is often provided in computer output for OLS regression (including SPSS). If we just used the unadjusted R^2, we would see that the fit always increased as the number of predictors in the model increased. The purpose of the adjusted R^2 is to make it harder for the fit measure to increase as more parameters are added to the model by introducing a penalty for each additional parameter included in the prediction equation. So, if one has a model with ten parameters that predicts as well as one with five, the one with five will have a higher adjusted R^2.

A similar correction is introduced in two other measures of fit: the Akaike (1974) information criterion (AIC) and the Schwartz (1978)

TABLE 9.12. CORRELOGRAM ANALYSIS OF SIMULATED SERIES WITH HIGHER SCORES ON WEEKENDS

Autocorrelations: Weekend Series

Lag	Auto- Corr.	Stand. Err.	-1	-.75	-.5	-.25	0	.25	.5	.75	1	Box-Ljung	Prob.
1	.049	.162						*				.092	.762
2	-.153	.160				***						1.008	.604
3	-.230	.157				*****						3.154	.368
4	-.208	.155				****						4.965	.291
5	-.257	.152				*****						7.813	.167
6	.177	.150						****				9.208	.162
7	.541	.147						*****.*****				22.742	.002
8	-.063	.144					*					22.933	.003
9	-.156	.142					***					24.140	.004
10	-.170	.139					***					25.645	.004
11	-.118	.136					**					26.392	.006
12	-.188	.133					.****					28.372	.005
13	.193	.130						****.				30.572	.004
14	.434	.127						****.****				42.172	.000
15	-.007	.124					*					42.175	.000
16	-.137	.121					***					43.462	.000

Plot Symbols: Autocorrelations *   Two Standard Error Limits .

Total cases: 35   Computable first lags: 34

Partial Autocorrelations: Weekend Series

Lag	Pr-Aut- Corr.	Stand. Err.	-1	-.75	-.5	-.25	0	.25	.5	.75	1
1	.049	.169						*			
2	-.156	.169				***					
3	-.220	.169				****					
4	-.231	.169				*****					
5	-.370	.169			*******						
6	.015	.169					*				
7	.431	.169						******.**			
8	-.204	.169				****					
9	-.152	.169				***					
10	-.072	.169					*				
11	.042	.169						*			
12	-.087	.169					**				
13	-.134	.169				***					
14	.193	.169						****			
15	.109	.169						**			
16	-.066	.169					*				

Plot Symbols: Autocorrelations *   Two Standard Error Limits .

Total cases: 35   Computable first lags: 34

TABLE 9.13. REGRESSION ANALYSIS OF SERIES WITH WEEKEND EFFECTS

Predictor	Unstandardized coefficients		Standardized coefficients		
	B	Std. error	Beta	t	Sig.
Constant	.994	.111		8.981	.000
D7	1.861	.271	.640	6.867	.000
D1	1.984	.271	.682	7.321	.000

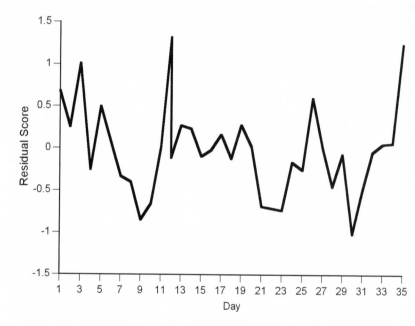

Figure 9.22. Adjusted weekend series after controlling for differences on Saturday and Sunday.

information criterion (SIC). However, these measures include more stringent penalties for increasing the number of parameters.

The formula for the AIC is

$$\text{AIC} = e^{2k/T} \left[(1/T) \, \Sigma(e_t)^2 \right],$$

where the summation is done over the entire set of residuals (e_t) in the model from 1 to T, and k represents the number of parameters estimated in the model. The summation term in the AIC, $[(1/T) \, \Sigma(e_t)^2]$, is actually the mean square error (MS_e) that is reported in OLS regression

TABLE 9.14. CORRELOGRAM ANALYSIS OF WEEKEND SERIES FOLLOWING REMOVAL OF WEEKEND TREND

Variable: Residuals in Weekend Series   Valid cases: 35

Autocorrelations: Weekend Series   Unstandardized Residual

```
     Auto- Stand.
Lag  Corr.  Err.  -1  -.75  -.5  -.25   0   .25   .5   .75   1   Box-Ljung  Prob.

 1   .236   .162                        *****.                    2.115     .146
 2   .164   .160                        ***                       3.171     .205
 3  -.145   .157                      .  ***                       4.019     .259
 4  -.275   .155                     .*****                        7.175     .127
 5  -.238   .152                     .*****                        9.627     .087
 6  -.094   .150                      .  **                       10.020     .124
 7   .044   .147                          *                       10.110     .182
 8  -.061   .144                       .  *                       10.286     .246
 9   .119   .142                          **                      10.996     .276
10  -.013   .139                          *                       11.005     .357
11  -.012   .136                       .  *                       11.013     .442
12  -.035   .133                       . *                        11.080     .522
13   .047   .130                          *                       11.208     .593
14   .109   .127                          **                      11.940     .611
15   .045   .124                          *                       12.069     .674
16  -.033   .121                        . *                       12.143     .734
```

Plot Symbols: Autocorrelations *   Two Standard Error Limits .

Total cases: 35   Computable first lags: 34

Partial Autocorrelations: Weekend Series   Unstandardized Residual

```
     Pr-Aut- Stand.
Lag  Corr.  Err.  -1  -.75  -.5  -.25   0   .25   .5   .75   1

 1   .236   .169                        *****  .
 2   .115   .169                        **
 3  -.221   .169                     . ****
 4  -.243   .169                     .*****
 5  -.091   .169                       .  **
 6   .039   .169                          *
 7   .048   .169                          *
 8  -.211   .169                     . ****
 9   .065   .169                          *
10  -.019   .169                          *
11  -.056   .169                        . *
12  -.049   .169                        . *
13   .079   .169                          **
14   .132   .169                          ***
15  -.048   .169                        . *
16  -.166   .169                      . ***
```

Plot Symbols: Autocorrelations *   Two Standard Error Limits .

Total cases: 100   Computable first lags: 34

output. The standard error of the estimate, which is also reported in OLS output, is the square root of the MSe. As a result, the AIC is a product of the exponential term and the MS_e. Even if MS_e declines as a result of adding more parameters (k) to a model, the exponential term ($e^{2k/T}$) will increase. The result is that the AIC can actually increase even if error of prediction declines. The goal in model fitting is to find a model that has no more parameters than necessary to explain the data. The lower the AIC, the better the model.

The SIC uses an even more stringent penalty for additional parameters:

$$SIC = T^{k/T}[(1/T) \, \Sigma(e_i)^2],$$

because $T^{k/T}$ increases more rapidly than $e^{2k/T}$ as k increases.

These fit measures provide some indication of the success of a model by allowing comparisons between alternative models. The AIC is designed to get smaller as the fit improves and to identify the best model if one has that model in one's consideration set. That is, if you are pretty sure that you have a correct model in your analysis pool, then the AIC will identify it.

However, if you do not know whether you have the correct model, then the SIC is designed to provide the better index because it will identify the best model of the ones you have. Often, the two will move consistently and give you the same conclusion. But sometimes they don't and you have to pick one of them as your guide. Because we seldom are confident about our models, many analysts use the SIC as the more diagnostic index (Diebold 2001).

As we examine different models from here on, we should keep track of the two criteria to see what they say about the fit of our models. SPSS does not provide the AIC or SIC for OLS regression, so you have to calculate it yourself. However, you can get it when using the ARMA program. Because the ARMA program uses maximum likelihood estimation, it uses a different measure of overall fit instead of the MS_e. This measure was discussed when we examined logistic regression analysis in Chapter 7. As a result, calculations of the AIC and SIC in the ARMA program are based on $-2LL$ (-2 times the log likelihood). However, the same interpretation is applied to these fit measures: the smaller the value, the better the fit.

TESTING FOR TRENDS THAT HAVE CAUSAL INTERPRETATIONS

To illustrate the use of the ARMA program for model building, we will apply it to test causal hypotheses about the effects of external events.

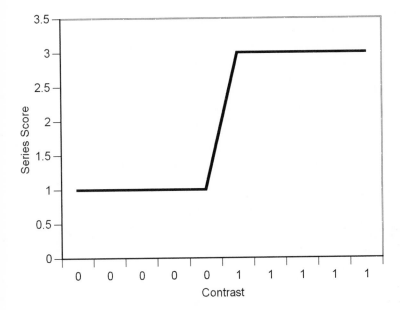

Figure 9.23a. Example of sharp discontinuity in a time series that can be predicted with a simple change contrast.

Let's look at the different types of external events that one might want to study.

One is just a variation on the trends we have already studied: the discontinuity or interrupted time series. This type of model assumes that there is an external event that dramatically changes the direction or elevation of a series. We usually know when the event occurred, and so we can test its effect on the series by comparing behavior before and after the event.

The simplest model for the interrupted time series is one in which we define a trend that is 0 before the event and +1 after the event (Figure 9.23a). If we think that the event should change the slope of the series, then we can test a nonlinear component that represents this slope change (Figure 9.23b). If there are enough time points in the series, we can test this hypothesis without worrying about AR components in the series. You can see the reason for this by comparing the interrupted time series with a hypothetical series that has cycles but is stationary (Figure 9.23c). If there are insufficient time periods in the dataset, then one might mistake the cycle for a discontinuity in the time series. For example, going from time 2 to time 5 might give the impression that the series

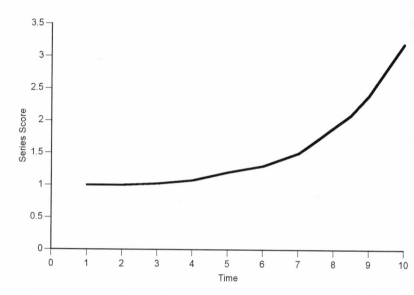

Figure 9.23b. Example of gradual change in the mean of a time series that can be predicted using a nonlinear curve-fitting procedure.

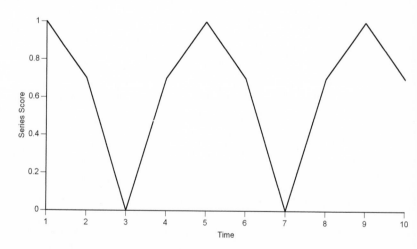

Figure 9.23c. Example of a stationary series that might be mistaken for change in the mean if a small time segment were examined.

as changed its mean. However, with enough time periods, one should see that the series has not changed its trend. With fewer than one hundred time periods, one should consider fitting an ARMA model to the nontrend components and then jointly estimating the trends and cyclic effects.

Another type of external event is one that occurs repeatedly but only has a short-lived effect, perhaps for a few days or a week after the event. However, the effects of this event may be confused with regular cycles that occur in the time series apart from the effect of the event. As a result, it will be important to control for these cycles when testing for the effects of the event.

We can explore the potential existence of these components by examining the residuals of the regression following removal of the event trend. If the correlogram and Box-Ljung statistic indicate the presence of serial correlation in the residuals, we can then test models using the ARMA program in combination with changes in the AIC and SIC.

We illustrate the use of this procedure to analyze a somewhat complicated set of external events that can influence the series of interest both instantaneously and with a lag: the case of debates during the 2000 primary season.

We have two measures of debate awareness during the primary period, item cFOl:

Have you heard or read anything about any debates (Starting 12/14/1999: or town hall meetings) among the candidates for president?
1 Yes
2 No

and item cFO2:

Have you watched any of these debates (starting 12/14/1999: or town hall meetings)?
1 Yes
2 No (+ Unaware of debates in cFOl)

To assess awareness and exposure to the debates, we can create a proportion for each day that represents the respondents who said they heard or saw a debate divided by the total number of respondents who were interviewed on that day. We can also define a trend that takes on the value of 1 whenever a debate or town meeting took place and 0 otherwise. This variable registers twelve different debates from January 3 to April 3. A list of these debates is contained in the calendar of political and media events on your CD-ROM. Plots of the two indexes are shown in Figures 9.24 and 9.25.

We begin with the awareness series by regressing the series on the

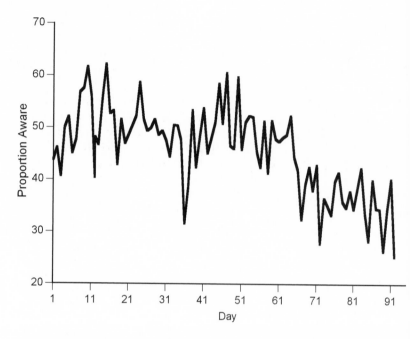

Figure 9.24. Proportion of respondents who were aware of debates between the major candidates during the year 2000 primary period.

debate predictor. However, we want to see if debates on any given day have effects that carry over to subsequent days. So, we create additional lagged versions of the debate variable that represent the delayed debate effect for up to six additional days. To do this, we use the lag transform in SPSS to create six versions of the debate variable representing six days of potentially delayed effects. It seems reasonable that the effect could last for a week. However, we could test alternative delay periods if we chose to do so.

We also want to rule out other calendar effects that might be related to the effects of debates. In particular, we can create dummy variables representing the six days of the week. If there was greater awareness of debates on certain days of the week, this could obscure or increase the actual effect of the debates.

Finally, we can also consider another effect, which is simply that awareness of debates declines as the primary period progresses. This effect would entail a significant predictor for the linear effect of days.

Entering all these variables into a multiple regression analysis yields the model shown in Table 9.15. There appears to be a strong day of

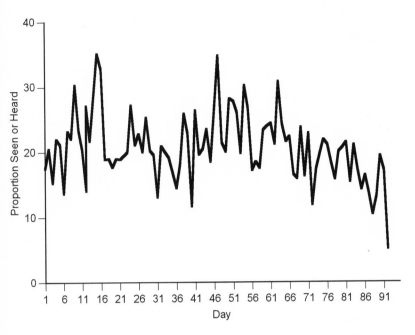

Figure 9.25. Proportion of respondents who reported watching or listening to a debate during the primary period.

debate effect as well as general decline in debate awareness as time during the primaries progressed. In addition, there is some evidence of greater awareness of debates on Fridays (day 6). This preliminary analysis enables us to obtain residuals that we can then examine for potential AR and MA components. A plot of these residuals is shown in Figure 9.26.

Examination of the correlogram for this series (Table 9.16) indicates the possible presence of an AR(1) and AR(5).

We therefore test an AR model with up to five lags using the ARMA program in SPSS. The solution in Table 9.17 indicates that debates have an immediate effect on the day they occur (debates) but that they also have a delayed effect three days later (debate 3). In particular, the solution indicates that there is an increase of 5.5 percentage points in awareness of debates on the day of the debate and an effect nearly as large three days later. We still see the Friday effect (D6) and a general decline in debate awareness as the primary period unfolded (Day). Finally, the analysis finds evidence of autoregression at lags 1 and 5.

We can try various alternative models with different numbers of lags

214   Daniel Romer

TABLE 9.15. MULTIPLE REGRESSION ANALYSIS OF DEBATE AWARENESS USING
LINEAR DAY, DAY OF WEEK (D1–D6) AND DEBATE EVENT PREDICTOR (DEBATES)
WITH LAGGED VERSIONS FOR SIX DAYS (LAG 1–LAG 6)

	Unstandardized coefficients		Standardized coefficients		
Predictor	B	Std. error	Beta	t	Prob.
Constant	51.175	2.619		19.540	.000
Day	−.191	.031	−.562	−6.066	.000
Debates	5.927	2.317	.204	2.557	.013
LAG(1)	2.765	2.245	.100	1.232	.222
LAG(2)	1.803	2.200	.069	.820	.415
LAG(3)	3.060	2.148	.121	1.424	.159
LAG(4)	.470	2.117	.019	.222	.825
LAG(5)	−.316	2.089	−.013	−.151	.880
LAG(6)	1.883	2.046	.077	.920	.361
D1	2.052	2.526	.084	.812	.419
D2	3.091	2.436	.127	1.269	.209
D3	1.779	2.431	.076	.732	.467
D4	1.798	2.450	.076	.734	.465
D5	.350	2.430	.014	.144	.886
D6	4.920	2.527	.202	1.947	.056

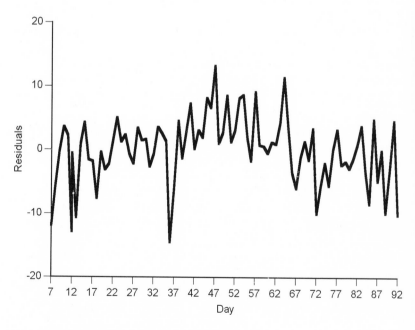

Figure 9.26. Residuals in awareness of debates.

TABLE 9.16. CORRELOGRAM ANALYSIS OF RESIDUALS IN DEBATE AWARENESS FOLLOWING REMOVAL OF TREND PREDICTORS

```
              Removal of Trend Predictors

Valid cases:  86

Autocorrelations:   Unstandardized Awareness Residual
```

```
     Auto- Stand.
Lag  Corr.  Err.  -1  -.75  -.5 -.25   0   .25  .5  .75  1    Box-Ljung  Prob.
```

Lag	Auto-Corr.	Stand. Err.	plot	Box-Ljung	Prob.
1	.273	.106	. |*** .*	6.612	.010
2	.040	.105	. |* .	6.755	.034
3	.094	.105	. |** .	7.563	.056
4	.156	.104	. |***.	9.807	.044
5	.327	.103	. |*** .***	19.772	.001
6	.225	.103	. |*** .*	24.580	.000
7	.199	.102	. |****	28.393	.000
8	.050	.102	. |* .	28.635	.000
9	.053	.101	. |* .	28.908	.001
10	.049	.100	. |* .	29.144	.001
11	-.004	.100	. * .	29.146	.002
12	.139	.099	. |***.	31.133	.002
13	.057	.098	. |* .	31.469	.003
14	.061	.098	. |* .	31.866	.004
15	.009	.097	. * .	31.875	.007
16	-.050	.096	. *| .	32.145	.010

```
Plot Symbols:     Autocorrelations *     Two Standard Error Limits .

Total cases:  119     Computable first lags:  85


Partial Autocorrelations:   Unstandardized Awareness Residual
```

```
     Pr-Aut- Stand.
Lag  Corr.   Err.  -1  -.75  -.5 -.25   0   .25  .5  .75  1
```

Lag	Pr-Aut-Corr.	Stand. Err.	plot
1	.273	.108	. |*** .*
2	-.037	.108	. * .
3	.101	.108	. |** .
4	.114	.108	. |** .
5	.283	.108	. |*** .**
6	.086	.108	. |** .
7	.153	.108	. |***.
8	-.076	.108	. **| .
9	.000	.108	. * .
10	-.117	.108	. **| .
11	-.121	.108	. **| .
12	.055	.108	. |* .
13	-.034	.108	. *| .
14	.071	.108	. |* .
15	.007	.108	. * .
16	-.012	.108	. * .

```
Plot Symbols:     Autocorrelations *     Two Standard Error Limits .
```

TABLE 9.17. OUTPUT FROM ARMA PROGRAM ASSUMING AN AR(5) MODEL ALONG WITH PREDICTORS FOR EFFECTS OF DEBATES (WITH SIX LAGS) AND DAYS OF THE WEEK (D1 – D6)

Number of residuals   86
Standard error   5.392536
Log likelihood   − 257.28202
AIC   554.56405
SIC   603.65099

Variables in the model:

	B	SEB	T-ratio	Approx. prob
AR1	.2491	.1205	2.0670	.0426
AR2	−.0997	.1223	−.8150	.4179
AR3	.1094	.1247	.8778	.3831
AR4	.0685	.1286	.5327	.5959
AR5	.3360	.1213	2.7686	.0072
DEBATES	5.4981	2.2017	2.4972	.0150
DEBATE_1	2.4472	2.1950	1.1149	.2689
DEBATE_2	2.2671	2.0097	1.1280	.2633
DEBATE_3	4.2964	1.8806	2.2846	.0255
DEBATE_4	1.4103	1.9133	.7371	.4636
DEBATE_5	−.4694	1.9788	−.2372	.8132
DEBATE_6	1.9255	1.9784	.9732	.3339
D1	2.3279	1.9431	1.1980	.2351
D2	3.0198	1.9671	1.5351	.1295
D3	1.9380	1.9800	.9787	.3312
D4	2.1622	2.0041	1.0788	.2845
D5	.1518	1.9568	.0776	.9383
D6	4.8884	1.9282	2.5351	.0136
Day	−.1817	.0639	− 2.8442	.0059
Constant	49.7555	4.2549	11.6936	.0000

in the autoregression function to see if the present model is the best solution. Table 9.18 shows values of the AIC and SIC for several alternative models. This analysis indicates that the present model is adequate (line in bold). Examination of the residuals from this model (Figure 9.27) also suggests that all cycles have been removed from the data. An examination of the correlogram indicates a similar conclusion. A comparison of the predicted and observed awareness series in Figure 9.28 indicates a fairly close fit. We leave the analysis of debates seen to the reader.

THE EFFECTS OF EVENTS ON PRESIDENTIAL APPROVAL

We can also illustrate the analysis of external events using the more traditional concept of the interrupted time series discussed earlier. In this

TABLE 9.18. VALUES OF AIC AND SIC FOR VARIOUS ALTERNATIVE MODELS OF DEBATE AWARENESS

Model	AIC	SIC
AR(4)	560.69	607.33
AR(5)	554.56	603.65
AR(6)	555.83	607.37
AR(5) MA(1)	555.01	606.56
AR(6) MA(1)	559.64	613.63
MA(5)	557.28	606.37
MA(6)	555.70	607.25

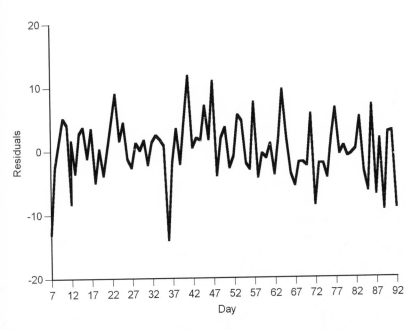

Figure 9.27. Residual plot in awareness of debates following removal of trends and AR(5) model for random component.

case, we examine both the long-term and short-term effects of several important events during the 2004 election year on approval of George W. Bush as President (see Winneg and Romer 2004 for a more detailed discussion of the analysis). One of the valuable assets of the NAES is the ability to examine the influence of events without knowing in advance when events might have an impact. In this example, we examine the

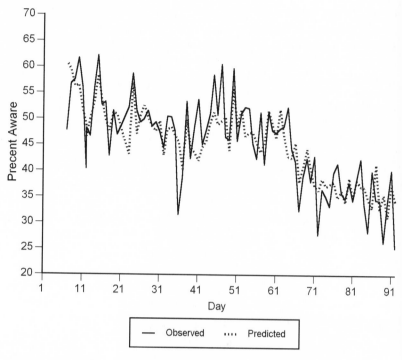

Figure 9.28. Predicted and observed scores for debate awareness.

influence of the unanticipated capture of Saddam Hussein on December 13, 2003, as well as political events that could be anticipated as part of the election (e.g., speeches at the Republican and Democratic conventions) or of the federal government's normal calendar (e.g., Bush's State of the Union address).

For each event, we examine both its short-term (5 days) and longer-term (until the election) influence on Bush's approval. Although we define a short-term effect as a discontinuity that only lasts for 5 days, one could test other periods to see if they predict as well or better. Our experience is that this time span adequately accounts for most short-term effects of events. To test for this discontinuity, we define a contrast that takes on the value 0 until the day of the event, 1 on the five days after the event, and 0 again for all other days. A long-term effect takes on the value 0 until the day of the event and the value 1 until the end of the series. This contrast tests the hypothesis that the event produced a more enduring change in the President's level of approval.

To test the influence of these events also requires consideration of at least two other sources of presidential approval. One is the longer-term flow of events that determines how a president is evaluated (see Zaller 1989 for a discussion of this process). During the election year, the president and the country was preoccupied with the situation in Iraq. Many events other than the dramatic capture of Saddam Hussein were relevant to this situation (e.g., prison abuse scandals, loss of troops, and discovery of looted arms caches). However, these events might only be a part of a broader narrative that unfolded during the year. This narrative focused on whether the war was worth fighting and if the president had the right strategy to win it. We examined the role of events by first identifying the major long-term trend in the president's approval over the period from October 10, 2003 to November 10, 2004 (381 days). We then examined the residuals in his approval to identify any AR or MA processes that might be mistaken for short-term effects of events. Finally, we tested an overall model that included long-term trends resulting from the accumulation of events that influenced evaluation of the president during the campaign, cycles in approval, and the short and long-term influence of several events.

LONG-TERM TREND IN APPROVAL

Figure 9.29 shows the predicted long-term trend in Bush's approval rating determined by fitting a cubic regression model. This curve indicates that the president's approval was on a downward trend throughout most of the period. It reached its lowest point just shy of 50% on day 313 (August 21) and rebounded from that point until the election.

Despite the presence of this long-term trend, it is also apparent that there are major deviations from the trend at various points during the election period. One possible source of these deviations is the presence of AR processes. An examination of the ACF and PACF indicated possible presence of an AR(3) and AR(7). Hence, we tested all potential events using the ARMA program to control for cycles in approval.

We tested the following events for both short- and longer-term effects: Saddam's capture (12/13/2003), Bush delivers State of the Union address (1/20/2004); senate begins hearings on the Abu Ghraib prison scandal (5/06/2004); Kerry addresses the Democratic Party convention (7/29/2004), and Bush addresses the Republican convention (9/02/2004).

Initial analyses of the above events indicated that all of them except Kerry's address were followed by changes in Bush's approval. However, after entering them into the ARMA program simultaneously with predictors for up to seven AR processes, only three remained significant (see Table 9.19): short term gain associated with Bush's State of the

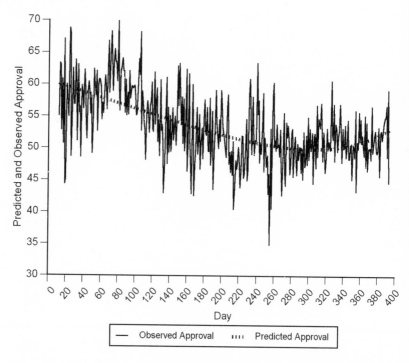

Figure 9.29. Predicted and observed approval based on cubic trend analysis of Bush's approval as president from October 19, 2003 to November 10, 2004.

Union address and long-term changes associated with Saddam's capture and Bush's State of the Union address. Controlling for AR processes removed what appeared to be evidence for effects of two of the events.

Figure 9.30 shows the predicted and observed series after the long-term trend shown in Figure 9.29 was removed. The series displays an obvious upturn following Saddam's capture that according to the ARMA analysis produced a long-term increase of over 5 percentage points in approval. There was also a sharp but short-lived upturn in the president's approval following the state of the union address that is mostly negated by a long-term drop in approval following the address. The long-term drop following the address may be the result of other events that occurred shortly after the address, such as the announcement by a major weapons inspector that no weapons of mass destruction were likely to be found in Iraq (1/25/2004). One could test this and other events to see whether they accounted for the long-term drop as well as or better than the state of the union address. What is clear, however, is that the boost that Saddam's capture gave the president was mostly

TABLE 9.19. ARMA ANALYSIS OUTPUT FOR PRESIDENTIAL APPROVAL

Number of residuals	381
Standard error	4.2733148
Log likelihood	−1088.6019
AIC	2199.2039
SIC	2242.5747

Variables in the model:

	B	SEB	T-ratio	Approx. prob.
AR1	.0270	.0516	.5233	.6010
AR2	.0197	.0517	.3814	.7030
AR3	.1157	.0520	2.2246	.0267
AR4	.0429	.0523	.8205	.4124
AR5	.0323	.0519	.6224	.5340
AR6	−.0434	.0518	−.8386	.4022
AR7	.1583	.0517	3.0578	.0023
Saddam	5.3052	1.2980	4.0872	.0000
State S	6.9690	2.0610	3.3813	.0007
State L	−4.3102	1.1085	−3.8882	.0001
Constant	−1.2897	.8478	−1.5213	.1290

Note: Event contrasts are long-term effect of Saddam's capture and State of the Union Address both short term (State S) and long term (State L).

negated in January 2004 by the events that followed his State of the Union address.

In summary, this example illustrates the need to separate the short-term effects of events from cycles in approval (AR processes) that might be correlated with those effects. By controlling for AR processes in the ARMA analysis, we can be more certain that short-term discontinuities are not the result of longer-term cycles. In addition, by first removing long-term trends (such as the cubic model of approval), we can also be more certain that long-term discontinuities are not correlated with pre-existing trends in an outcome.

Testing Hypotheses About Causal Relations Between Time Series

We have used the ARMA procedure to model the random component in an analysis of external events. However, we may be interested in a different problem, namely, the relation between two time series.

For example, if we were interested in the relation between a candidate's favorability thermometer rating and the candidate's perceived viability as a nominee for the party, should we regress one of these variables on the other?

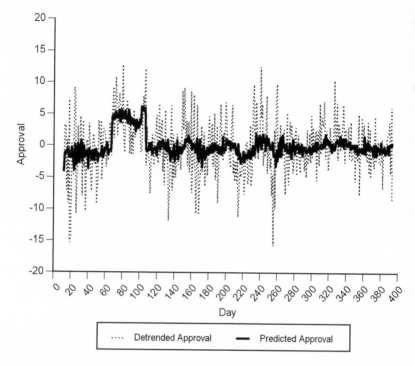

Figure 9.30. Detrended actual and predicted Bush approval resulting from ARMA analysis with up to AR(7) and three event predictors (Saddam long term, State of the Union address long and short term).

In particular, suppose we hypothesized that viability was a cause of rating. Could we create a series for each variable and do OLS regression analysis with rating as the dependent variable Y_t and viability as the independent variable X_t to see how they relate to each other over a period of interest? The model for this analysis would be

$$Y_t = aX_t + e_t,$$

where e_t is the random component in series Y_t and a is the coefficient of the linear relation between the two series.

The first consideration is that if e_t has autoregressive (AR) or moving average (MA) components, then standard errors of the coefficients and the coefficients themselves may be biased. As a result, the confidence intervals may be incorrect, and we will end up with an invalid model.

There have been several solutions suggested to this problem over the years. One examines a statistic that is sensitive to the presence of AR(1) in the dependent variable: the Durbin Watson or d.

If we regress Y_t on X_t and calculate residuals from the regression model (e), then

$$d = \Sigma(e_t - e_{t-1})^2 / \Sigma (e_t)^2.$$

If the dependent variable contains an AR(1) process with a coefficient p, this statistic will equal

$$2(1 - p).$$

If there is no autocorrelation, then $d = 2$. If p is > 0, then d falls in the range of from 0 to 2. If p is < 0, then d is in the range from 2 to 4. The statistic has a complicated sampling distribution, but as it approaches either 0 or 4, one is advised to consider the presence of autocorrelation and hence to disregard the tests of coefficients for predictors.

Although the d statistic has long been associated with time series analysis, it is designed to have maximal power to detect only first order autocorrelation. If a series has no first order autocorrelation but does have higher order correlation, d may not detect it. We recommend the use of the Box-Ljung test and examination of the correlogram to determine presence of autocorrelation. But this procedure requires detrending the series to make it stationary before examining the correlogram.

The second thing to consider is that regressing one series on another is a very weak test of the relationship between them. Any number of explanations would predict a correlation between the two variables without there being a causal relation between them. The best evidence for causal influence in time series is the lag-lead relationship, in which a lagged value of a variable predicts the current value of another variable with the lagged value of the dependent variable held constant:

$$Y_t = b_1 Y_{t-1} + a_1 X_{t-1} + e_{1t}.$$

This model is similar to the panel study approach we examined in the section using OLS regression approaches to panel designs (Chapter 8). Furthermore, if the residual in the equation is normally distributed white noise, we can estimate the equation using OLS regression. However, this analysis requires both series to be stationary. To achieve this condition, we may either difference each series (if each represents a random walk) or, more likely, remove the time trend using OLS regression.

A second test of causal order is to regress X on previous values of itself

224   Daniel Romer

and Y. If X causes Y, then earlier values of Y should not predict later values of X:

$$X_t = d_1 X_{t-1} + c_1 Y_{t-1} + e_{2t}.$$

To pursue this analysis strategy, it is critical to know how many lags of each variable to introduce into the models predicting each variable. This is critical because we want to include as many lags as are needed to identify potential relations between the series. As a result, before exploring this method of analysis, we will examine another preliminary analytic technique known as the cross-correlation function. This analysis is similar to the autocorrelation; however, in this case, it is the relation between two detrended series (i.e., series that have been made stationary) that are correlated at different lags.

AN ARTIFICIAL EXAMPLE OF CROSS-CORRELATION

Let's look at an example that is constructed from simulated data. For one variable X, we have constructed a time series that is a direct function of white noise: $X_t = Z_t$, that is, Z_t is a normal random deviate $(0,1)$. This series could then be considered in relation to another series, Y_t, that is defined as a function of the lag in X_t: $Y_t = X_{t-1} + W_t$, where W_t is a different normal random deviate $(0,1)$.

Because the two series are defined so as not to have any trends, we can use the cross-correlation function to observe relations between the series at different lags. This function tells us how the series relate to each other as both lagged and lead functions. However, one can only use this procedure if both series are stationary; that is, after any trends have been removed. The cross-correlation function is read as showing the correlation between the series at different lags for each series. At lag 0, we have the correlation between the series with no difference in lags. As the analysis indicates, the two series are not contemporaneously correlated. This is what we would expect from correlating two randomly generated series. The confidence bands use the standard error of the correlation $2(1/\sqrt{N})$ to indicate potentially significant relations between series. The significant relation at lag 1 refers to the fact that if one were to correlate the first series (X_t) at lag 1 with the other series at lag 0, the correlation would be .722, a value consistent with the fact that we constructed the second series to be a function of the lag of the first series (plus white noise). This says that Y_t leads X_t by one lag, as it should since it was constructed to have the lagged relation (see Table 9.20). There is also some evidence of a relation at lag -2. We know that this is spurious because the model was not designed to contain this relation. But if we did not

TABLE 9.20. CROSS-CORRELATION OUTPUT FROM SPSS FOR ANALYSIS OF X_t AND Y_t

```
Cross Correlations:     Xₜ
                        Yₜ

        Cross Stand.
Lag     Corr.  Err.  -1  -.75  -.5  -.25   0   .25   .5   .75   1
                       ├──┼───┼───┼───┼───┼───┼───┼───┼──┤
 -7     .115   .104                        .  **  .
 -6    -.166   .103                     . ***  .
 -5     .107   .103                        . |**  .
 -4    -.010   .102                        . *   .
 -3    -.002   .102                        . *   .
 -2    -.241   .101                   * .***|  .
 -1    -.100   .101                     . **|  .
  0     .024   .100                        . *  .
  1     .722   .101                        . |*** .**********
  2    -.046   .101                        . *  .
  3    -.075   .102                        . *  .
  4    -.157   .102                     .***|  .
  5     .069   .103                        . |*  .
  6     .065   .103                        . |*  .
  7     .017   .104                        . *  .

Plot Symbols:     Autocorrelations *     Two Standard Error Limits

Total cases:   100    Computable 0-order correlations:   100
```

know this, we would be wise to consider this possibility in our subsequent analyses. The interpretation of this coefficient is that the first series, X_t, leads the second with a negative relation at lag 2. This analysis is a helpful initial procedure to determine potential relations between series. It will tell us if they have a contemporaneous relation (the zero lag cross-correlation) and if they have lagged relations. If there is only evidence of a contemporary relation, it will be unlikely that we can identify a lag-lead relation between the series. However, if we find any evidence of cross-correlation beyond the contemporaneous, we will want to test the relations in both directions to see if we can find evidence of causal priority. Hence, the cross-correlation function is a very useful diagnostic tool for first examining the relation between two series.

INTERPRETATIONS OF CONTEMPORANEOUS RELATIONS BETWEEN TIME SERIES

Our strategy of detrending time series to create stationary series often raises questions in the minds of readers who are new to time series analy-

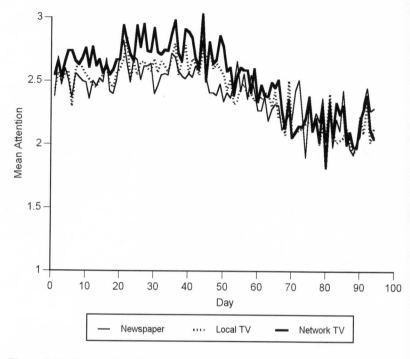

Figure 9.31. Time series of attention to news about the presidential primary on national (cEO3) and local television news (cEO7) and in newspapers (cEl4) from January 3 to April 30, 2000.

sis. One question that is asked concerns the validity of the remaining variation in the series. If we correlate time series with each other after detrending, we often find sizeable relations between them. For example, all three measures of attention to news (on national television, local television, and newspapers) about the presidential primaries in 2000 exhibited a similar time path during the primary period (see Figure 9.31).

After detrending each series using the procedure followed earlier, we obtained three series that still appear to follow the same time trends. Indeed, the correlation between local and national television news was .55 ($p < .01$) (see Figure 9.32).

An important question is whether the remaining covariation in these measures could merely reflect measurement error rather than anything substantive. To answer this question, we can examine the causal diagram shown in Figure 9.33.

This diagram represents a plausible interpretation of the relations between two news measures (attention to election news on network and

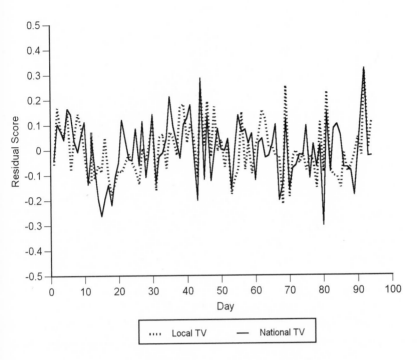

Figure 9.32. Residual series in attention to national and local television news.

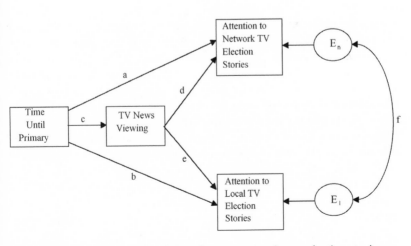

Figure 9.33. Potential causal relations between attention to election stories on network and local television news.

on local television news) and the effects of time during the primary period. We assume that with the approach of a major primary, news media will report stories about it. These stories will increase in intensity as the primary approaches and will come to the attention of television news viewers. As a result, respondents will report seeing more of those stories on both types of news sources (paths a and b). At the same time, people's overall use of television news may also be related to time (path c) and this in turn may influence attention to news about the election (paths d and e). As a result, another influence on attention to election news is the sheer amount of time that people spend watching either news source. When time is taken out of the trend in exposure to campaign news in each news source, one source of correlation between attention to the two news sources may be errors of measurement in each variable (path f). Another may be correlation produced by valid influence on each news source. Unless we have a direct measure of potential influence on the two news sources, we cannot separate correlation between the unknown components from measurement error. Fortunately, one potential source of correlation that is measured is news viewing in general (paths d and e).

On each day of the survey, we may see variation in news viewing. The trends shown in Figure 9.34 suggest a pattern of slowly declining news use during the primary period. The detrended series for each type of television news (Figure 9.35) follows a similar time path. Indeed, they are correlated very highly: $r = .61$, $p < .01$. If detrended viewing of television news predicts detrended variation in the two election news measures, then the correlations we find between different measures of exposure to election news could represent this source of valid news use. If, however, the correlations are the result of measurement error, then the residuals in each news measure will be unrelated to attention to television news in general.

When we combine the residuals in national and local television news use to create a general television news viewing index, we see that this score correlates with both measures of attention to news about the primary: $r = .36$, with detrended attention to primary stories on national television news, and $r = .57$ with the same detrended attention to local television news. As a result, news viewing on television accounts for a substantial amount of the relation between the attention to primary election stories on the two television news sources.

This analysis suggests that the relation between residual scores in attention to news stories about the primary is valid variation that could be explained by other factors, such as general use of news sources. The more people pay attention to television news, the more likely they are to be exposed to stories about the primary.

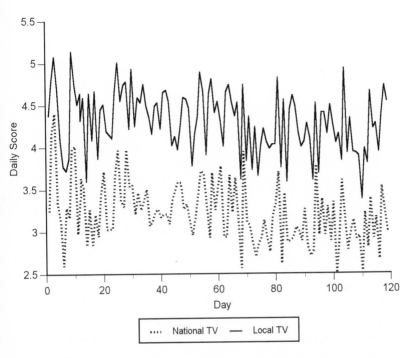

Figure 9.34. Time series for days in the last week that news was obtained from two sources: national television news (cEO1) and local television news (cEO6).

It is plausible therefore that correlations between detrended scores in the NAES reflect sources of valid variation unrelated to time trends. Indeed, we are going to use this variation to isolate causal relations between time series.

THE STRATEGY FOR ISOLATING CAUSAL RELATIONS BETWEEN TIME SERIES

The diagram in Figure 9.36 shows potential relations that might underlie a causal relation between two detrended times series, X and Y. Just as in the panel design, we are going to use the prior status of X as represented by the L operator to predict the subsequent status of Y.

We omit paths from the lagged versions of each predictor to its unlagged version because we will remove all AR components from each series prior to conducting the analysis. Nevertheless, our analysis will hold constant the prior relation between each series (r_1) so that we can estimate the unique contribution of each predictor to the final status of

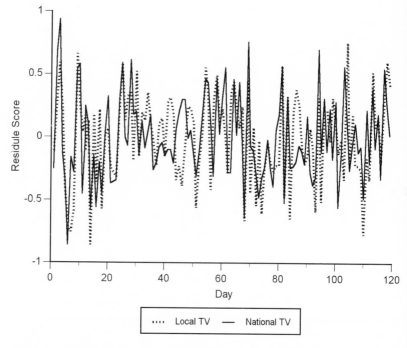

Figure 9.35. Residuals in news viewing on national and local television.

each variable. If X leads Y by one lag, then $L(X)$ will predict Y. This path can be called the *cross-correlation* between the lag of X and Y. In addition, if the relation is unidirectional, then $L(Y)$ will not predict X. This is a stronger requirement that rules out the possibility either that X and Y are either jointly determined by some other factor or that each affects the other, a result that is called *feedback*.

This type of causal pattern is called *Granger* causality in the economic literature, after the person who first identified it (Granger 1969). Lazarsfeld pioneered a similar approach in the analysis of political data (1948). In psychology, the approach is very similar to the cross-lagged panel correlation identified by Campbell (1963). In any case, the idea is that causality from X to Y implies that prior information in X will predict subsequent status of Y, holding constant prior information in Y.

There is no path directly linking X and Y in Figure 9.36. If either X or Y causes the other contemporaneously (within the limits of the time periods used to measure the variables), then there is also the possibility of contemporaneous causality in the system. Since the purpose of the analysis is to find evidence of Granger causality between the variables, it

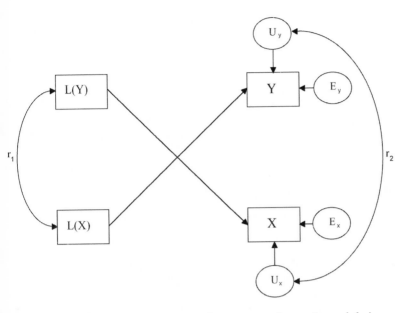

Figure 9.36. Causal diagram of relations between two time series and their lagged values.

is best not to make any assumptions about contemporaneous relations between them. However, the diagram does allow the possibility that the unknown components in X and Y are correlated (r_2). This assumption is weaker because it predicts that X and Y are correlated but not necessarily because of a causal relation between them.

To summarize the possible relations between two time series, one can distinguish four possible combinations of outcomes in a Granger causality analysis: (1) X can Granger cause Y; (2) Y can Granger cause X; (3) both X and Y can Granger cause each other (feedback); and (4) either X or Y may be correlated with the other contemporaneously.

ANALYSIS OF GRANGER CAUSALITY

In the model shown in Figure 9.36 for the possible relation between two variables, X and Y, we can estimate the relations between the variables using a procedure known as vector autoregression, or VAR for short. The most basic model is one with a VAR(1) structure. The procedure involves estimating one regression equation for each variable in the system. Since in our example there are two variables, we will have two equations:

$$Y_t = b_1 Y_{t-1} + a_1 X_{t-1} + e_{1t},$$
$$X_t = c_1 Y_{t-1} + d_1 X_{t-1} + e_{2t}.$$

The residual terms in these equations, e_{1t} and e_{2t}, are assumed to be white noise processes with means of 0 and standard deviations of σ_1 and σ_2. They can be treated as white noise because the model includes all sources of autocorrelation in each variable. At the same time, the residual terms can be correlated with each other. This condition is likely when Y_t and X_t are correlated.

CONSIDERATIONS IN FITTING A VAR SYSTEM

There are two issues in estimating a VAR system. One concerns the number of lags to include in the model. To help identify a plausible start for a VAR model, we will use the cross-correlation function that is available in SPSS to determine if the two series are correlated across the lags of either variable.

The cross-correlation function should only be used on detrended series that are stationary. Otherwise, it will give misleading results. The function will provide some evidence of the range of lags that are potentially influencing each series. This is a good first step for defining the model that we will use to identify potential causal lags in time series.

A second issue that must be resolved in constructing a VAR model is the interpretation of the correlation between the residual terms in the model (r_2 in Figure 9.36). If the correlation between the series is 0, then problems in interpretation are minimal. However, the two series are often correlated at lag 0 apart from any causal influence that earlier lags introduce. In this case, it is unclear whether the correlation is the result of third causes that influence each series or of a contemporaneous causal relation between the series at lag 0. Of course, the whole point of conducting the VAR analysis is to gain an understanding of potential causal relations between the series. If we have to make assumptions about such causal relations, we are putting the cart before the horse.

Fortunately, there is one case in which a relation between the series at lag 0 ($r_2 \neq 0$) is not problematic. If neither series contains any AR processes, then the interpretation of the VAR analysis is more straightforward. As shown in Figure 9.36, if there are no AR relations between lags of the same series, we can interpret the cross-correlations as evidence for Granger causality. To see this, consider the possibility of a path from $L(Y)$ to Y and the correlation between Y and X represented by r_2. This sequence of paths is not a direct influence of $L(Y)$ on X, but it could be the source of any observed effect of $L(Y)$ on X in a VAR analysis. However, if the relation between $L(Y)$ and Y is zero (there is no AR(1) in Y), then this path will not contribute to the relation between $L(Y)$ and X.

When any series in a VAR has AR processes, its apparent influence on the other series may be misleading. If one took the outcome of the analysis at face value, one would conclude that Y causes X in the Granger sense when in actuality, it only predicts itself by virtue of an AR relation (also see Mark 1979 for a discussion of this problem). To reduce this possibility, it is helpful first to remove all AR processes from each series, a process known as *prefiltering* (Chatfield 1999).

Let's use an example that is relevant during the primaries: estimates of candidate viability (likelihood of gaining the party's nomination) and respondent feelings of favorability toward the candidate (thermometer ratings). Bartels (1988) argues that perceptions of viability are important factors in primaries because they influence the likelihood that voters will consider a candidate and view the candidate favorably. His approach would suggest that changes in viability should influence attraction to a candidate.

We can test this prediction during the primary period in the 2000 NAES dataset. Figure 9.37 shows mean favorability ratings for Bush (cAO1) and McCain (cA21) from January 3 to April 30, and Figure 9.38 shows the viability ratings of each candidate for the same period (cNO1 and cNO2).

There is not much evidence in these plots to suggest that viability drives ratings of either Bush or McCain. But first let's take differences of each pair of measures so we can see changes in the relative standing of the two candidates. Figure 9.39 suggests that the candidates did not differ much in favorability over this period. However, Bush always had higher viability ratings, especially after Super Tuesday (March 7).

An examination of the favorability series suggests no change in either the mean or variability of the series; hence it seems likely that the series is already stationary. But before examining the viability correlogram, we first have to detrend the series. In examining the viability curve, it is apparent that there are at least four turning points in the viability status of the two candidates. Bush remains high until the New Hampshire primary (February 2 or Day 30), when he drops precipitously until Super Tuesday (Day 65), when he quickly bounces back. From then on his viability advantage is so great that the survey does not continue to measure differences in the viability of the candidates.

To detrend the viability series, we fit a model using event predictors for both the New Hampshire (NH) and Super Tuesday (ST) primaries. These predictors included both a short-term effect of five days and a long-term effect that lasted until the end of the time series. The model also included a predictor representing linear change in time (Day). The

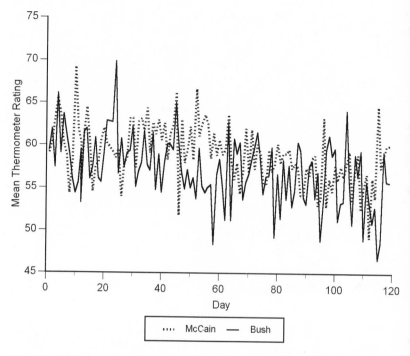

Figure 9.37. Time series for Bush and McCain favorability ratings from January 3 to April 30, 2000.

regression solution shown in Table 9.21 produced a good fit to the series, $R^2 = .923$. A plot of the residuals of the detrended model and the original series is shown in Figure 9.40.

The detrended series contains many of the same cycles as the original series, but it is now stationary. An examination of the correlogram for the viability series suggests the presence of an AR(1) (Table 9.22). The correlogram for the favorability series indicates very little evidence of any serial correlation in the series (Table 9.23). This pattern of results suggests the need to filter the viability series. This is easily accomplished by regressing the detrended viability series on a lagged version of itself to remove the AR(1) component. The residual from this analysis contains the filtered series. If higher-order autoregressive components had been detected, we would need to remove those as well.

A comparison of the standardized favorability and filtered viability series is in Figure 9.41. There is some indication that favorability differences lead viability differences. The cross-correlation function shows evidence of correlation between the series at the first lag, $r = .212$ (Table

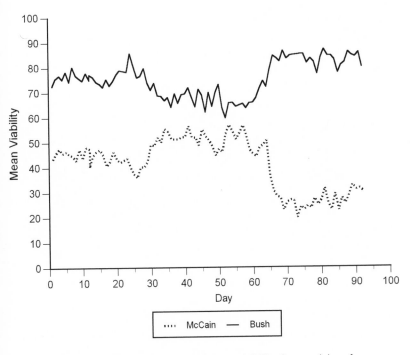

Figure 9.38. Time series for Bush and McCain viability for receiving the nomination of the Republican Party.

9.24). This relation suggests that favorability leads viability by one lag. The correlation at lag 0 is not significant ($r = .125$), a finding that indicates no evidence of contemporaneous correlation. The lack of correlation at lag 0 also reduces the importance of filtering out any AR processes in either series. However, we continue the analysis using the filtered version of the viability series.

The next step is to generate lagged versions of both variables so we can enter them into a vector autoregression model for each dependent variable. There is some uncertainty about the number of lags to include in this analysis. The cross-correlation function suggests that one lag may be sufficient, so we illustrate the analysis with a VAR(1). We also know that there is a relatively large but nonsignificant correlation at lag -4 ($r = .197$). We will pursue this possibility as well by testing VAR models with lags from 1 to 4.

To determine the order of the VAR, we compare goodness of fit indices for VAR models ranging from one to four lags. Table 9.25 shows that for the AIC and SIC, the solution with one lag seems to provide the best

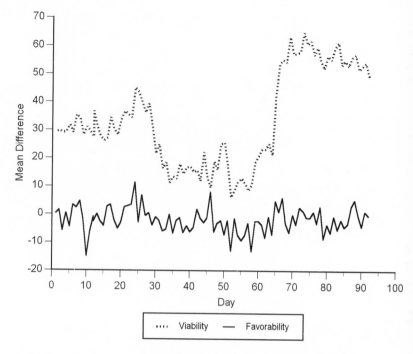

Figure 9.39. Time series for differences in favorability ratings and viability estimates for Bush and McCain (Bush-McCain).

TABLE 9.21. REGRESSION ANALYSIS OF VIABILITY DIFFERENCE SCORE WITH PRIMARY EVENTS AND DAY AS PREDICTORS

Predictor	Unstandardized coefficients		Standardized coefficients		
	B	Std. error	Beta	t	Prob.
Constant	30.202	1.369	22.061	.000	
Day	0.166	0.069	.253	2.417	.000
NH Short	5.299	2.632	.072	2.013	.047
NH Long	−22.167	2.688	−.615	−8.248	.000
ST Short	−1.141	2.571	−.016	−0.444	.658
ST Long	35.946	2.493	.956	14.419	.000

fit to the data. The adjusted R^2 index is the least sensitive of the three indices in that it does not distinguish between one and two lags for the model with favorability as the dependent variable.

The results of the regressions for VAR(1) shown in Table 9.26 indi-

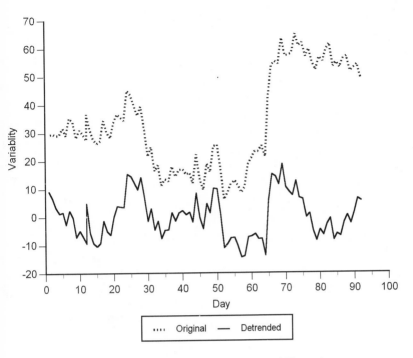

Figure 9.40. Comparison of original and detrended viability series.

cate that the lagged version of viability does not predict favorability ratings ($p = .278$) but that lagged favorability ratings predict viability ($p = .046$).

Hence, the interpretation of this analysis is that only favorability ratings have a causal influence in the Granger sense. Furthermore, the patterns of the original time series in Figure 9.39 indicate that viability undergoes dramatic changes that are not mirrored in favorability ratings. As a result, there is evidence in both the original series and the detrended versions that viability does not influence attraction to a major candidate during the primary period.

Summary

Our review of time series analysis indicates that we can decompose daily variation in NAES variables into white noise, AR and MA components, as well as trends attributable to external events (e.g., debates). We can also examine relations between series to identify Granger causality. We have argued that it is critical to detrend a series before detecting AR

TABLE 9.22. CORRELOGRAM ANALYSIS OF DETRENDED VIABILITY

Autocorrelations: Residual Viability

```
        Auto-  Stand.
Lag     Corr.   Err.  -1  -.75  -.5 -.25   0   .25   .5   .75   1   Box-Ljung   Prob.
         ├────┼────┼────┼────┼────┼────┼────┤
  1     .411   .104                    .     |*** .****               15.553     .000
  2     .197   .104                    .     |****                    19.155     .000
  3     .083   .103                    .     |** .                    19.805     .000
  4    -.038   .102                        . *|  .                    19.942     .001
  5    -.001   .102                        . *|  .                    19.942     .001
  6    -.045   .101                        . *|  .                    20.144     .003
  7    -.055   .101                        . *|  .                    20.439     .005
  8    -.194   .100                       ****|  .                     24.219     .002
  9    -.134   .099                       .***|  .                     26.026     .002
 10    -.101   .099                        . **|  .                    27.080     .003
 11    -.025   .098                        . *|  .                     27.146     .004
 12    -.042   .098                        . *|  .                     27.328     .007
 13     .059   .097                        .  |*  .                    27.697     .010
 14     .005   .096                        .  |*  .                    27.699     .016
 15    -.287   .096                      ** .***|  .                   36.728     .001
 16    -.263   .095                       * .***|  .                   44.412     .000
```

Plot Symbols: Autocorrelations *   Two Standard Error Limits .

Total cases: 119   Computable first lags: 88

Partial Autocorrelations: Residual Viability

```
        Pr-Aut- Stand.
Lag     Corr.   Err.  -1  -.75  -.5 -.25   0   .25   .5   .75   1
         ├────┼────┼────┼────┼────┼────┼────┤
  1     .411   .106                    .     |*** .****
  2     .033   .106                    .     |*  .
  3    -.011   .106                        . *  .
  4    -.089   .106                        . **|  .
  5     .051   .106                        . |*  .
  6    -.055   .106                        . *|  .
  7    -.022   .106                        . *  .
  8    -.199   .106                       ****|  .
  9     .030   .106                        .  |*  .
 10    -.030   .106                        . *|  .
 11     .059   .106                        .  |*  .
 12    -.091   .106                        . **|  .
 13     .135   .106                        .  |*** .
 14    -.096   .106                        . **|  .
 15    -.344   .106                      *** .***|  .
 16    -.127   .106                       .***|  .
```

Plot Symbols: Autocorrelations *   Two Standard Error Limits .

Total cases: 119   Computable first lags: 88

TABLE 9.23. CORRELOGRAM FOR FAVORABILITY RATINGS

Autocorrelations: Favorability Ratings

Lag	Auto-Corr.	Stand. Err.	-1 -.75 -.5 -.25 0 .25 .5 .75 1	Box-Ljung	Prob.
1	.101	.091	. ** .	1.247	.264
2	.104	.090	. ** .	2.584	.275
3	.058	.090	. * .	3.005	.391
4	.010	.089	. * .	3.017	.555
5	.108	.089	. ** .	4.482	.482
6	.016	.089	. * .	4.514	.607
7	-.007	.088	. * .	4.521	.718
8	-.048	.088	. * .	4.822	.776
9	-.061	.087	. * .	5.306	.807
10	.116	.087	. ** .	7.092	.717
11	-.066	.087	. * .	7.681	.742
12	-.028	.086	. * .	7.788	.801
13	-.083	.086	.** .	8.718	.794
14	-.120	.085	.** .	10.693	.710
15	-.005	.085	. * .	10.697	.774
16	-.124	.085	.** .	12.831	.685

Plot Symbols: Autocorrelations *   Two Standard Error Limits .

Total cases: 119   Computable first lags: 118

Partial Autocorrelations: Favorability Ratings

Lag	Pr-Aut-Corr.	Stand. Err.	-1 -.75 -.5 -.25 0 .25 .5 .75 1
1	.101	.092	. ** .
2	.095	.092	. ** .
3	.040	.092	. * .
4	-.009	.092	. * .
5	.100	.092	. ** .
6	-.005	.092	. * .
7	-.029	.092	. * .
8	-.057	.092	. * .
9	-.049	.092	. * .
10	.131	.092	. *** .
11	-.079	.092	. ** .
12	-.032	.092	. * .
13	-.068	.092	. * .
14	-.085	.092	. ** .
15	.005	.092	. * .
16	-.100	.092	. ** .

Plot Symbols: Autocorrelations *   Two Standard Error Limits .

Total cases: 119   Computable first lags: 118

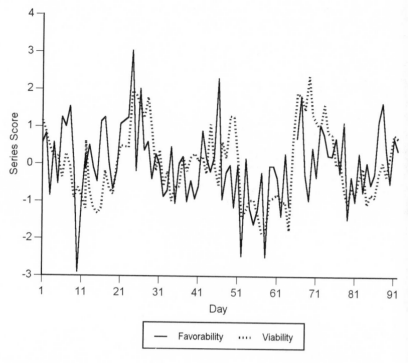

Figure 9.41. Standardized values of the filtered residual viability series and favorability series.

or MA components. It is also critical to include potential AR and MA components in any models that test for external events. The VAR approach can be used to test for Granger causality between time series. However, in using this analysis, it is also important to first filter out any AR components that might appear to give a series the ability to predict the status of another series by going through contemporaneous relations at lag 0.

Exercises

Analyze the public's awareness and viewing of the presidential debates using the same techniques employed to study the influence of debates during the primaries.

Analyze the relation between viability perceptions of Bush and McCain and vote intentions in the 2000 election.

Analyze the relation between viability perceptions of Bush and Kerry and favorability ratings using the 2004 Election file.

TABLE 9.24. CROSS-CORRELATION ANALYSIS BETWEEN FAVORABILITY RATING
AND DETRENDED AND FILTERED VIABILITY RATING

```
               Viability Rating

Listwise deletion.    Missing cases:  27    Valid cases:  92

Cross Correlations: Favorability Rating
                    Detrended Viability Rating Filtered


      Cross Stand.
Lag   Corr.  Err.  -1  -.75  -.5 -.25    0   .25  .5   .75   1
                    ├───┼───┼───┼───┼───┼───┼───┼───┤

 -7   .030   .111                    .    *
 -6   .144   .110                    .   ***.
 -5  -.038   .110                    . *  .
 -4   .197   .109                    .   ****
 -3  -.014   .108                    . *  .
 -2   .040   .108                    . *  .
 -1   .108   .107                    .  **.
  0   .125   .107                    . ***.
  1   .212   .107                    . ****
  2   .063   .108                    . *  .
  3   .106   .108                    . ** .
  4   .136   .109                    . ***.
  5   .032   .110                    . *  .
  6  -.077   .110                  . **  .
  7   .092   .111                    . ** .

Plot Symbols:     Autocorrelations *     Two Standard Error Limits

Total cases:   119    Computable 0-order correlations:   88
```

References

Akaike, Hirutugu. 1974. A New Look at the statistical Model Identification. *IEEE Transactions on Automatic Control* AC-19: 716–23.

Bartels, Lawrence M. 1988. *Presidential Primaries and the Dynamics of Public Choice.* Princeton, N.J.: Princeton University Press.

Campbell, Donald. T. 1963. From Description to Experimentation: Interpreting Trends as Quasi-Experiments. In *Problems in Measuring Change*, ed. C. W. Harris. Madison: University of Wisconsin Press.

Chatfield, Chris. 1999. *The Analysis of Time Series: An Introduction.* New York: Chapman and Hall/CRC.

Diebold, Francis X. 2001. *Elements of Forecasting.* 2nd ed. Cincinnati, Oh.: South-Western.

Enders, Walter. 1995. *Applied Econometric Time Series.* New York: John Wiley.

TABLE 9.25. GOODNESS OF FIT INDICES FOR FOUR DIFFERENT VAR MODELS

Lag/index	Viability as dependent variable	Favorability as dependent variable
1 Lag		
Adj. R^2	.047	.004
AIC	19.57	21.80
SIC	22.70	23.69
2 Lags		
Adj. R^2	.004	.008
AIC	21.11	22.79
SIC	24.32	26.25
3 Lags		
Adj. R^2	−.017	−.017
AIC	22.87	24.58
SIC	27.83	30.04
4 Lags		
Adj. R^2	−.014	.001
AIC	24.14	25.62
SIC	31.02	32.91

TABLE 9.26. REGRESSION ANALYSIS OF VIABILITY AND FAVORABILITY VARIABLES

Model	Unstandardized coefficients		Standardized coefficients		
	B	Std. error	Beta	t	Prob.
Viability as dependent					
(Constant)	.445	.507		0.877	.383
LAG(Viability)	−.043	.109	−.043	−0.396	.693
LAG(Favorability)	.231	.124	.135	2.029	.046
Favorability as dependent					
(Constant)	−1.921	.531		−3.616	.001
LAG(Viability)	.108	.113	.102	0.950	.345
LAG(Favorability)	.115	.108	.115	1.069	.288

Granger, C. W. J. 1969. Investigating Causal Relations by Econometric Models and Cross-Spectral Methods. *Econometrica* 37: 424–38.

Harvey, Alexander. C. 1990. *The Econometric Analysis of Time Series.* Boston: Philip Alan, Hemel Hempstead, and MT Press.

Mahajan, Vijay and Robert A. Peterson. 1985. *Models for Innovation Diffusion.* Beverly Hills, Calif.: Sage.

Lazarsfeld, Paul. F. 1948. The use of panels in social research. *Proceedings of the American Philosophical Society* 92: 405–10.

Mark, Melvin. M. 1979. The causal analysis of concomitancies in time series. In *Quasi-Experimentation: Design and Analysis Issues for Field Settings,* ed. T. D. Cook and D. T. Campbell. Boston: Houghton Mifflin.

Schwarz, G. 1978. Estimating the dimension of a model. *Annals of Statistics* 6: 461–64.

Winneg, Kenneth and Daniel Romer. 2004. The impact of events on Bush approval. Accessed online (June 12, 2005), www.annenbergpublicpolicycen ter.org/naes/2004–03

Zaller, John. 1989. Bringing Coverse Back In: Modeling Information Flow in Political Campaigns. *Political Analysis* 1: 181–234.

Chapter 10

The Power of Numbers: Examining Subpopulations with the NAES

DANNAGAL GOLDTHWAITE YOUNG, RUSSELL TISINGER, KATE KENSKI, AND DANIEL ROMER

This chapter explores how the National Annenberg Election Survey (NAES) can be used to examine subgroups in the population. Because of the large number of interviews conducted with adults in the U.S., the NAES provides researchers an opportunity to analyze subpopulations that are often too small to capture with a moderate-sized probability sample. The national sample can be used as one very large cross-section or be divided into several smaller cross-sections, giving researchers access to probability samples large enough to obtain meaningful descriptions of subgroups that comprise as little as one percent of the country's overall population.

Consider the following groups about whom researchers often want to know more: Native Americans, individuals who are unemployed, members of the National Rifle Association, gun owners, or audiences of particular films, television, or radio programs. The size of the NAES provides researchers with the statistical power to draw meaningful conclusions about these relatively small groups. Furthermore, given the random sampling scheme employed by the NAES, samples of these small groups are more likely to be representative of their populations than samples obtained through "snowball" or other methods of recruitment.

The cumulative 2004 NAES national RCS dataset collected between October 7, 2003, and November 16, 2004, includes a total of 81,422 interviews. Even a subgroup that comprises as little as 0.5 percent of the country's population would be represented by over 400 cases in this dataset. The cumulative 2000 NAES national RCS dataset collected between December 14, 1999, and January 19, 2001, includes a total of 58,373 respondents. Consider the research questions one could address with a probability sample large enough to include over 1,000 Native

TABLE 10.1. SAMPLE SIZES IN THE 2000 AND 2004 NATIONAL ANNENBERG
ELECTION SURVEY NATIONAL RCS FOR VARIOUS SUBGROUPS

Subgroup	2000 RCS	2004 RCS
Hispanic	4,676	6,155
Mexicans	2,442	3,452
Puerto Ricans	556	707
Cubans	170	286
Other Hispanic	1,418	1,581
African Americans	5,087	6,606
Asians	981	1,265
Native Americans[a]	—	1,010
Noncitizens	1,990	2,639
Households with firearms[a]	—	31,082
Households with NRA members[a]	—	6,115
Evangelical Christians	21,378	28,934
Unemployed	1,004	2,758
Late-night comedy viewers	2,923	23,702
Rush Limbaugh listeners	4,350	6,871
Howard Stern listeners	496	883
Viewers of *Fahrenheit 9/11*[a]	—	737

[a] Not asked in 2000.

Americans, over 6,000 Hispanics, almost 29,000 evangelical Christians, over 6,000 households with National Rifle Association members, or over 2,600 noncitizens residing in the United States. These are the sample sizes available in the 2004 NAES national RCS dataset. Table 10.1 presents the number of respondents in the 2000 and 2004 datasets from various subgroups in the population that might be of interest to researchers in the areas of political science, communication, and sociology.

Time Series Versus Repeated Cross-Sectional Samples

One approach to examining subpopulations was described in Chapter 7. There it was suggested that time could function as an independent variable using repeated cross-sections of the dataset. In addition, one could compare change over time across different subpopulations. For example, one could study increases in knowledge about candidates' election positions as a function of time and exposure to news. In that analysis, subgroups defined by differential news exposure were studied to determine if they acquired knowledge at different rates during an election campaign.

The use of a repeated cross-sectional analysis is particularly appropriate when the prediction about time follows a simple linear rule. However, one may not be able to specify in advance how an outcome, such as knowledge, will vary over time. It may increase linearly with time, or it may follow some other trend. The advantage of using a daily time series to study change is that it does not presuppose any particular time trend. In this chapter, we illustrate how to identify and compare time trends across different subpopulations using the time series methods that were introduced in earlier chapters.

To illustrate the types of analyses that could be conducted with the NAES, the two sections that follow explore changes in political knowledge among subgroups in the population. Because the success of democratic elections depends in part on the electorate's acquisition of accurate information about the candidates, we chose political knowledge as the focus of these analyses. In the first section, we analyze trends in candidate recognition and perceived learning among residents of early versus late primary and caucus states. We use the 2004 NAES national RCS as well as the separate New Hampshire primary RCS to explore the hypothesis that the intense campaign activity in early contest states enables residents of those states to learn more about the candidates. In the second section, we examine the levels of knowledge and trends in knowledge acquisition among viewers of late-night comedy programs, including *The Daily Show with Jon Stewart*, in 2004. This section responds to the ongoing debate between journalists, scholars, and late-night comedy show hosts regarding whether late-night comedy viewers are learning about the campaign from the shows or whether they are simply more politically knowledgeable in the first place. Both of these sections are designed to demonstrate the types of research questions one can address with the NAES and illustrate the benefits of working with such a large sample.

Candidate Recognition and Perceived Learning in Early and Late Contest States

How much citizens learn is dependent, in part, on the levels of campaign activity in a given state (Jamieson et al. 2000; Dutwin 2000). Because the presidential primary and caucus schedule is spread out over several months, states that hold their primaries or caucuses earlier in the campaign season receive much more attention from the candidates and the media than those states that hold their primaries or caucuses later (Patterson 2002). These regional differences in involvement produce differences in the acquisition of political knowledge about the presidential primary candidates. Kathleen Hall Jamieson and her colleagues argue that, "Whether a campaign happens in a voter's own state or not, whether it is a contested primary or not, makes a difference in what a voter learns" (2000, 15). With this in mind, an examination of the 2004

irvey should reveal that Democratic voters in early contest states
arned more about the presidential nominees than did voters in the
ter contest states. We use the term "contest" to include both primary
lections and caucuses. While an easy hypothesis to test in principle,
ich a test requires a large sample of voters from early and late presiden-
al contest regions.

The NAES 2004 is particularly well suited for this analysis because it
as a large sample for the entire nation during the nomination cam-
aign season. The survey contained interviews with 21,302 citizens[1]
etween October 21, 2003, and March 2, 2004. In addition, a state-
pecific study of New Hampshire adults was conducted prior to the New
Iampshire Primary between January 8 and February 3, 2004 ($N = 3,386$
itizens). Since New Hampshire is the first state to hold a presidential
rimary, this dataset is particularly relevant for our test of the early ver-
us late contest hypothesis. Effective comparisons of New Hampshirites
o residents of other states could not be drawn, for example, from a
noderate-sized random national sample, because New Hampshire resi-
lents compose a very small part of the adult population. It is estimated
hat on July 1, 2004, New Hampshire had 994,506 residents who were 18
ears or older, which translates into 0.45 percent of the adult population
U.S. Census Bureau 2005). Consequently, a moderate-sized random
national sample of 1,500 adults would yield less than 7 residents on
verage.

We began our analysis by categorizing states as either early or late con-
ests using the Democratic presidential primary/caucus schedule (Project Vote Smart, 2004). States holding their primaries or caucuses on or
before March 2, Super Tuesday, were classified as early contest states.
Before proceeding, we should note that while prior research suggests
hat early contest states possess a more stimulating communication envi-
onment than late contest states, this hypothesized effect did not hold
rue in 2000 for Iowa, a caucus state. For example, Waldman (2000)
ound that, although the Iowa caucuses were held before the New
Hampshire primary in 2000 and the residents of both states experienced
'retail" campaigning, Iowa voters were not as involved in the campaign
is New Hampshirites. Only about 10 percent of Iowans voted in a caucus
compared to the 44 percent of New Hampshire residents who voted in
their primary (Waldman 2000). Nevertheless, we included both primary
and caucus states in our analyses. Of citizen respondents in our national
sample, 56.7 percent lived in states considered early contests, and 43.3
percent lived in states considered late contests.

To examine the differences in knowledge acquisition by early and late
contest states, we focused on two types of political knowledge: candidate
recognition and perceived learning about the election. Candidate rec-

ognition is perhaps the most fundamental type of election knowledge
In our study, candidate recognition was obtained from the so-calle
"feeling thermometer" questions that asked respondents to rate a pe:
son on a favorability scale ranging from 0 to 10. Respondents who pr(
vided a rating were considered to have heard of the candidate. Whe:
respondents said that they could not rate the candidate, they were aske(
whether they had heard of the candidate or not. Respondents who sai(
that they had heard of the candidate but could not rate him or her wer
also coded as recognizing the person. We focused on awareness of Dea:
(cAC26), Edwards (cAC04), and Kerry (cAB01) as our gauge of cand
date recognition. The percentage of respondents recognizing all thre
of these candidates was analyzed as a dependent variable across time.

In comparison to candidate recognition, perceived learning is a mucl
more subjective measure that relies on the voter's assessments of his o
her own personal competence. Respondents who had not expressed a:
intention to vote in a Republican or third party presidential primary o
caucus, and thus were potentially eligible to vote in a Democratic pri
mary or caucus, were asked: "So far have you learned enough about th(
Democratic presidential candidates and the issues to make an informe(
choice among the candidates, or have you found it difficult to choos(
because you feel you have not learned enough?" (cFF12). A postelectio:
version of this question was asked of those survey participants who ha(
voted in a Democratic presidential primary or caucus (cFF13).

Our knowledge variables were tracked across time, because w(
assumed that there was a dynamic component to knowledge acquisitio:
about candidates, with acquisition increasing as the primaries and cau
cuses took place. Table 10.2 presents the daily sample sizes from th(
national and New Hampshire samples for the knowledge variables
While the sample size of the NAES is impressive overall, the daily sam
ples can be small at times, producing wide sampling variation that car
obscure time trend comparisons between subgroups. Consequently, w(
smoothed the data using a seven-day centered moving average t(
remove the sampling variation.

CANDIDATE RECOGNITION

Figure 10.1 shows the levels of Democratic candidate recognition in the
separate New Hampshire file as well as in the subpopulations of the
national file corresponding to early and late contest states. Consisten!
with findings from the 2000 primary election (Hagen, Johnston, Jamieson, Dutwin, and Kenski 2000), New Hampshire voters were much more
aware of the candidates than everyone else in 2004. The differences
between early and late contest states, however, appeared to be practically

TABLE 10.2. DAILY SAMPLE SIZES FOR THE CANDIDATE RECOGNITION AND PERCEIVED LEARNING VARIABLES IN NEW HAMPSHIRE, EARLY CONTEST, AND LATE CONTEST STATES.

	Average daily N	Smallest daily N	Largest daily N
Candidate recognition			
Early contest sample	92.33	30	142
Late contest sample	70.49	20	121
New Hampshire sample	125.41	33	243
"So far have you learned enough about the Democratic presidential candidates and the issues to make an informed choice among the candidates, or have you found it difficult to choose because you feel you have not learned enough?"[a]			
Early contest sample	64.77	36	90
Late contest sample	50.42	26	86
New Hampshire sample	87.93	17	183

[a] Only citizens who had not expressed an intention to vote in a non-Democratic Party primary or caucus were asked this question. Those who had already voted in a Democratic primary or caucus state residents were asked the postelection version of this question.

nonexistent until January, when a small gap emerged. Residents in late contest states, however, began to catch up by the second week of February. Candidate recognition improved as caucuses and primaries took place, and this improvement occurred in both early and late contest states.

According to our visual examination of time trends in candidate recognition, the divide between early and late contest states was not striking during the 2004 nomination season. Although New Hampshire residents appeared to display dramatically higher levels of candidate recognition, early and late contest states both displayed gradual increases that were not particularly distinguishable in the smoothed data. Nevertheless, it would be desirable to identify time trends in each series so that statistical tests of the differences between the two types of states could be performed.

The smoothed data indicate that growth in candidate recognition did not begin to appear in either type of state until late December. From that point onward, it appears that steady growth in recognition occurred in both types. To explore this further, we examined the time trends from December 24, 2003, to February 17, 2004, a period encompassing 56 days. We defined a variable called Day that ranged from 1 to 56 during this period and used it to predict candidate recognition in the two types of states. Figure 10.2 shows the unsmoothed time series for each type of state. It appears that recognition grew rapidly during this period before leveling off at about 90 percent in early February. This pattern of growth most closely resembles the media diffusion model described in Chapter

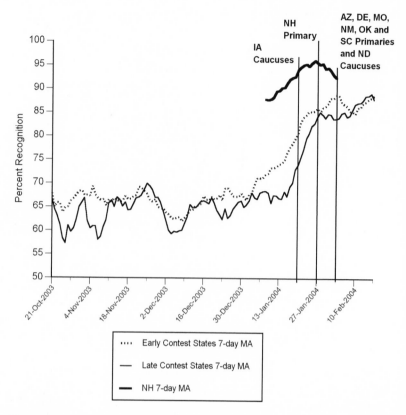

Figure 10.1. Percentage of citizens recognizing Howard Dean, John Edwards, and John Kerry in New Hampshire, early contest states, and late contest states from October 21, 2003 to February 17, 2004 (MA, moving average).

9, in which growth levels off as it approaches the maximum achievable (asymptote) in the population. Because this growth pattern has direct theoretical and analytic relevance, we estimated this model for both the early and late states. If this model provides a good fit to the data, we can then compare the parameters of the fitted trends to see if they represent different rates of growth.

The media diffusion model can be written as

$$Y^* = 100 - Y = C^*/e^{r\text{Day}},$$

where Y^* is the inverse $(100 - Y)$ of the percentage of respondents that recognizes the three presidential candidates (Y). In addition, C^* is a constant that is the inverse of the starting point of the series $(100 -$

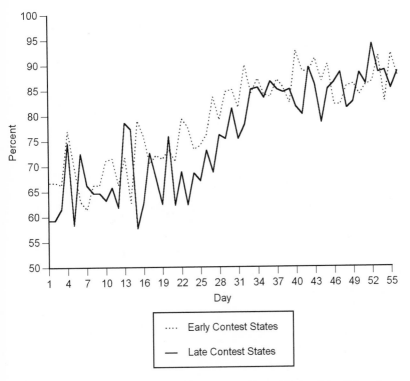

Figure 10.2. Percentage of citizens recognizing Howard Dean, John Edwards, and John Kerry in early and late contest states from December 24, 2003 to February 17, 2004.

C), and r is a rate parameter for the exponential function that represents the speed of diffusion in days during the primary. The model states that the percentage of persons who do not recognize the candidates approaches zero as an inverse exponential function of time (see Figure 9.16). We can estimate this equation using the exponential curve fitting routine in SPSS with Y^* as the dependent variable as defined as above.

When the diffusion model is applied to each series, we find that the model accounts for about 70 percent of the variance in recognition. The output from these analyses is shown in Table 10.3. The accompanying plots show the fit of each model to the inverse of recognition scores (Figure 10.3). Nevertheless, the rate parameters of the models are identical to those of the diffusion curve as defined by Y. Indeed, the two curves in Figure 10.4 show the predicted scores after subtracting the fitted scores from 100. It is noteworthy that although the intercept for the

TABLE 10.3. REGRESSION ANALYSIS OUTPUT FOR EARLY AND LATE
CONTEST STATES IN 2004 USING AN EXPONENTIAL PREDICTION OF
CANDIDATE RECOGNITION

	Recognition early		Recognition late	
Analysis of Variance	Sum of squares	Mean square	Sum of squares	Mean square
Regression (df = 1)	8.00	8.002	8.88	8.877
Residuals (df = 54)	3.16	0.059	3.12	0.058
R^2	.717		.739	
Variables in each equation				
Variable	B	SE	t	Prob.
Day (Early)	−0.0234	0.0020	−11.69	<.001
Constant (Early)	37.0800	2.4307	15.26	<.001
Day (Late)	−0.0246	0.0020	−12.39	<.001
Constant (Late)	44.3214	2.8880	15.35	<.001

early states is higher than for the later states, the slope for the later states is steeper than for the early states. By the end of the time period, the two types of states are virtually indistinguishable. This pattern suggests that the early states held an advantage prior to the beginning of the time period under analysis (late December 2003), but that this advantage slowly dissipated as campaigning in both sets of states increased early in 2004.

An analysis of the residuals of the fitted models indicated no evidence of AR or MA components in either series. Hence, it is possible to test the statistical significance of the trends we see in Figure 10.4 by comparing the slopes and intercepts of the two fitted equations presented in Table 10.3. The difference in slopes (B_1 versus B_2) can be compared using a t test according to the following formula:

$$t = (B_1 - B_2) / S_{B_1 - B_2},$$

where the denominator is the *standard error of the difference* in slopes. This value is calculated using the *pooled* mean square error (MS_E) in the analysis of each equation. The MS_E is the mean square of the residuals in the analysis of each series in Table 10.3 (defined on page 206). When one is comparing two regression analyses for the same time period, the pooled MS_E is simply the sum of the values for each equation, in this case .0586 + .0579 = .1165. The standard error of the difference in slopes is calculated using the following formula:

$$(10.1) \qquad S_{B_1 - B_2} = \frac{\sqrt{(MS_{E_1} + MS_{E_2})}}{V_D(N - 1)}$$

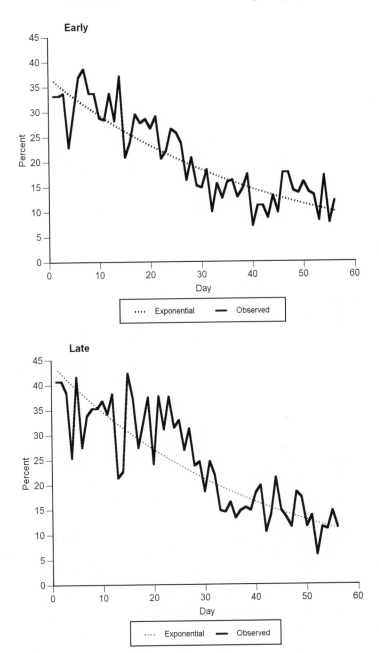

Figure 10.3. Predicted and observed exponential trends in candidate recognition for early and late contest states from December 24, 2003 to February 17, 2004

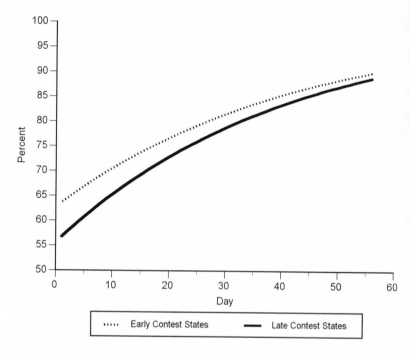

Figure 10.4. Predicted recognition for early and late contest states in 2004.

where V_D is the variance in the predictor (Day) and N is the number of days in the series (56). Substituting the various values in the formula for $S_{B_1 - B_2}$ yields a value of 0.0028. The difference in the two values of B is -0.0012, which produces a t ratio of only 0.42. This t is clearly not significant. But if it were larger, one could evaluate it using 108 degrees of freedom, calculated by adding the number of days in each series (112) and subtracting 2 degrees of freedom for each model (4).

This statistical test of slopes fails to find that the later states displayed faster growth than the early states during this time period. It is also possible to test the difference in intercepts between the two series, $C_1 - C_2$. The intercepts represent the starting values in the two series. The constants in the regression output represent the inverse of the starting values, $C^* = 100 - C$. After subtracting each value from 100, we see that the early states started at a higher value than the later states (62.9 versus 55.7). A different t test is required to test the difference between C_1 and C_2. Specifically, the denominator of the t is

$$(10.2) \qquad \sqrt{(MS_{E_1} + MS_{E_2})} \left[\frac{1}{N} + \frac{M_D^2}{V_D(N-1)} \right]$$

where M_D is the mean of the predictor, in this case the variable Day, and N and V_D are defined as in equation (10.1). Substituting the various values into this formula yields a t value of 35.2 that is highly significant with 108 degrees of freedom.

One might also ask whether the series are significantly different during the period prior to the observed diffusion in candidate recognition. Visual inspection of the smoothed series suggests that there is little growth in recognition for either series during this period. One could verify this by regressing each series on the 64 days in this period. If one did so, one would indeed find that neither series had a significant slope greater than zero. In that case, the mean of each series (66.2 and 64.0) would provide the best estimates of recognition during this early period. To test the difference in these means, one could conduct a t test of the paired differences in recognition for the 64 days in each series. The difference of 2.20 percentage points is statistically reliable, $t(63) = 2.36$, $p = .02$, indicating that the early states held a small but observable advantage in recognition during this early period in the nomination process.

PERCEIVED LEARNING ABOUT THE ELECTION

The dynamics of perceived learning are graphed in Figure 10.5, where it is very clear that New Hampshirites were more inclined than residents of the other primary states to say that they had "learned enough" to make an informed decision. The levels of perceived learning between citizens in early and late contest states were almost indistinguishable until a few days before the Iowa caucuses, when citizens in early voting states began to express more confidence in their learning.

Despite the apparent lack of differential learning between the early and late contest states, it is again possible to fit trends to each series in order to conduct more sensitive tests of potential differences in rates of growth. Inspection of the growth in learning in Figure 10.5 suggests that perceived learning increased exponentially with time. It is not surprising that the learning needed to make a decision would behave differently from candidate awareness. Although awareness grows as a simple diffusion process, learning requires evaluation of candidate positions, a process that requires considerably more effort and steps than simple awareness. This difference is apparent in the lower levels and more gradual growth of perceived learning in Figure 10.5 than candidate awareness in Figure 10.1.

Even though New Hampshire residents display powerful growth in learning, the pattern of this growth does not resemble simple media diffusion. Rather, it appears to follow an S-type pattern that is common for

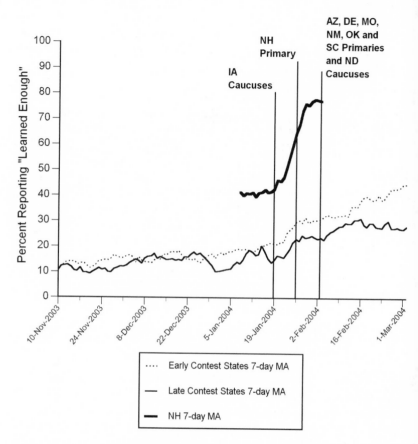

Figure 10.5. Perceived learning among those citizens who potentially were going to vote in a Democratic primary/caucus by New Hampshire residents, early contest states, and late contest states from November 10, 2003 to March 2, 2004 (MA, moving average).

diffusion mediated by interpersonal processes (Mahajan and Peterson 1985). In this diffusion process, growth occurs at an exponential rate at first and then slows as it reaches asymptote for the population. However, because the early and late states never approach the asymptotic levels seen in New Hampshire, we can model change in those series using exponential growth characteristic of the first half of S-shaped diffusion.

To test the hypothesis that learning grows exponentially, we can use the SPSS curve-fitting program for the exponential function. Indeed, application of this program indicates that an exponential function fits the data quite well. In the case of the early states, R^2 is 0.66, and for the

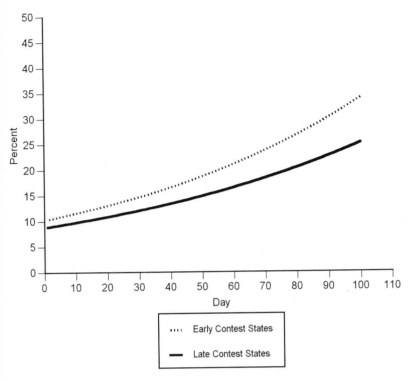

Figure 10.6. Predicted trends in perceived learning in the Democratic primaries for early and late states from November 10, 2003 to March 2, 2004.

later states, it is 0.41. These relatively good fits suggest that learning during the primaries grows as a percentage of existing levels of learning in the population. This might occur because people discuss the candidates with each other, thereby building confidence in their ability to make a decision. The higher the proportion of the population that has learned enough to make a decision, the greater the chances that others will be exposed to such persons and learn to make a decision as well.

We can also test the difference in slopes between the two series to see whether this learning process grows more rapidly in early contest states. As seen in Figure 10.6, the two trends appear to be different, with the early states exhibiting faster growth. However, a test of the difference between the two slopes (.0119 versus .0105) indicates that we cannot reject the null hypothesis that the early states grew at the same rate during this period, $t(224) = 1.00, p > .15$.

Nevertheless, a test of the difference in constant terms (10.36 vs. 8.81) indicates that the early states did begin the process at a more advanced level, $t(224) = 16.32$, $p < .001$. As a result, the advantage they gained early on was maintained throughout the primary period.

In summary, residents of late contest states were able to recognize candidates almost as well as early contest residents. However, residents of both types of states were less able to do the more difficult work of making an informed decision about the candidates. Furthermore, late contest citizens showed lower levels of confidence about candidates than those who resided in earlier states that received most of the campaign and media attention, and this difference tended to grow as the season progressed. Residents of New Hampshire stood in even sharper contrast to all the other states in that they had very high levels of both outcomes. These findings have important implications for the validity of the nominating process in presidential elections. Citizens in both early and late contest states have only limited ability to learn enough about the candidates to make a choice, and the early contest states face even greater challenges. Our evidence from 2004 suggests that the concerns about the contemporary presidential nomination process put forth by Jamieson et al. (2000) and Patterson (2002) should not be dismissed.

Late Night Comedy Program Audiences and Political Knowledge

Another set of subgroups that are often difficult to capture, but about whom much as been written in the popular press, are the audiences of late-night comedy programs. With reports of growing numbers of young people citing late night comedy shows as sources of political information (Pew 2000, 2004), the question of whether or not late night jokes teach people about politics has become a favorite topic of journalists and scholars (Baum 2003; Prior 2003; Young 2004). Using the NAES, not only can we explore the characteristics of these individual audiences, but we can also track them over time to understand their comparative rates of knowledge acquisition during the presidential general election campaign.

When this is discussed in the popular press, journalists have often endowed late-night comedy shows with the power to both teach and influence. "The punch line here is that voters—particularly young ones—get their political educations from TV comedians," wrote Rainey of the *Los Angeles Times* (2004, E1). A lengthy piece in *Business Week*, for instance, states, "TV comics like Letterman, NBC's Jay Leno, HBO's Dennis Miller, and ABC's Bill Maher have emerged as politically influential voices—particularly among independent-minded younger voters" (Dunham 2000).

In contrast to the assumption of many journalists that late-night comedy programs inform their audiences, late-night hosts have tended to deny having any such impact. In July 2004 *The Daily Show* received the Television Critics Association Award for "best news and information program," and their postpresidential debate coverage after the first Bush-Kerry debate beat out some of their "real" news competition in the ratings, drawing an audience of 2.4 million viewers (de Moraes 2004). However, Jon Stewart, the show's host, has never accepted the proposition that his show provides viewers with political information they do not already possess. In 2000, for example, Stewart argued that his viewers needed to "know something before [he] even makes a joke about it" (Bettag 2000). Stewart believed his viewers came to the show with a certain awareness of politics and current events. This suggestion predicts that *Daily Show* viewers are more likely to follow politics in the news media than the average citizen and therefore come to the show with more knowledge to begin with.

In this section, we explore the relationship between viewing *The Daily Show* and knowing specific facts from the presidential campaign. First, we use the dataset as one large cross-section to maximize sample size and explore characteristics of the *Daily Show* audience. Second, we use the RCS component of the dataset to create visual representations of *Daily Show* viewers' acquisition of campaign facts over time compared with the same rates in other subpopulations. Using the RCS component of the dataset helps to address the question of whether viewers of *The Daily Show* were obtaining political information at a faster rate than viewers of other programs, or whether they came to the program with a higher level of political knowledge from the start.

To analyze the characteristics of *The Daily Show* audience using one large cross-section from the survey, we chose the period from July 15 through September 19, 2004. This time period included both party conventions and ended before debate season began. Weighting this particular cross-section to the population gave us 19,013 respondents, of whom 5,269 reported watching at least one day of late night comedy programming in the previous week (cEA19). Of those who watched late night comedy, 37 percent reported watching Jay Leno most often, 34 percent watched Letterman most often, and 15 percent reported watching *The Daily Show* most often. In spite of the fact that only about 4 percent of the sample had watched late-night comedy *and* cited *The Daily Show* as their most viewed late-night program, we were still left with 812 *Daily Show* viewers during this period.

The following analysis explores how viewers of *The Daily Show* compared to other respondents in their knowledge of one campaign issue: Bush's position on Social Security. One question (cCC34) asked during the entire period of study was, "Who favors allowing workers to invest some of their Social Security contributions in the stock market? George W. Bush, John Kerry, both or neither candidate" [Correct = Bush]. To compare three popular late night comedy shows (viewers of *The Daily Show*, viewers of *The Tonight Show* with Jay Leno, viewers of *The Late Show* with David Letterman) against people who reported not watching late-night comedy in the previous week, we calculated independent sample *t*-tests. Results indicated that knowledge of Bush's Social Security position was significantly higher ($p < .001$) among individuals who viewed late-night comedy programs (at least once in the previous week) than among those who did not (48% versus 43%). Furthermore, viewers of *The Daily Show* scored significantly higher (55%) than viewers of Leno (49%), Letterman (47%) or heavy viewers of network news (50%).

The finding that viewers of *The Daily Show* were more likely to know Bush's position on investing Social Security contributions than heavy viewers of network news suggests that they were indeed more knowledgeable than other television viewers. To verify that this discrepancy was not due to factors such as education, following of the campaign, or other forms of media use, we conducted a multivariate logistic regression analysis predicting the probability of answering this knowledge item correctly. Predictor variables in the model included gender (cWA01), age (cWA02), party identification (cMA01, cMA02, cMA03), years of education (cWA03), following the campaign (cKA01), attention to campaign stories in national and cable news (cEA05) and days in the past week the respondent watched national network news (cEA01), cable news (cEA03), read the newspaper (cEA10), and obtained news online (cEA24). The model also included three dummy variables denoting most viewed late-night comedy program (*The Daily Show*, *The Tonight Show*, and *The Late Show*, cEA20) where the reference category referred to respondents who reported watching no late-night comedy in the past week (72% of entire sample) or who reported watching a late-night comedy program other than those three (4% of entire sample).

According to the results of the logistic regression model shown in Table 10.4, the strongest predictor of knowing that Bush supported this plan was preference for viewing *The Daily Show*, where viewers had odds to know this fact that were 1.66 times greater than nonviewers of late night comedy shows. This finding adds further support to the hypothesis that *The Daily Show* informs viewers better than other shows, even after controlling for other relevant variables. Indeed, the second strongest predictor was following the campaign, where each step on the four-point scale increased one's odds of answering this item correctly by 50 percent. Other significant positive predictors of knowing this fact were gender, age, education, identifying as a Republican, attention to campaign news stories, online news use, and cable news use. Network news viewing

TABLE 10.4. LOGISTIC REGRESSION MODEL PREDICTING KNOWLEDGE OF BUSH'S SUPPORT FOR THE INVESTMENT OF SOCIAL SECURITY CONTRIBUTIONS IN THE STOCK MARKET, JULY 15–SEPTEMBER 19, 2004

Predictor	B	SE B	Exp(B)
Constant	−4.41	.25	.01***
Gender (1 = male, 0 = female)	.38	.07	1.47***
Age (years)	.02	.00	1.02***
Party identification (1 = strong Republican,7 = strong Democrat)	−.03	.01	.97*
Education (years)	.13	.01	1.14***
Following the campaign (0 = not closely at all, 1 = not too closely, 2 = somewhat closely, 3 = very closely)	.41	.04	1.50***
Attention to campaign stories in news (0 = none, 1 = not too much, 2 = some, 3 = a great deal)	.19	.04	1.21***
Days in the past week the respondent reported:			
Watching national news	−.04	.01	.96**
Watching cable news	.05	.01	1.05***
Reading newspaper	.00	.01	1.00
Accessing news online	.08	.02	1.08***
Late-night viewers who preferred:			
The Daily Show	.50	.16	1.66**
The Tonight Show with Leno	.13	.10	1.14
The Late Show with Letterman	.07	.111	.07
Nagelkerke R^2	.19		
N	4530		

***$p<.001$; **$p<.01$; *$p<.05$; #$p<.1$.

was negatively associated with knowledge of this fact ($p < .05$) when the other variables were held constant.

Despite the evidence supporting the role of *The Daily Show* in increasing viewers' political knowledge, we still have not examined time trends in this knowledge. Is it the case, for instance, that viewers of *The Daily Show* were more likely to know certain candidate issue positions earlier in the campaign than viewers of *The Tonight Show* or viewers of network news? Or, were viewers of *The Daily Show* acquiring these facts at a steeper rate during this period of the campaign than viewers of the other programs? If the latter of these two possibilities were true, it would be consistent with the proposition that viewers of *The Daily Show* acquired information from viewing the program. If, on the other hand, Jon Stewart was correct in his assessment that viewers of *The Daily Show* already had extensive political knowledge coming into the show, we should find that the percentage of respondents who knew certain facts from the campaign was higher among *Daily Show* viewers earlier in the campaign than it was among the general population or among viewers of other programs. Furthermore, we would expect that rate of growth in knowledge would be comparable to that of other types of viewers.

Figure 10.7 shows the percentage of respondents who knew that Bush favored allowing workers to invest some of their Social Security contributions in the stock market. The figures include four different trend lines: one that tracks the national RCS including all respondents to the survey, a second line that tracks those respondents who viewed late night comedy programming in the previous week and who cited *The Daily Show* as their most viewed program, a third that tracks those who watched late-night comedy and cited *The Tonight Show* with Jay Leno as their most viewed program, and a fourth line that tracks those respondents who reported watching four or more days of national network news broadcasts in the previous week. These trend lines represent the percentage of respondents who answered the Social Security question correctly within each group from July 20 to November 1. Rather than showing the raw data, the trend lines in the figure have been smoothed using a 13-day centered moving average to remove random noise.

According to the figure, throughout the late summer and fall, people who cited *The Daily Show* as their most viewed late night comedy program were more likely to answer this knowledge item correctly than were Americans on average, viewers of Jay Leno, and respondents who reported watching four or more days of network news broadcasts in the previous week. All subgroups represented in the figure increased their likelihood of answering this question correctly over time, particularly during the Republican National Convention and after the first presidential debate on September 30. However, even before the Democratic National Convention began on July 26, viewers of *The Daily Show* were more likely to know that Bush favored this plan. In mid-July about 45 percent of Americans and 50 percent of network news viewers answered this question correctly, compared to almost 60 percent of *Daily Show* viewers. By Election Day, almost 60 percent of the American population answered this question correctly, compared to about 65 percent of news viewers and viewers of Jay Leno, and over 70 percent of *Daily Show* viewers.

The trend lines in Figure 10.7 suggest that viewing *The Daily Show* did not increase the rate of acquiring political knowledge. However, other factors confounded with one's self-selecting into or out of *The Daily Show* or other audiences could also have played a role in affecting knowledge. For example, it is possible that the national network news recruited audience members over the course of the campaign who were more interested in the presidential election than viewers of *The Daily Show*. As a result, news viewers might appear to have gained knowledge at the same

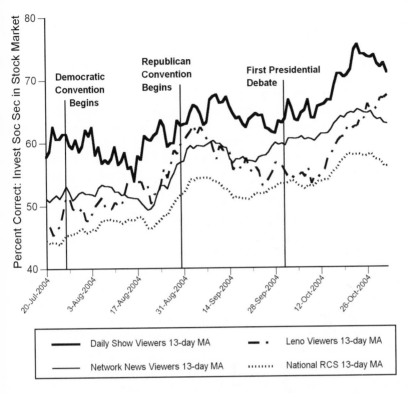

Figure 10.7. Percentage of respondents correctly identifying Bush as the candidate who favors allowing workers to invest some of their Social Security contributions in the stock market among *Daily Show* viewers, Leno viewers, national news viewers, and national average from July 20, 2004 through Election Day (MA, moving average).

rate as Jon Stewart's audience, but this might not be the result of the content of the news. To test this possibility, we examined differences in demographic characteristics as well as indicators of attention and interest in the presidential campaign for viewers of *The Daily Show* and national television news. For the purposes of this exercise, we focused only on these two series.

Table 10.5 contains mean differences for daily demographics (age, gender, and education) as well as political interest and knowledge indicators between viewers of *The Daily Show* and the national television news over the period of July 21 to November 3, 2004. A test of whether these scores were different from zero (dependent *t*-tests) is also included in the table. These tests indicate that the Daily Show audience was more male, younger, and better educated. In addition, *The Daily Show* had viewers who paid more attention to news about the election, who followed the campaign more in general, and who also had more knowledge about Bush's Social Security position. To determine if these differences might have changed over the course of the summer and fall of 2004, we correlated the difference scores with time (day) in this period as well as differences in knowledge. These correlations, shown in Table 10.5, show no evidence of a linear relationship between time and any of the difference scores. If one or the other type of audience differentially gained members who were more knowledgeable, we would expect the differences to be related to time. The analysis suggests that the differences in demographics and political interest did not change differentially for the two audiences over the period prior to the election. However, there is an indication that differences in age predicted knowledge. This finding suggests that demographic differences may have had some influence on differences in knowledge.

Figure 10.8 shows the difference scores in knowledge plotted over the time period from July until the election. We know from the analysis in Table 10.5 that the mean of the series is significantly greater than zero. This plot suggests that the knowledge advantage displayed by *Daily Show* viewers remained constant throughout the period under study. An autocorrelation analysis indicated no evidence of AR or MA components in the series. The variance in the series does appear to decline slightly with time, and this is attributable to the larger sample sizes that were obtained in the NAES as the election neared. To determine if the mean of the series remained stable, we can regress the series on time holding constant demographic and interest variables. This analysis was conducted in steps to see first if there was a significant change in the slope of the series and then to see if any of the demographic or interest variables might enter the equation.

As seen in Table 10.6, there was no significant linear time trend in the knowledge series in the first step of the analysis. In the second step, only differences in age entered into the equation ($p < .05$), and this variable did not change the relation between time and knowledge. Indeed, once age differences were entered, the constant in the prediction equation increased from 0.07 to 0.19. This finding suggests that the advantage shown by *Daily Show* viewers would have been even larger if age differences in the audiences were controlled (the younger viewers of *The Daily Show* should be less knowledgeable about politics).

Our analyses indicate that in the case of respondents' knowledge of Bush's plans for Social Security, the audience of *The Daily Show* was more likely to know the facts about this campaign issue earlier in the campaign than other respondents and maintained this difference right until

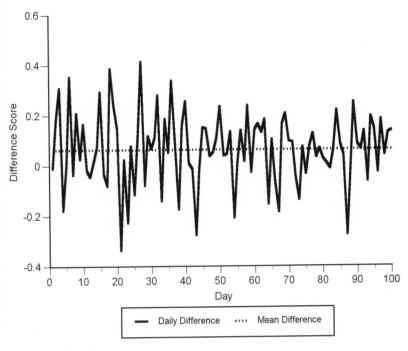

Figure 10.8. Differences in knowledge of Bush's position on Social Security between viewers of *The Daily Show* and national network news from July 15 to November 1, 2004.

the election. It appears that viewers of *The Daily Show* were more politically knowledgeable than the general population, than Leno viewers, and even than national network news viewers from the beginning of the campaign. *Daily Show* viewers were more likely to follow the campaign throughout the period under study, and this difference could explain their greater knowledge about issues such as Bush's plans for Social Security. There was no evidence that *Daily Show* viewers became differentially more knowledgeable over the course of the campaign compared to network news viewers. Hence, there was no evidence that *The Daily Show* differentially increased knowledge compared to national television news in general. Perhaps Jon Stewart was correct in his assessment that viewers of *The Daily Show* need to know about the campaign to understand the show's humor in the first place; otherwise, they simply would not find it funny. While this analysis provides evidence that viewers of *The Daily Show* are more knowledgeable *to begin with*, it certainly does not address the question of how the show's content might affect viewers'

TABLE 10.5. Mean Differences in Demographics, Attention, and
Knowledge Between Viewers of *The Daily Show* and National Network
News, July 15–November 1, 2004 and Correlations of Those Differences
with Linear Time (Day) and Knowledge

Characteristic	Mean difference	t-ratio	Correlation with day	Correlation with knowledge
Gender (% male)	16.10	11.9[a]	-0.047	0.105
Age (years)	-14.63	34.6[a]	0.130	0.198[b]
Education (years)	0.84	13.6[a]	0.155	-0.140
Attention to campaign stories in news (0 = none, 1 = not too much, 2 = some, 3 = a great deal)	0.08	3.4[a]	-0.041	0.099
Following the campaign (0 = not closely at all, 1 = not too closely, 2 = somewhat closely, 3 = very closely)	0.06	2.1[b]	-0.104	0.066
Knowledge (% correct)	6.55	4.7[a]	-0.029	

[a]$p < .01$; [b]$p < .05$

TABLE 10.6. Regression Analysis of Knowledge Differences between
Viewers of *The Daily Show* and National Network News,
July 15–November 1, 2004

Model		B	SE	t-ratio	Probability
1	Constant	.073	.028	2.58	.011
	Day	.000	.000	−.29	.772
2	Constant	.178	.058	3.09	.003
	Day	.000	.000	−.56	.574
	Age	.007	.003	2.09	.040

opinions. It is quite possible that viewers of the show obtain a different
perspective on "the facts" and that this influences their voting intentions. Further analyses of the influences of programs such as *The Daily
Show* would surely be needed to answer such questions.

Conclusion

By examining knowledge acquisition between residents of early and late
contest states and among late-night comedy viewers, we demonstrated
the capacity of the NAES to provide insights into relatively small groups
that most datasets do not have a large enough sample size to examine.

The first section showed that in 2004, residents in early primary/caucus states (apart from New Hampshire), who were more likely to be visited by candidates and be addressed through advertising, exhibited an early advantage in candidate recognition compared to the later states. However, this difference declined as the campaign period continued. The diffusion of candidate awareness rapidly caught up in the later states. Nevertheless, residents of the earlier states were more likely to express confidence in their ability to make a choice in the primaries, and this difference was maintained throughout the period of study.

The second section examined levels and trends in knowledge acquisition among viewers of late night comedy programs and suggested that *Daily Show* viewers were more knowledgeable than viewers of other programs and the nation overall. It also illustrated that rather than obtaining knowledge from viewing *The Daily Show*, viewers were more likely drawing on preexisting knowledge to enjoy the program. Both of these sections illustrate ways to analyze subgroups of the NAES over time to draw conclusions about the influence of campaigns on different segments of the population. In the analysis of different states, we saw that trends can be compared in terms of slope and intercept parameters to draw conclusions about differential growth over the course of the presidential campaign. In the analysis of different television audiences, we saw that differential changes over time between two audiences could be analyzed to identify trends and to control for other differences that might distinguish audiences as a campaign progresses.

This chapter barely scratches the surface of the NAES dataset's capabilities with regard to analyzing subgroups of the U.S. population. The NAES contains sufficient sample size and statistical power to provide information about a myriad of other groups that would likely be too difficult to measure reliably with most datasets. This affords researchers the opportunity to view differences in less explored areas, like consumption of particular television programs or films (e.g., people who saw the movie *Fahrenheit 9/11*) and economic situation (e.g., the unemployed). The data even include a sample of families with members who have served or are serving in the armed services. Researchers equipped with NAES data have a unique opportunity to explore differences between groups and to chart how those differences change over time. It is through just these kinds of analyses that one can gain a richer understanding of social and political trends that might influence an election.

Note

1. Variables cWC04 and cWC05 were used to screen for citizenship.

References

Baum, Matthew. 2003. Soft News and Political Knowledge: Evidence of Absence or Absence of Evidence? *Political Communication* 20: 173–90.

Bettag, Tom. 2000. *Nightline.* New York: ABC News, September 18.

De Moraes, Lisa. 2004. The Debate with Something for Everyone. *Washington Post,* October 2, C7.

Dunham, Richard. 2000. Where Bush Is beating Gore: As the Butt of Late-Night Zingers. *Business Week,* September 11. Retrieved April 1, 2004, from http://www.businessweek.com/bwdaily/dnflash/sep2000/nf20000911_085.htm

Dutwin, David. 2000. Knowledge in the 2000 Primary Elections. *Annals of the American Academy of Political and Social Science* 572: 17–25.

Hagen, Michael G., Richard Johnston, Kathleen Hall Jamieson, David Dutwin, and Kate Kenski. 2000. Dynamics of the 2000 Republican Primaries. *Annals of the American Academy of Political and Social Science* 572: 33–49.

Jamieson, Kathleen Hall, Michael G. Hagen, Dan Orr, Lesley Sillaman, Suzanne Morse, and Kim Kirn. 2000. What Did the Leading Candidates Say, and Did It Matter? *Annals of the American Academy of Political and Social Science* 572: 12–16.

Mahajan, Vijay and Robert A. Peterson. 1985. *Models for Innovation Diffusion.* Beverly Hills, Calif: Sage.

Patterson, Thomas E. 2002. *The Vanishing Voter: Public Involvement in an Age of Uncertainty.* New York: Knopf.

Pew Research Center for the People and the Press. 2000. *Audiences Fragmented and Skeptical: The Tough Job of Communicating with Voters.* Retrieved April 1, 2005, from http://people-press.org/reports/display.php3?ReportID=200

———. 2004. *Cable and Internet Loom Large in Fragmented Political News Universe.* Retrieved April 1, 2005, from http://people-press.org/reports/display.php3?ReportID=46

Prior, Marcus. 2003. Any Good News in Soft News? The Impact of Soft News Preference on Political Knowledge. *Political Communication* 20: 149–71.

Project Vote Smart. 2004. *State Primary Dates.* Retrieved April 1, 2005, from http://www.vote-smart.org/election_president_state_primary_dates.php

Rainey, James. 2004. Just How Powerful Is a Comic's Punch? Late-Night Hosts Weave Politicians into a Lot of Laugh Lines—Humor That Can Hinder or Help. *Los Angeles Times,* May 19, E1.

U.S. Census Bureau. 2005. Table 1-RES: Estimates of the resident population by selected age groups for the United States and states and for Puerto Rico: July 1, 2004 (SC-EST2004-01-RES), February 25. Retrieved April 1, 2005 from http://www.census.gov/popest/states/asrh/tables/SC-EST2004-01Res.xls

Waldman, Paul. 2000. Political Discussion in Primary States. *Annals of the American Academy of Political and Social Science* 572: 29–32.

Young, Dannagal Goldthwaite. 2004. Late-Night Comedy in Election 2000: Its Influence on Candidate Trait Ratings and the Moderating Effects of Political Knowledge and Partisanship. *Journal of Broadcasting and Electronic Media* 48: 1–22.

Appendix of Technical Terms

Chapters 3 and 4

Descriptive research questions   Questions focus on the characteristics of a population based on the sample. The emphasis is on the accuracy of the estimate. For example, what proportion of the public intended to vote for Bush in the 2000 presidential election, and how much error surrounds the estimate? This is often the focus of press reports about elections.

Associative research questions   These questions ask whether there is a relationship between two variables. For example, is intention to vote for Bush related to age?

Causal research questions   These questions ask whether change in one variable affects or causes change in another. For example, does age affect intention to vote for Bush?

Variable   A quantity that takes on two or more values. These values can be quantitative (e.g., political ideology) or qualitative (e.g., party identification).

Constant   A quantity that has only one value. It does not vary.

Independent variable A variable that is thought to be the cause or predictor of another variable.

Dependent variable   A variable that is analyzed as the result or outcome of another variable.

Covariation   Relation between two variables usually indexed by the covariance or correlation coefficient.

Confounding variables Variables that may explain the relationship between other variables but that are not explicitly acknowledged in an analysis. For example, level of education may explain why readers of newspapers have more knowledge about politics. Unless education were held constant, the relation between newspaper use and knowledge may be misleading.

Intervening variables   Variables that help explain the causal relation between two variables. The independent variable causes variation in the intervening variable, which in turn produces variation in the dependent one. For example, the finding that men know more about the issue positions of the candidates than women may be explained by their greater tendency to discuss politics with friends. People who engage in more discussion about politics tend to have better recall of political information than those who do not. As a result, the relation between gender and political knowledge can be explained in part by the intervening variable of discussion. Holding constant people's discussion with others will reduce the relation between gender and ability to accurately recall the positions of candidates.

Operationalization   The method by which variables are defined in measurement in contrast to their meaning in theory. In surveys such as the NAES, decisions are made about how to ask questions that assess such variables as knowledge of the candidates, perceptions of the candidate's personalities, and importance of certain issues. The survey questions used to assess these variables are operationalizations of the concepts they are intended to measure.

Reliability   The ability of a measure to give the same results if nothing has changed in the underlying variable. In the NAES, the reliability of a question is the extent to which it would give the same answer if it were asked again a short time later. A measure that gives researchers different results on different occasions even though nothing else has changed is not reliable.

Validity   The ability of an operationalization to measure the concept it is intended to capture. A valid measure is one that adequately assesses the meaning of the variable the researcher wants to measure. Validity can be demonstrated by showing that a variable correlates with other measures that should be related to the concept. For example, we can assess the validity of measures of candidate knowledge by correlating the measures with attention to news about the election. If those who pay more attention to campaign news score better on the knowledge measures, this supports their validity.

Content validity   Asks whether the measures used in the study appear on their face to correspond with the concepts they are intended to measure. Sometimes called face validity.

Construct validity This type of validity concerns the adequacy with which our measures actually assess the concept we are measuring. To the degree different measures of a variable correlate with each other, we have increased confidence that they assess the same variable.

Random error   Error in the measurement of a variable that does not occur in a systematic way. To the degree random error influences a score, it will as likely increase the score as decrease it. As a result, averaging across observations will tend to cancel out random errors and make estimates less subject to the influence of error. The influence of random errors is reduced as the number of observations increases.

Bias   Error that influences scores systematically. Averaging observations will not remove this source of error from estimates. For example, if people overstate their previous voting behavior, then our estimates of this behavior will be biased upward no matter how large our sample.

Internal validity   The accuracy of a claim that one variable causes another. In analyses of the NAES, we find that respondents' party identification influences their evaluations of the candidates. To the extent this finding is based on sound measurement, analyses, and statistical inference, we can say that it has internal validity.

External validity   The ability to generalize a finding to alternate ways of measuring the concepts and across people, times, and settings. In our example of party identification affecting candidate evaluation (see internal validity), if this finding generalizes across different measures of party identification and candidate evaluation and, in addition, if it represents the way different people behave no matter where or when they are questioned, then the finding has external validity. If, however, there were something in our survey procedures that produced this finding that would not be found using different procedures, then the finding's external validity might be questioned. A finding may have internal validity, but may lack external validity.

Census   A study or survey of an entire population.

Sample   A subset of a population that is selected for study.

Random sample   A subset of a population that is selected for study based on a sampling plan that gives each population member an equal chance of being selected.

Sample frame   Members from a population who have a chance of being selected into the sample.

Nonresponse bias   A bias that occurs when the individuals who have been selected for interviewing decline to participate in the survey or participate but do not complete the entire survey and differ from those individuals who do complete it. In the NAES, missing data are infrequent. However, it is wise when conducting analyses with variables that have missing scores (e.g., income) either to use a valid method of imputation for missing data or to ensure that the missing scores do not bias one's analyses. Response rates in the NAES are comparable to other major national telephone surveys (about 25%). Although the rate is relatively low, the survey is still relatively representative of the U.S. population (see Chapter 2) and should produce generalizeable results.

Statistical conclusion validity   The ability of a study to draw conclusions about the data based on the size of the sample, the sensitivity of the measurement, and the appropriateness of the statistical tests used to make inferences about the data. The larger the sample, the more sensitive the measurement, and the more appropriate the statistical tests, the greater the statistical conclusion validity.

Cross section   Data that have been collected at a single point in time.

Repeated cross-sectional design   A design in which the data have been collected at two or more points in time. The collected data are different samples drawn from the same population.

Panel design   A design in which the same individuals are interviewed at two or more points in time.

Rolling cross-section (RCS) design   A design that involves taking a series of cross sections over a period of time and employing a sampling protocol used to ensure that each cross section is equally representative of the population. Each cross section is equally spaced across the time period of interest. In the NAES, every effort was made to keep response rates and respondent characteristics constant across each day of interviewing. Hence the data can be analyzed by day without controlling for sampling variability. It is important to note that the interviews were conducted at the end of the day, so each day's data are the result of previous days and the effects of what happened during the daytime and early evening of the interview date.

Ecological fallacy   Making invalid inferences about individual-level processes from group-level data.

Replicates   Random subsamples of the telephone numbers targeted for interviewing in a rolling cross-sectional study such as the NAES.

Chapter 5

Variable distribution   A table or graphical display that shows the frequency or percentage of cases for each value of a variable.

Cumulative distribution   A table or graphic display that shows the frequency or percentage of cases below or above a certain value of a variable.

Unimodal distribution   A distribution that has the most cases in a single region of the variable.

Bimodal distribution   A distribution that has two regions of values with the most cases. For example, ratings of attraction to political candidates are often bimodal, with many persons liking candidates and many disliking the same candidates.

Uniform distribution   A distribution with scores that are approximately equally frequent for all values.

Symmetric distribution   A distribution that has approximately the same proportion of scores above and below the midpoint of the variable.

Skewed distribution   A distribution that has a higher proportion of scores at one end of the continuum than at the other end.

Unimodal, symmetric distribution   A distribution that has both a single modal region and is symmetric around this region. The normal distribution has these characteristics.

Levels of measurement   Characteristics of measurement scales that define the quantitative information contained in the scale values.

Nominal scales   Scales that only contain information about identities, such as persons who prefer one candidate over another or who live in one section of the country versus another. No information about order is assumed.

Ordinal scales   Scales that provide rank-order information, such as the order of preference for candidates. The values do not contain information about the magnitude of differences between scores. The difference between ranks of 1 and 2 may be quite different from the difference between ranks of 2 and 3.

Interval scales   Scales that not only provide rank-order information but also contain information about the distances between values. The most frequent case is a scale with equal distances between scores, the classic example being the temperature scale. Many variables in the NAES are somewhere between ordinal and interval; however, treating them as interval scales often creates little distortion in results.

Variable transformations   Rescaling of variables to make them linearly related to other theoretically relevant variables.

Descriptive statistics   Summary scores that describe a distribution, including the mean, median, mode, and measures of variability, such as the interquartile range and standard deviation.

Mean   A measure of the center of a distribution calculated by taking the sum of all scores divided by the number of scores.

Mode   The most frequent score in a distribution.

Median   The score that corresponds to the case just past 50% of the cumulative distribution. In large distributions, it is the score at the 50th percentile. The median is a more sensitive measure of central tendency for skewed distributions because the mean is more influenced by extreme scores.

Interquartile range   The range of scores between the 25th and 75th percentile in the cumulative distribution of scores.

Variance   A measure of dispersion of a distribution defined by the mean of the squared deviations of each score from its mean, $(X_i - M)^2$. The square root of the variance is the **standard deviation**.

Crosstabulation   A procedure for examining the relation between two variables in which all values of the variables are arrayed in a table with one in the rows and the other in the columns. The cells of the table contain the number of cases defined by the rows and columns of the variables and the percentage of cases in either the row or column.

Statistical significance   An assessment of whether a statistic describing a distribution is likely to occur by chance. To the degree the statistic is *unlikely* to have occurred by chance, it is said to be statistically significant. Chance is often defined as occurring more often than 5% of the time.

Degrees of freedom   A quantity that defines a parameter of a statistical distribution that is critical for determining statistical significance

Pearson chi-square statistic   A measure of the relation between variables in a crosstabulation calculated by taking the sum of the squared differences between the observed and expected cell frequencies divided by the expected frequency. The value, written as χ^2, can be evaluated for significance by comparing it to the expected distribution of the chi-square statistic. The statistic can be calculated for variables of any scale type.

Gamma statistic   A measure of the relation between two ordinal scales that assesses the degree of relation on a scale of -1 to $+1$. Scores with an absolute value of 1 are perfectly **monotonically** related, meaning their rank orders are perfectly matched. Scores of zero indicate no relation between the variables. The gamma statistic is particularly helpful for assessing relations between highly skewed variables.

Pearson correlation coefficient   A measure of relation between two variables that have been standardized to a mean of zero and a standard deviation of 1 (z scores). The correlation is the mean of the products of the paired z scores, $Z_X Z_Y$. The correlation ranges from -1 to $+1$. An absolute score of 1 means that the variables are perfectly linearly related. A score of zero means they are not linearly related.

Independent sample *t* test   A measure of the relation between two variables that assesses whether two means of one variable defined by the values of a second variable are statistically different. The statistic is assessed for significance by comparing the obtained value to the expected value of the *t* distribution.

Chapter 6

Smoothing   A graphical presentation technique that permits examination of daily variation in a time series while minimizing the contribution of random variation. Smoothed scores are not typically analyzed using regression or other quantitative techniques. To analyze a time series quantitatively, it is recommended that the regression procedures discussed in Chapters 8 and 9 be employed.

Centered moving average   A smoothing technique that pools data by calculating an average for a given point in time with a specified number of values surrounding it. For example, a seven-day centered moving average assigns the average value of the day plus the values of the three days preceding it and the three days following it.

Prior moving average   A smoothing technique that pools data by calculating an average for a given point in time with a specified number of values preceding it. For example, a seven-day prior moving average assigns the average value of that day plus the values of the six days preceding it in the series.

Chapters 7 and 8

Ordinary least squares (OLS)   A method of parameter estimation in linear regression for dependent variables that are measured on quantitative scales, such as ratings of candidates. The method identifies parameter values that minimize the variance of prediction errors (mean squared error).

Logistic regression analysis   A method of parameter estimation for dependent variables that are dichotomous at the individual level, such as yes versus no responses. The method uses maximum likelihood estimation procedures to identify predictors of the log of the odds of a response. These procedures maximize the log likelihood of the prediction function, and this value is frequently provided in computer output from the procedure.

Log likelihood   A measure of fit that is maximized in the method of maximum likelihood estimation. A transform of this measure, $-2 \times$ log likelihood ($-2LL$), is used to evaluate goodness of fit and to test the significance of additional parameters in a model. When prediction residuals are normally distributed, maximum likelihood and ordinary least squares estimation produce identical results.

Residuals   Deviations from prediction in a regression model. They contain both measurement error and effects of unknown variables. A common assumption is that the residuals are normally distributed. If they are, one can use standard tests of significance on the parameters, such as t-tests. Residuals that are not normally distributed can be estimated using maximum likelihood techniques, such as in the case of logistic regression.

Covariance   A measure of relation between two sets of paired scores calculated by summing the product of the deviations of each pair of scores from its mean, $(X_i - M_x)(Y_i - M_y)$, and then taking the mean of this sum. A covariance of zero means the variables are not linearly related.

Mean squared error (MS$_e$)   The variance of the residuals in a regression model. OLS regression minimizes this value to identify the parameters of the model. The standard error of the regression is simply the standard deviation of the MS$_e$. Both statistics are typically contained in regression analysis output.

R^2   A measure of goodness of fit ranging between zero and 1 for OLS linear regression models. It is the square of the correlation between the predicted and observed scores. It increases as the mean square error of the prediction equation declines. The larger its value, the better the fit. Computer programs also provide estimates of R^2 for logistic regression models. These values provide an estimate of goodness of fit, but they do not have the same interpretation regarding mean square error.

Unknown regression components   Factors in a regression model that are not measured but that influence the scores in the model. Because they are not measured in the model, their weights are unknown and they might influence the weights of the known predictors if they were included. Unknown components may also produce correlations between the residuals of dependent variables.

Measurement error   Unmeasured random variation in a regression model that is attributable to unstable components in the measurement of the dependent variable. This source of variation is often assumed to be uncorrelated across dependent variables. In the NAES, measurement error could reflect unstable reactions to questions because the respondent is not paying attention to a question or samples recollections from memory that are not stable. See also random error in Chapters 3 and 4.

Contrast-coded variable   A transformation of an independent variable such that the mean of the variable is zero. The transformation enables easier interpretation of the coefficients in a regression model.

Dummy-coded variable   A variable in a regression model that is coded to the value of 1 to represent the value of a subclass and zero for all other members of the class. For example, one could recode political party into two dummy variables: 1 for Republicans and zero for everyone else, and 1 for Democrats and zero for everyone else. Any class of J members can have $J - 1$ dummy variables to represent its effects in a regression model.

Interaction variable   Variables created from existing variables in a regression model to represent predictions for any variable that depend on the values of other variables. Often the product of two variables is used to represent the effect of an interaction between them. A variable that interacts with another is often called a moderator of the effects of the other variable.

***B* weight**   The unstandardized coefficient of a variable in a regression equation. It measures the change in the dependent variable as a function of a one-unit change in the independent variable. The constant term is also a *B* weight; however, it is simply a parameter in the model. Each *B* weight (other than the constant term) has a corresponding Beta weight that is the value of the coefficient applied to the variables when they are standardized (z scores).

Standard error (SE)   A deviation measure that defines the range of likely values that a parameter in a model can assume. The smaller the

SE, the more sensitively the parameter can be estimated. The larger the sample size and the value of R^2 for the model, the smaller the SE. The ratio of the parameter to the SE in OLS regression defines the t test that is used to measure the probability that the parameter is in the range of zero. A p value of .05 is usually taken as a cutoff for defining a statistically significant result, although this is only a convention.

t-test   A test of statistical significance defined by the ratio of a parameter to its standard error. The test is used in linear regression analysis to identify significant B weights in the model. Values greater than 2 in absolute size identify parameters that are significant at the $p < .05$ level in samples greater than size 60.

Wald test   A test of statistical significance defined by the square of the ratio of a parameter to its standard error. The test is used in logistic regression analyses to identify significant B values using the Chi-square distribution. A value of 3.84 is significant at $p < .05$ for a single parameter.

Chapter 9

Autocorrelation   The correlation between a series at lag 0 and the same series at a different lag.

ACF   Autocorrelation function, a graph of the autocorrelation for successive lags of the same series is called the ACF. The analysis should only be conducted with detrended series.

Partial auto-correlation (PAC)   The standardized regression coefficient for the pth lag holding constant all earlier lags.

PACF   Partial autocorrelation function, the graph that shows successive values of the PAC. In an AR(p) model, all PACs greater than lag p will be zero because by controlling the earlier lags, there will be no significant relation between the series remaining.

MA(q)   The moving average time series model with q lags, a function of the present and q previous random components. It has no memory beyond the q lags of previous influence. Its coefficients are restricted to values less than 1 in absolute value.

AR(p)   The autoregressive time series model with p lags, a function of the present random component and p previous lags of the series. Its memory can extend beyond the p lags that directly influence its value because each lag contains information from all previous lags. Its coefficients are restricted to values less than 1 in absolute value.

White noise   A time series that is entirely composed of successive random components with a mean of zero, constant variance, and no relation between terms.

Stationary series   A time series that has a constant mean, standard deviation, and covariance between lags. White noise is an example of a stationary series. AR and MA processes are stationary as well. Any series with a trend that changes the mean or variability of the series is not stationary.

Random walk   An AR(1) series in which the autoregressive weight is 1. A random walk is not stationary, but taking the first difference of the series will produce a series that is stationary.

Box-Ljung test   A chi-square test that assesses the presence of autocorrelation for the first p lags of the ACF. For example, if one evaluates autocorrelation for the first three lags of a series, then the Box-Ljung test is evaluated with three degrees of freedom.

Correlogram   The ACF graph with confidence bands for the values of the autocorrelations. A correlogram analysis is an examination of the ACF and PACF.

Standard error bands   A pair of lines in the SPSS correlogram output that defines the range of the autocorrelation that is within two standard-error deviations of zero. Values that lie outside of the band are individually significant predictors of the series at the $p < .05$ level of significance.

Lag   In correlating a time series with prior values of itself, the lag refers to the number of prior time periods in the correlation. A lag of one refers to a series one time period back in time. A lag of zero is simply the series itself. Negative lags refer to the number of succeeding time periods that are correlated with a series. Negative lags are used in the output of the cross-correlation program in SPSS. The lag operator L moves a series ahead one time period so it can be compared with the original at lag 0. In this case, lag is used as a verb. To lag a series one time period is to perform the lag operation on the series. In SPSS, one can create a lagged version of a series using the time series transforms.

Cross-correlation function   An analysis of the correlations between different lags of two series. The output in SPSS shows a graphic representation of the correlations and their confidence bands to allow ready detection of significant correlations at different lags of either series. The analysis should only be conducted on detrended series.

Adjusted R^2   A measure of goodness of fit based on R^2 that ranges between zero and 1. It adjusts for the number of parameters in the model to take account of increases in R^2 that can occur simply because additional parameters have been added to the model. Hence, the larger its value, the better the fit.

ARMA analysis   A program that uses maximum likelihood estimation of AR and MA components in a time series and that allows simultaneous estimation of seasonal and other trends.

AIC   The Akaike information criterion, a measure of goodness of fit for regression models that declines as the fit improves. It uses a harsher penalty for the addition of parameters than the adjusted R^2, and hence is regarded as a more sensitive test of model fit. In combination with the SIC, it allows one to evaluate alternative models for time series using either OLS regression or ARMA analysis.

SIC   The Schwarz information criterion, a measure of goodness of fit for regression models that also declines as the fit improves. It uses an even harsher penalty than the AIC. It is regarded as more sensitive to model adequacy especially when little is known about the modeling domain. In combination with the AIC, it allows one to evaluate alternative models for time series using either OLS regression or ARMA analysis.

Durbin Watson statistic, d   A statistic that has been used to assess the presence of first order autocorrelation in the residuals of time series data. Presence of autocorrelation in the residuals has been taken as a signal that the solution may be biased. However, it is limited in its ability to detect higher-order correlation in time series. A value less than 2 in the range between 2 and zero is regarded as a sign of positive autocorrelation.

Granger causality   A concept of causation applied to time series analysis in which one series X is said to Granger cause the other Y, if information contained in the lags of X can predict Y holding constant comparable lags in Y.

Feedback in Granger causality   A possible outcome of Granger causality tests in which both series can predict the future status of the other.

Contemporaneous causality   A possible situation in Granger causality testing in which either series can cause the other at lag 0. It is a possibility whenever the two series are correlated even after removing all cross-correlation from lags of each variable.

Index

Page references followed by f and t refer to figures and tables, respectively

Acknowledgments

The National Annenberg Election Survey and this volume owe their success to many people. The inaugural wave of the survey in 2000 benefited from the active participation of Richard Johnston of the University of British Columbia as well as many members of the Annenberg Public Policy Center (APPC) staff and students. Mary McIntosh of Princeton Survey Research helped guide the implementation of the survey in its first year. Christopher Adasiewicz has continued in his role as codebook and data manager for both waves of the survey. The interviews were conducted by Schulman, Ronca, & Bucuvalas, Inc. Jon Stromer-Galley created the CD-ROM. Michael Hennessy of the APPC and Frank Diebold of Penn's Department of Economics provided helpful comments on the first version of this book.

Kenneth Winneg took over as managing director of the 2004 version of the survey. The survey also benefited from the participation of Adam Clymer, former Chief Washington Correspondent for the *New York Times*, who assisted in the design of the questionnaire throughout the field period and wrote the press releases that informed the public about important findings. Shiloh Krieger assisted in compiling these releases for the CD-ROM. Kate Kenski, Erika Falk, Dannagal Goldthwaite Young, Russell Tisinger, and Natalie Jomini Stroud also assisted in the design of the questionnaire and survey analysis during the project. Gordon McDonald provided assistance during the campaign. Nicole Franklin provided data analytic support for the releases and for this book, and Shira Gordon proofread the codebook. Eian More provided staff support for the production of the book. Kathleen Hall Jamieson orchestrated the entire project.